CENSUSES, SURVEYS AND PRIVACY

CENSUSES, SURVEYS AND PRIVACY

Edited by

Martin Bulmer

Lecturer in Social Administration
London School of Economics and Political Science

HOLMES & MEIER PUBLISHERS, INC.

New York

First published in the United States of America 1979 by
HOLMES & MEIER PUBLISHERS, INC.
30 Irving Place, New York, N.Y. 10003

Library of Congress Cataloging in Publication Data

Main entry under title:

Censuses, surveys, and privacy.

    Includes bibliographical references.
    1.   Confidential communications—Social surveys—
Addresses, essays, lectures.   2.   Confidential
communications—Census—Addresses, essays, lectures.
I.   Bulmer, Martin.
HN29.C42   1979   323.44   79–9292
ISBN 0–8419–0536–3

ISBN 0–8419–0536–3

PRINTED IN GREAT BRITAIN

Contents

Preface

Privacy is a contemporary issue of increasing general concern. Pressure groups, the media, politicians and the public are from time to time exercised about it. The continuing growth of big government and corporate industry, together with the invention and development of the electronic computer, have created potential threats to privacy on a hitherto undreamt of scale. Yet these same trends produce ever-increasing requests for personal information from the citizen, for purposes as various as taxation, employment, credit-rating, automobile registration and many others. As a result, society's 'need' to know these personal particulars has to be balanced against the individual's claim to privacy about his personal affairs. Striking this balance is a delicate and intractable task to which there is no easy solution.

Social research and inquiry constitutes one kind of request for personal information directed to the citizen. In social surveys and population censuses, members of the public are asked questions about their social and economic characteristics, their personal histories, their social attitudes and their social behaviour. Public co-operation is forthcoming for several reasons, including a belief that the results of research will be of public benefit and a willingness to talk about oneself. Also very important is a tacit recognition of the integrity of social scientists and statisticians conducting the research. Such inquiries are conducted according to certain rules.

The most important of these are that all *individual* data collected in social research are confidential, and information about identifiable individuals is never published from censuses and surveys. The social investigator is interested only in the *aggregate*, or general, picture. In addition, data collected are held in confidence by the person or persons collecting them, are kept secure once they are collected, and are not released in identifiably individualised form outside the research organisation. In the case of censuses, there are strong legal safeguards to ensure both the privacy of the information given and its absolute security thereafter.

Social research and statistical inquiries are ultimately justified in terms of the greater good which will result, in the long term, from greater knowledge and information about the state of society and its workings. For example, knowledge about the size and structure of the population, as well as how it is changing, is basic to the planning of social services such as education, housing and health. Public policy, to be well informed, needs adequate data about the condition of the population. Yet population censuses and social surveys have aroused concern about encroachments on privacy. The censuses held in several countries in 1970–71, in particular, produced protests of a kind not hitherto encountered by census-takers. Some of this concern was of an exaggerated and even demagogic kind, exploited for political ends. But whatever its quality, such protests cannot be ignored by those who do social research. The conduct of surveys and censuses depends ultimately on public co-operation. This is a necessary condition for their existence and continuation.

This book examines the problems which censuses and surveys pose for preserving privacy, and which privacy poses for the conduct of censuses and surveys. It is divided into four sections. Parts 2 and 3 consider specifically social surveys and population censuses. Part 1 is a general discussion of the problem of privacy as it affects social research. Part 4 considers means by which the existing safeguards for privacy in the conduct of social research may be strengthened. The contributors are all themselves professional social scientists, social researchers or government statisticians, all with first-hand acquaintance with their subject. Their concern with privacy problems reflects the fact that it is the members of the social-research community themselves who are at the forefront of moves to safeguard privacy in social research.

Privacy and social research are both very large fields. Several features of the present book should be noted. Firstly, it is intended as an *introduction* to the subject accessible to the non-specialist; its content is not highly technical. Secondly, it focuses upon quantitative research by means of censuses and surveys. Experimental research on the one hand and observational and ethnographic studies on the other are not covered. Nor is it primarily concerned with the protection of statistical data derived from administrative records in bureaucracies, recently treated in D. H. Flaherty's important five-country study, *Privacy and Government Data Banks* (London, Mansell Scientific, 1979). The large literature on privacy and computing is included in the Further Reading section at the end, but this is not primarily a study of that field.

The material brought together here provides some new perspectives, from quite different standpoints, upon a difficult problem. It is one which continues to exercise the social science and statistical communities, as major international conferences at Paris in 1974, Hasselby Slott in 1976, Bellagio in 1977 and Cologne in 1978 on different aspects of privacy and social-research data demonstrate. This is a continuing discussion, which is likely to intensify as the 1980–1 round of population censuses approaches. It is one which has major implications for the public acceptability of social science and social inquiry.

Carrying out censuses and surveys is specialised work for highly-trained technical experts. Social surveys and censuses, however, also depend upon the co-operation of the individual respondent, who probably knows nothing whatever about these technical matters but does have views of his own about research, however vague. Even in census-taking, respondent co-operation cannot be taken for granted today to the extent that it could in the past. Critics of censuses, in particular, have alleged that such inquiries are unnecessarily extensive, intrusive and onerous, and that the data collected are not necessarily secure. The onus is now upon those who conduct censuses and surveys to show that they take privacy problems seriously, and that they have effective means of safeguarding the interests of the individual citizen at all stages of the research process. The argument of this book, and the material which it contains are intended to show that they do.

September 1978   MARTIN BULMER

Contributors

DR ROBERT F. BORUCH is Professor of Psychology and Director of Methodology and Evaluation Research at Northwestern University, Evanston, Illinois. A statistician and psychologist by training, his principal research interest is in the design and analysis of field experiments for testing social policy. His publications include *Social Experimentation* (with H. W. Riecken, 1974), *Experimental Testing of Public Policy* (with H. W. Riecken, 1975), *Assuring Confidentiality in Social Research* (with J. S. Cecil, 1979), more than thirty journal articles and contributions to symposia on applied social research, and a forthcoming monograph on *Secondary Analysis of Evaluative Data*. He was the second President of the Council for Applied Social Research, of which he remains a member of the Board of Directors, and is current Chairman of the Social Science Research Council Committee on Program Evaluation. He gave evidence on behalf of the American Psychological Association to the Privacy Protection Study Commission.

MARTIN BULMER lectures in the Department of Social Science and Administration at the London School of Economics and Political Science. His main teaching and research interests are in the methodology of social research and the application of social research to public policy. His publications include *Social Policy Research* (editor, 1978), *Sociological Research Methods* (editor, 1977), *Mining and Social Change* (editor, 1977) and *Working Class Images of Society* (editor, 1975).

DR ROBERT O. CARLSON is Dean of the Schools of Business at Adelphi University, Garden City, New York, and was for many years Chairman of the Editorial Board of the *Public Opinion Quarterly*. For eighteen years he worked on management problems for Standard Oil Company (NJ) (now EXXON) in the Middle East, Africa, the Far East and Europe. He is a past President of the American Association for Public Opinion Research, former Executive Officer of the American Sociological Society, and a former President of the Public Relations Society of America. He has taught at Columbia, Fairfield and New York Universities and was a consultant to the Rand Corporation. He is the editor of *Communications and Public Opinion* (1975).

DAVID R. COPE is lecturer in Social Planning at the Institute of Planning Studies, University of Nottingham, where he teaches population studies, urban sociology, forecasting, computing and social statistics to postgraduate students. He is Treasurer of the Census Research Group, a national organisation of researchers using census data, and is a member of the Office of Population Censuses and Surveys Research Advisory Committee on the 1981 Census. Apart from privacy and official statistics, his main research interests are the sociology of fertility and the environmental and social consequences of coalmining in the East Midlands. He has published on these topics in journals such as *New Society, Nature, The International Journal of Environmental Studies* and *Futures*.

DR C. HAKIM is Principal Research Officer in the Department of Employment, London, but was previously on the staff of the Office of Population Censuses and Surveys, London. Her research work has included studies of education and employment in developing and industrialised societies.

DR ERIC JOSEPHSON is Director of the Center for Socio-Cultural Research on Drug Use at Columbia University, New York City, and Senior Research Associate at its School of Public Health. His main research interests lie in the field of deviant behaviour and social policy. Among his publications are *Drug Use: Epidemiological and Sociological Approaches* (with Eleanor E. Carroll) and *Man Alone: Alienation in Modern Society* (with Mary Josephson).

DR WILLIAM PETERSEN is Robert Lazarus Professor of Social Demography at Ohio State University. Previously he taught in the Department of Sociology at the University of California, Berkeley. One of America's leading social demographers, his main research interests are public policy on population growth and the relation of ethnic composition to social structure. His publications include *Planned Migration* (1955), *The Politics of Population* (1964), *Population* (1969) and *Japanese Americans: Oppression and Success* (1971).

EDWARD SHILS is Distinguished Service Professor of Sociology and Social Thought at the University of Chicago. He is also a fellow of Peterhouse, Cambridge University. He founded and edits *Minerva: a review of science, learning and policy*. His publications include *Center and Periphery: Essays in Macrosociology* (1975), *The Intellectuals and the Powers* (1972), *The Torment of Secrecy* (1956) and *Towards a General Theory of Action* (co-editor with Talcott Parsons, 1951).

DR CONRAD TAEUBER has been Professor and Director of the Center for Population Research, Georgetown University, Washington, DC, since 1973. Previously, from 1951 to 1973, he was Associate Director of the United States Bureau of the Census. A former President of the Population Society of America, his main research interests are in demography and allied statistical fields. His publications include *The Changing Population of the United States* (1958) and *The People of the United States in the Twentieth Century* (1971).

Part One

Introduction

1 The Impact of Privacy upon Social Research

Martin Bulmer

Introduction and Definitions

This book is about the impact of one social, political and moral issue – privacy – upon contemporary social science. As social inquiry extends its scope, questions about the legitimacy of its inquiries and the rights of the individual citizen to be left alone are posed with increasing sharpness. Is it justifiable to ask members of the public questions in censuses and surveys about sensitive and private topics such as income or sexual behaviour? Is it justifiable to allow social scientists access to medical records in hospitals or doctors' surgeries in order to advance science? Should different sets of records be linked together for purposes of statistical analysis, even though the individual citizens who originally provided the information believed that it would be treated as confidential? What legal safeguards are there to prevent the release or legal seizure of social-research data collected under promises of confidentiality?

These and other questions relating to social research and privacy will be considered in the following pages. Together, they amount to a formidable battery of questions about the place of social science in modern society and the conditions under which it can be carried on. Privacy is not an issue which can be pushed on one side. It is a matter which the social-science community must consider and come to terms with if it is to maintain the legitimacy of what it is doing. By the same token, privacy is not an issue confined to social science. Indeed, many of the more controversial privacy issues – intrusiveness by the press and radio and television, the legality of the activities of private investigators, the scope of credit-rating agencies, or industrial espionage – have arisen in other fields altogether, away from the problems in social research.

This work considers privacy in relation to quantitative social research. It seeks to determine what are the principal issues, what choices and dilemmas are posed for social scientists to resolve, and how great a threat social science may be to individual privacy, or privacy may be to research. It does so by means of a careful examination of certain general issues, and then a discussion in detail of two types of quantitative social research – social-survey research and population censuses. The majority of contributors are themselves professional social scientists, and the tone of their contributions is that of reasoned and critical assessment of these problems. Privacy is a subject which arouses fierce passions, not infrequently generating more heat than light. A determined attempt has been made here to avoid such polemical excesses.

A good starting point to the discussion is to attempt to define what is meant by 'privacy'. It has been loosely defined as 'the right to be left alone' or 'keeping other people out of your affairs, not being pestered or pried on'.[1] This implies being free from searching inquiries about oneself and one's activities. A more formal definition, by Alan F. Westin, is: 'the claim of individuals, groups or institutions to determine for themselves when, how and to what extent information is communicated to others.'[2] This implies the ability to control information about oneself, whether to give it free circulation, limited circulation or no circulation at all.

An alternative definition, with a slightly different emphasis, is in terms of the right to participate in a meaningful way in decisions about what information will be collected and how that information will be used.[3] Westin's definition implies that there will be some disclosure of information, and the individual providing the data should decide the nature and extent of disclosure. This alternative definition recognises that individuals share many kinds of data with record-keeping institutions and seeks to give them a right to participate in a meaningful way in decisions about what information is gathered and how it is used.

A common feature of all three definitions is that privacy is an *interactional* concept, always referring to privacy of the individual, group or institution vis-à-vis other individuals, groups or institutions. Privacy is only an issue where interaction, perception and communication are possible. As a concept, it refers to *information transfer;* this distinguishes the concept of privacy from concepts such as solitude, loneliness and isolation. The concept refers to the extent to which an individual, group or institution controls the dissemination of information about oneself or itself to others. A concern with privacy in social research highlights the mutuality in the relationship between researcher and the subject of research. Voluntariness on the part of the person or persons whose privacy is in question is an essential component.[4]

'Privacy' is distinct from 'confidentiality'. The latter refers to the conditions of use and disclosure of data once it is collected. Thus the form used in the 1971 British Census of Population stated: 'The information you give on this form will be treated as CONFIDENTIAL and used only for compiling statistics. No information about named individuals will be passed by the Census Office to any other Government Department or any other authority or person.'[5] An assurance of confidentiality says that data will only be disseminated in a particular way. In social research, this assurance is most commonly given in the form that no *individual* data will be released, and that only *aggregate* statistical data (which does not permit the identification of a named individual) will be published. Unlike the concept of privacy, confidentiality pertains to the conditions, safeguards and security under which the person collecting the research data keeps that data. Though assurances are given to the subject of research, the person giving information to the researcher can have no control over the subsequent fate of that data once it is collected from him or her.

Clearly, privacy and confidentiality are closely linked, although distinct. In particular, the extent to which confidentiality can be guaranteed is likely to influence public perceptions of privacy as an issue. A good deal of the discussion about social research and privacy in fact concerns confidentiality. In relation to censuses, for example, there has probably been somewhat more public concern about the confidentiality of data as it is collected, stored and published than about the intrusion upon privacy represented by the asking of particular questions in the census schedule.[6]

If confidentiality cannot be assured, or the safeguards are less than watertight, the individual citizen can assert his right to privacy and withhold information asked for in a census or survey. (He can do so anyway, but is less likely to do so if adequate assurances about confidentiality are offered and adequate safeguards are known to exist.)

It is useful to distinguish the concepts of privacy and confidentiality (with which this book is concerned) from the concepts of secrecy and freedom of information (with which it is not). The differences between these concepts is related to the difference between society and the state; or between a focus upon the private citizen and his personal life, as distinct from the political system and public life. *Privacy* refers to the control of individuals over information about themselves. Disclosure of information is possible if the individual wishes it. *Secrecy* refers to a condition in which disclosure or acquisition of information beyond a certain boundary is prohibited. If this boundary is breached, sanctions are invoked.[7] There is, for example, a clear distinction between the decisions of individual citizens whether they will tell survey interviewers what their income is (a matter, even in the aggregate, of privacy) and the imposition by a government on its defence personnel of a rule not to release information about weapons systems (a matter of secrecy with associated sanctions). Although the study of privacy necessarily involves the relationship between the individual and the state (and the possible invasion of privacy by the state in search of social data), this is quite distinct from secrecy in the political arena, on the part of those in power and their agents. Secrecy relates primarily to the political realm;[8] privacy to the social realm more generally.

The distinction between confidentiality and freedom of information parallels the distinction between privacy and secrecy. 'Freedom of information', an issue much discussed in industrial societies in recent years,[9] relates to the political and public sphere and, in particular, to what proportion of information held by governments should be released to the public, usually on request. What degree of open government is desirable? Confidentiality, on the other hand, although it may be invoked as a rule prohibiting release of information in systems which are based on official secrecy, is once again a broader category pertaining to the conditions under which all types of social data (not just the policy papers and 'secrets' of government departments) are held. Most important for the present discussion, in societies where freedom of government information operates, this does not affect the maintenance of confidentiality of individualised data held by the government (and others). 'Freedom of information' does not entail the right to invade individual privacy or breach confidentiality; rather, it refers to the opening up of what were hitherto official 'Secrets'.

The Expansion of Empirical Social Research

A necessary condition for privacy to become an important public issue in relation to social research is that social research should be sufficiently visible to matter. During the twentieth century, social research has grown enormously. What at the end of the nineteenth century was the pursuit of a few socially-minded upper-middle-class people of leisure in Britain and the United States had become, by the last quarter of the twentieth century, a vast industry spread across universities, independent institutes, commercial firms and governments.[10] It is true that in the nineteenth century, governments maintained census and vital registration offices, but even they functioned on a modest scale by comparison with their size and importance today.

To define formally the types of research with which this book is concerned: *Population censuses* are complete, 100 per cent enumerations of a given population to gather demographic and social data, carried out throughout a given territory at one point in time, by the government of that territory, and compulsory for the citizen to answer. The usual form of collecting census data is a self-completion questionnaire, filled in usually by the head of the household, but distributed and collected by a census enumerator. *Social surveys* are inquiries directed to only a sample of a given population, usually a small proportion of it, to gather social data on a particular topic or topics. Participation in a social survey is voluntary. Data is usually collected either by personal interview, where the interviewer completes a schedule, or by mail questionnaires filled in by the respondent. *Administrative data*, unlike census and survey data, is data not collected *initially* for research purposes at all. It is data collected as part of an administrative process, which may then be used for research and statistical analysis. An example would be medical records about patients kept by a family doctor or hospital. Providing such data is usually 'compulsory' in the sense that it is obligatory in order to complete the administrative process. But at the time of giving the information, the administrative body may not know (or may not reveal) that this data will subsequently also be used for research.

An important distinction to bear in mind, which will be returned to in Part 4, is the distinction between data collected solely for statistical and research purposes and data collected for administrative purposes. Census and survey data is of the former kind, administrative data of the latter kind. But the *research* use of administrative data is different from its *administrative* use. Such data is used in administrative action to reach a decision about a named individual, who is identified. The research use of the same data is aimed to build up an *aggregate* picture of a collectivity, not to identify named individuals. Thus, though the *input* to research may be an administrative record, within the data-processing operation the record acquires anonymity and retains it in the statistical *output*. Thus a common characteristic of all the research discussed in this book is that, whatever its source, it conceals individual identities in the published results and does not violate the confidentiality of the individual returns.

Of the types of social research discussed in this book, social surveys are almost entirely a twentieth-century development, becoming established as a large-scale activity only after the Second World War.[11] Censuses have a longer history, but their size and importance for policy-making is greater in the twentieth century than in the nineteenth. The more general category of record-keeping and the compilation of administrative data is one of man's oldest activities, but the nature of the problems encountered – and the use of such data in social research – are qualitatively different today due to the growth of government and the computer revolution. To quote merely one example, James Rule has estimated that the number of entries in the Metropolitan Police main fingerprint collection increased from 150,000 in 1910 to 2,150,000 in 1970, a more than fourteen-fold increase in sixty years.

The growth of social research is not autonomous or self-generating. It derives from a number of sources. One is the sheer growth of government activity and intervention in industrial societies. Propelled by the experience of two world wars, governments have steadily extended their influence in most spheres of life – the financial, the industrial, the educational, the medical, and so on. Although significant differences remain between societies, even in the United States federal government intervention is far greater today than in 1900. In the wake of such increasing intervention comes a demand for better data about these spheres of extending government activity.

Not only has government intervention increased, and with it the size of the bureaucracy, but it has expanded particularly rapidly in 'social' fields – education, health, housing, social security etc. Therefore the demand for social data and the findings of social research have correspondingly increased. Linked to the expansion of higher education, and within higher education the very rapid expansion of the social sciences, this has led to growing demands for social research from government and other bodies, and the creation of an academic community of social scientists able and eager both to undertake such research (whether as helper or social critic) and to train new generations of social scientists to work outside the universities, and further strengthen the demand for social research in the future.

In the recent past, the development of new forms of research fusing action with inquiry (whether called action research, social experimentation or evaluation research) has brought social research even closer to the process of policy-making and to decisions about the distribution of resources. Data gathered in the course of such inquiries may therefore have very direct consequences for its subjects, unless their privacy can be safeguarded.

This outline sketch of the growth of social research is meant simply to underline the growing demand for social data, not only from governments. The serious media, for example, are important consumers of it, seeking in their commentaries upon contemporary events to back up their analyses with hard data upon current social trends. Increasingly, other groups such as employers associations and trade unions, pressure groups and community groups seek data on which to base decisions and policies, and to influence opinion, in their respective spheres of interest. Privacy is therefore made a more salient issue simply to the extent that the quantity of social research being undertaken is growing. But this is not the only contributory cause.

Technological Change: the Computer Revolution

A most powerful influence upon both social research itself and concern with privacy has been the advent of the electronic computer. It is salutary to recall that this is a development of the very recent past, going back little further than 1950.[12] The ubiquity of the computer in the present-day world is a very recent development and has had an immediate influence upon privacy issues. One polemical work on the subject has indeed claimed that 'of all the threats posed to privacy in a rapidly changing and developing world, none is more sinister in its potential, more far reaching in its implications, than the computer'.[13]

What is it about computers which makes them so important? A few brief points will be made, since the subject is sometimes invested with a certain mystique. The first one is a negative one: the computer is not a 'mechanised brain', or a substitute for human thought. It does not substitute for the capacities of the human mind, rather it extends the human capability for storing information and performing certain operations upon it. It is probably most helpful to think of the computer as a means of *storing* information and *communicating* such information through a network. Additionally, the computer can perform certain simple comparing and calculating tasks with very high reliability and at extremely high speed.[14]

Thus, for example, a computer can store a record of several million pieces of information and search its files for one of these pieces (and find it) in a fraction of a second. But the information must be fed into it in a certain way, stored in a certain way and retrieved in a certain way.

It is simplest for the present discussion to treat the computer as a 'black box', into which data and signals are fed and out of which information is obtained in the form of output. There are several distinct stages in the operation of a computer system. Firstly, *input* must be prepared, often in numerical form and always in a pre-determined format for entry by machine. All information stored in a computer ultimately must be reduced to ones or zeros, and much of the work of computer specialists is in putting data (especially non-numeric data) in a form which the machine can accept. *Storage* of computer data inside the machine takes various forms. Basically, it is stored in *files*, which are sets of records about people in a particular category (for example, all people with criminal convictions). In this respect, these files are similar to the manually-maintained files of many bureaucratic organisations, except that they are stored in electronic form, must be accessed through the machine, are held in a very much smaller space, and require a name or some other personally identifiable label in order to retrieve them. *Processing* of data, and the *production* of *output*, takes place in response to orders given to the machine by computer programmers, who write instructions in a form acceptable to the machine with its binary logic. Output may be in printed or visual form (the latter on a display screen), and in modern computer systems can be provided at any point in the computer network, which may be physically remote from the actual computer where data is stored and calculations carried out.

What is so important is the enormously superior power which the computer offers for the convenient storage of masses of data and for speed in gaining access to, or in processing, such data. None of these functions are different in principle from those which can be performed manually by an army of clerks, maintaining written or printed records in hand-operated files. What makes computer systems qualitatively different is the size of the files which can be maintained, coupled with speed and ease of access. This speed, coupled with the capacity to store, combine, retrieve and transfer data, its flexibility and low unit cost, has major significance for privacy concerns.

Specifically, the advent of computer-handling of information makes easier the maintenance of extensive record systems, easily accessible from many distant points. They make it possible for data to be transferred quickly from one information system to another, much easier and more quickly than can be accomplished manually. They make it possible for data to be combined in ways which might not otherwise be practicable. And because the data are stored, processed and often transmitted in electronic form which is not directly intelligible, few people may know what is in their records or what is happening to them.[15]

The general implications of these developments for privacy are clearly considerable, though too broad to be dealt with here.[16] Their impact upon social research, which involves the processing and storage of a particular kind of information, is of interest for our subject and is considered in more detail in Part 4, but several general points need to be made at this stage. The impact of computers upon social research is not confined to record-keeping and the analysis of administrative data. The introduction of electronic data processing has also transformed data analysis of censuses and social surveys. Therefore, the devising of safeguards for computerised data applies to censuses and surveys as much as to administrative data. The need to devise and implement such safeguards is itself a difficult and technical question, with which a good deal of the literature is concerned. Public commissions in both Britain and the United States have examined these issues.

In addition to these discussions among specialists, there is a need to communicate safeguards to the general public. For example, in the 1981 British census, heads of households will be required to enter the name and address of each person on the census schedule. This information is required to check the completeness both of the enumeration and of information on each individual. However, these names and addresses will not be entered on the computer for data analysis.[17] Yet this will not be immediately apparent to the individual citizen completing the census, unless the point is also emphasised in the associated census publicity. As so often in safeguarding privacy, social researchers need to take steps to safeguard privacy and confidentiality *and* to be seen to be doing so. Not infrequently are they criticised when in fact they are doing the former without enough attention to the latter.

Public Concern About Privacy as an Issue

It is conceivable that the growth of social science and the computer revolution could have remained of narrow interest to technical specialists without raising public issues about privacy. It could have done so, but it did not. Privacy is today a public issue. Several contributors to this book comment on the public interest which there has been in the last twenty years in privacy *in general* as a social question. This must go some way to explaining why it has also become an issue in relation to social research.

A number of popular books, on both sides of the Atlantic, have appeared in the last fifteen years with titles such as *The Privacy Invaders, The Naked Society, The Invasion of Privacy, The Death of Privacy, The Data-Bank Society* and so on.[18] A number of more academic works have come out with titles such as *The Assault on Privacy, Privacy & Freedom, Data-Banks in a Free Society* and *Private Lives and Public Surveillance.*[19] This growing literature reflects increasing sensitivity by politicians, pressure groups, the media and the academic community to the general issue of privacy.

In Britain, for example, interest was sharply focused by the report of the government's committee on privacy (known as the Younger Committee, after its chairman), which was appointed in 1970 and reported in 1972.[20] This made a survey of privacy issues in a number of fields (including medical research but not specifically on social research) and also commissioned a social survey to investigate the importance of privacy in the public eye.

This survey, although only an appendix to the main report, is of interest in providing evidence of the importance attached, by a sample of the British public in 1971, to privacy as a social issue. The survey was conducted by OPCS in conjunction with a market research firm, interviewing a probability sample of 2000 people. A weighted sample of 1596, based on 1635 successful interviews, was used in the analysis.

One has strong methodological and conceptual reservations about the reliability and precision of the data, but they do support *prima facie* the argument that privacy is seen by the public as an important social issue. The relevant findings are shown in Tables 1.1 and 1.2, which also contain an explanation of the questions on which the data are based.

Forty-five per cent of respondents thought that protecting people's

TABLE 1.1 *Importance accorded to privacy in a national sample, 1971, compared to other general issues*

General issues (a)	Rating (b)		
Keeping down prices	4.42		
Reducing unemployment	4.22		
Stopping strikes	4.21		
Raising the old-age pension	4.01	*Protecting people's privacy*	
Improving health services	3.60	Extremely imp.	16%
Building more houses	3.55	Very imp.	29%
Protecting people's privacy	**3.39**	Quite imp.	38%
Building more schools	3.37	Not very imp.	15%
Protecting freedom of speech	3.19	Not at all imp.	3%
Providing more university places	2.52		

Notes

(a) Fixed-choice question listing items and asking respondents firstly to rank each item in order of importance and then, for each item, to answer the question: 'How important would you say . . . is at the moment? Would you say it is: extremely important; very important; quite important; not very important; not at all important?'

(b) The rating scores are averages for all respondents (total weighted sample = 1596) on the five-point scale, where

$$
\begin{aligned}
\text{extremely important} &= 5 \text{ points} \\
\text{very important} &= 4 \text{ points} \\
\text{quite important} &= 3 \text{ points} \\
\text{not very important} &= 2 \text{ points} \\
\text{not at all important} &= 1 \text{ point}
\end{aligned}
$$

Source: Social Survey carried out for the Younger Committee on Privacy, *Report of the Committee on Privacy*, Cmnd. 5012, London, HMSO, 1972, esp. pp. 230–1 and 245–6.

privacy was extremely important or very important. On average, privacy was rated more important than building more schools, protecting freedom of speech and providing more university places, and nearly as important as building more houses. Privacy as a general issue is clearly of great concern to many people. When seven specific social issues were posed, privacy was rated (Table 1.2) the most important of all seven, more important than protecting freedom of speech and protecting the freedom of the press, or of giving equal rights for women. Again, this provides further evidence that privacy is seen as an important social value in Britain.

TABLE 1.2 *Importance accorded to privacy in a national sample, 1971, compared to other social issues*

(A separate list to that in Table 1.1, again read out to respondents and scored in the same way.)

Social issue	Rating
Protecting people's privacy	**3.76**
Improving race relations	3.60
Protecting freedom of speech	3.64
Protecting the freedom of the press	3.42
Giving equal rights for women	3.12
Improving prison conditions	2.76
Ensuring fair treatment for gypsies	2.68

Source: as Table 1.1.

Evidence from the United States, summarised by Westin and Baker,[21] shows that privacy is an issue on which a substantial minority did feel concerned. In a Louis Harris poll of 1970, in answer to the question: 'Do you ever tend to feel that sometimes your sense of privacy is being invaded or not – that people are trying to find out things about you that are not any of their business?', thirty-four per cent said 'Yes', 62 per cent said 'No' and 4 per cent were undecided. When asked to specify violations of privacy which they had experienced personally, no one problem was pre-eminent. The breakdown shown in Table 1.3 is nevertheless of interest.

Out of ten possible privacy violations, two – the census and polling – are directly treated in this book, and two others– government tax returns and computers – relate to social research and privacy generally. It is significant that 14 per cent of respondents regarded the census as a violation of privacy, and 10 per cent public-opinion polling. This is consistent with more detailed evidence about the impact of privacy concerns upon social-survey research and censuses which is presented in Parts 2 and 3. Falling response rates to social surveys are attributed in part to concern about privacy. The public controversy which accompanied the conduct of population censuses in several countries in 1970/1 was a further indication that privacy and confidentiality are live issues in the conduct of contemporary social research.

TABLE 1.3 *Personal experiences with privacy invasions*

Violation of privacy	Is violated (percentage)	Not violated (percentage)	Not sure (percentage)
Computers which collect a lot of information about you	19	71	10
Business which sells you things on credit	19	76	5
Government tax returns	17	79	4
People looking in your windows	17	80	3
People listening in to your telephone conversations	15	81	4
People eavesdropping on your conversations with others	15	81	4
The government when it takes a census	14	84	2
Employment interviews	11	83	6
Neighbours who gossip about your family	10	86	4
Public-opinion polltakers	10	86	4

Source: Louis Harris International Poll, 1970, quoted in A. F. Westin and M. A. Baker, *Databanks in a Free Society*, New York, Quadrangle Books, 1972, p. 477.

Further light is thrown on public attitudes, less directly, by answers to a further question (in the Younger Committee's social survey) about the sensitivity of particular types of information. The respondents were asked: 'I would like to ask you about how you would feel if certain types of information were known about you. Would you object to any of the following being available to anyone who wanted to know?' The distribution of replies is shown in Table 1.4.

Striking a Balance Between Privacy and Social Inquiry

The present work seeks to analyse increasing concern with privacy

TABLE 1.4   *Sensitivity of different types of information*
in a national sample, 1971

Would object to availability of information about own	Percentage of respondents
Sex life	87
Income	78
Medical history	51
Political views	42
Telephone number	34
Address	33
Religious views	28
(Wife's) maiden name	18
Education	17
Occupation	12
Racial origin	10
Nationality	8

(Total weighted sample = 1596)

Source: Reports of the Younger Committee on Privacy, in *Databanks in a Free Society*, pp. 257–8 and 271–2.

issues in relation to the specific examples of social surveys and population censuses. In both, these concerns have affected, and will in future affect, the conduct of research and the feasibility of carrying out further work. What principles should guide research policy in weighing up the relative claims of the individual's right to privacy and the general right to free social scientific inquiry? This is not a work of moral philosophy nor of practical prescriptions. It does not, therefore, contain a statement of how the balance could or should be made. It may, nevertheless, be useful to enter a note of caution.

For in seeking to reconcile the claims of privacy with the claims of social science, one is struck by the intractable nature of the dilemma which this poses. The benefits which flow from science and from social science are frequently proclaimed by their practitioners. The importance of both is shown by the increasing resources directed to both by modern governments. Yet the claims of privacy are also strong. This is put most eloquently by Edward Shils in the last paragraph of Chapter 2: 'Intrusions on privacy are baneful because they interfere with an individual in his disposition of what belongs to him ... [They] belong to him by virtue of his humanity and civility. A society that claims to be both humane and civil is committed to their respect.'

However it is expressed, the antinomy is present. How does one 'strike a proper balance between the individual's personal privacy interests and society's information needs'?[22] What is the 'appropriate balance between the individual's fundamental right to privacy and society's need to know'?[23] 'The claim to privacy will always be embattled – its collision with the community's need to know is classic and continuous. Man has always lived in a community, and the community has always required some forfeiture of freedom, including that of privacy . . . At one time or another, privacy has yielded – as it must – to the positive group needs for security, for order, for sustenance, for survival.'[24]

There may be no simple solution to the striking of such a balance. As Martin Rein has pointed out, there are inherent difficulties in defining coherent social purposes in public policy. There are competing paradigms among those who interpret and investigate policy, and no satisfactory way of resolving differences between paradigms.

> There is no central, abiding, over-arching guiding principle that can fill the gaps in understanding, resolve the quandaries of action, order the conflicts of human purposes or resolve the conflicting interpretations of action which competing frameworks pose . . . these dilemmas are desirable because they pose moral choices and permit a debate about moral purposes. If there were no dilemmas in social action, there would be no opportunities for meaningful moral discourse in human affairs.[25]

An influential American statement of 1967 on privacy and behavioural research observed: 'neither the principle of privacy nor the need to discover new knowledge can supervene universally. As with other conflicting values in our society, there must be constant adjustment and compromise, with the decision as to which value is to govern in a given instance to be determined by the weighing of the costs and the gains – the cost in privacy, the gain in knowledge.'[26]

Though the tone is perhaps slightly pompous, Ruebhausen and Brim catch the dilemma precisely: 'Absolute rules do not offer solutions to conflict in values. What is needed is wisdom and restraint, compromise and tolerance, and as wholesome a respect for the dignity of the individual as the respect accorded the dignity of science.'[27] They go on to argue that the balance will not just find its own equilibrium. Regulation is necessary to achieve balance and sensitive awareness. 'It is not enough to be optimistic about the tensions be-

tween science and privacy. It is incumbent upon lawyer and scientist
to accommodate the goals of science with the claim to privacy, and to
help articulate the rules and concepts that will maintain both the productivity of science and the integrity of personality.'[28]

Principles Governing the Conduct of Social Research

How to safeguard social-research data against breaches of privacy
and confidentiality is discussed in detail in Part 4. The conclusion to
this introduction will consider briefly whether any general principles,
to form a backdrop to the chapters which follow, can be introduced to
anticipate that discussion. The responsibility of the social scientist in
this respect is clear, due primarily to the fact that 'the individuals,
groups and communities that provide the data for social research are
deficient in power relative to the other participants in the research
process'.[29] This is true of the research subject's position within the society at large and within the organisation conducting the research. It
is also true of his position of relative disadvantage in the research situation itself – face-to-face with the interviewer or census enumerator,
for instance.

The two most widely-canvassed general principles to provide guidance for the proper conduct of social research have been those of
informed consent to participate in research and adequate safeguards
for the confidentiality of data once it is collected.

Informed consent refers to the agreement of the research subject to
participate in the research. It was first enunciated at the Nuremberg
Trials, in relation to the notorious medical experiments on concentration camp inmates, in which, for example, subjects were immersed
in icy water for long periods to 'test' the possible survival of fighter
pilots brought down in the sea. The first Nuremberg principle is that
'the voluntary consent of the human subject is absolutely essential'.[30]
According to this principle, the subject must be competent, informed
about the purposes of the research, understanding or comprehending
of what he or she is told, and giving consent voluntarily and not under
any form of duress. The duty of conveying information about the research and ascertaining the quality of the consent rests with the investigator.[31]

The Nuremberg principles have been the main guide for codes relating to clinical research in medicine, where the principle of informed
consent has been most fully elaborated. That the issue is still a live one

is shown by the furore over the Tuskegee syphilis study in the United States in 1972, and the establishment by the Department of Health Education and Welfare of the National Commission for the Protection of Human Subjects in Biomedical and Behaviour Research.[32] In the social and behavioural sciences, the issue has been most carefully examined in relation to psychological experiments in the laboratory, and psychologists have been among the leading commentators on the problem.

The principle has clearly applicability to social research of other kinds, though its application is not without difficulty. In the first place, inquiries where legal compliance is required – notably the census – are not compatible with the principle. In practice, census-taking authorities and their political masters scrutinise particularly carefully the content of each census to ensure its public acceptability. In this respect, public scrutiny and accountability are a surrogate for individual consent. The census, however, is something of a special case. Difficulties about obtaining informed consent also arise in research where co-operation is voluntary and the inquiry is under the control of the investigator.

These difficulties are of at least three kinds. One is that to inform the subject fully about the purposes of the research may affect the reliability and validity of the data which is collected. Unlike most medical research, where treatment has a physical basis (for example, the taking of a drug), social research relies on observed behaviour or oral and written statements. Telling subjects the purpose of an experiment or the content of an attitude survey may affect their behaviour in the experiment or their verbal response to the survey. Examples are experimental studies of persuasibility and influence, and surveys of sensitive topics such as racial prejudice. A second difficulty is that of explaining adequately to the lay subject the technical content of the inquiry. Many technical features of research – for example, the measurement of personality by questionnaire methods or the multi-variate analysis of survey data – cannot be easily explained in lay terms. The third difficulty is what constitutes consent. When is it informed, when is it freely given? Like freedom, is it negative or positive? Is consent given by the absence of refusal to co-operate, by tacit acquiescence, by oral agreement or by written statement?[33]

These questions are further discussed in the chapters which follow, for example in Part 2 on survey research. It is clear, however, that a rigid and literal insistence on formal consent is in some circumstances unrealistic. Where attempts to obtain fully-informed individual consent are incomplete or not possible, public judgment must act as a surrogate for this. This is often of two kinds, obtaining the consent of representatives of the subjects of research (for example, from trade-union officials in employment research), and obtaining the approval or authorisation of one's scientific peers. Scrutiny by fellow-professionals to ensure the safeguarding of the well-being of human subjects is now well established in the medical field. The extent to which these practices can be extended to social research and how consent can be formalised and codified is touched on in Part 4. It is clear, nevertheless, that the proper conduct of research rests to a great extent on a relation of trust between subject and researcher, and upon the integrity of the researcher.

> Consent to participate in a study must be the norm before any subject embarks on the enterprise. Since consent must sometimes be given despite an admittedly inadequate understanding, the right to discontinue participation at any point must be stipulated in clear terms. When full information is not available to the subject and when no alternative procedures to minimise the privacy problem are available, the relationship between the subject and the scientist (and the latter's institution) must be based upon trust. This places the scientist and the sponsoring institution under a fiduciary obligation to protect the privacy and dignity of the subject who entrusts himself to them.[34]

Whether fully-informed consent as such is obtained or not, the scientist and his sponsoring institution must insure privacy by the maintenance of confidentiality.

This is the second principle of general importance. If the relationship between subject and researcher rests on trust, one important element in that relationship is the assurance that individual information will be treated confidentially and only published in aggregate form. An explicit or tacit assurance that the data provided in a census or survey are kept confidential is an integral part of securing public co-operation. In the case of the census, these assurances are of a particularly strong and legally binding kind, as is shown in Part 3.

Securing confidentiality can be achieved and ensured by various means. One is through the personnel conducting the research. In the case of the census, staff are legally obliged to maintain confidentiality of data. In other types of research, the integrity of the professional social scientist will assure both his informants and society at large that he will be responsible and will maintain the confidence of any individualised information given him. Scientific training and membership of a scientific community are means of imparting and reinforcing this integrity.

Other means of ensuring confidentiality are technical. In surveys, the name and address of respondents may not be entered on the interview schedule. In the census, the name and address may not be entered on the computer file. If total anonymity is not possible, the identity of individuals may be coded and separated from the set of responses. This code may be kept under very tight conditions of security. In certain cases, data may be destroyed after analysis, although the growth of data banks discourages this.

Issues relating to the legal protection of research data will be raised in Part 4. Social scientists by training are professionally opposed to making *individual* research data available to people such as journalists, police officers, private detectives or government agents. But there have been cases in which legal attempts have been made to subpoena such data, to compel social scientists to release individual data.[35] The question therefore arises whether social-research data other than census data require legal protection from revelation to third parties.

This links to the question of how best to regulate the scientific community, for infractions of confidentiality have occurred and will inevitably occur in future. Is professional self-regulation a sufficient safeguard? Or is some more public form of regulation, such as a data commission, more appropriate? These issues will be further examined in Part 4.

Conclusion

If one rejects either an out-and-out defence of privacy as an absolute value, or an unheeding belief that the search for knowledge overrides all else, then there are no simple solutions to the questions posed in this book. These dilemmas are considered from different points of view in the two chapters which follow. Edward Shils considers conceptual and developmental aspects.[36] The report of a study group from the British Association for the Advancement of Science asks: does research threaten privacy or does privacy threaten research?

2 Privacy in Modern Industrial Society*

Edward Shils

The idea of privacy is a vague one and difficult to get into a right perspective. Numerous meanings crowd in on the mind that tries to analyse privacy: the privacy of private property; privacy as a proprietary interest in name and image; privacy as the keeping of one's affairs to oneself; the privacy of the internal affairs of a voluntary association or of a business corporation; privacy as the physical absence of others who are unqualified by kinship, affection, or other attributes to be present; respect for privacy as respect for the desire of another person not to disclose or to have disclosed information about what he is doing or has done; the privacy of sexual and familial affairs; the desire for privacy as a desire not to be observed by another person or persons; the privacy of the private citizen in contrast with the public official; and these are only a few. But not only are there many usages of the concept of privacy; there are also the numerous related and contrasting terms: freedom, autonomy, publicity, secrecy, confidentiality, intimacy, and so forth. In the ensuing paragraphs, I will attempt to state a little more clearly what I mean by 'privacy' and to place it in relationship to other concepts.

* Reprinted with permission from a symposium on *Privacy* which appeared in *Law and Contemporary Problems*, **31,** Spring 1966, pp. 281–306, published by the Duke University School of Law, Durham, North Carolina. ©1966 Duke University.

Privacy is a 'zero-relationship' between two persons or two groups or between a group and a person. It is a 'zero-relationship' in the sense that it is constituted by the absence of interaction or communication or perception within contexts in which such interaction, communication, or perception is practicable – that is, within a common ecological situation, such as that arising from spatial contiguity or membership in a single embracing collectivity such as a family, a working group, and ultimately a whole society. Privacy may be the privacy of a single individual, it may be the privacy of two individuals, or it may be the privacy of three or numerous individuals. But it is always the privacy of those persons, single or plural, vis-à-vis other persons.

In any society, most of the population is private in a certain sense vis-à-vis most of the rest of the population. Mutual ignorance obtains; interaction is impossible because no structural or spatial context of interaction exists. But this separateness is not privacy in our sense. The phenomenon of privacy exists only in contexts in which interaction, communication, or perception is physically practicable and within the range of what can be expected of human beings. The situation must, therefore, be one in which the abrogation of privacy by intrusion from the outside or by renunciation from the inside is practically possible.

Thus, it is relevant to speak of privacy only where the isolation of a person or a group can be breached. We speak of privacy only where there is a feasible alternative to privacy, namely, where actions or words can be either withheld or disclosed, where a space can be inviolate or intruded on, where a situation can be disregarded or observed. Thus privacy presupposes the prior existence of a system of interaction among persons in a common space – it might be face-to-face interaction within a household, a neighbourhood, or village or within a unit in a corporate body such as a firm, an army, or a congregation; the presupposed system of interaction might be one in which there is ordinarily no face-to-face interaction between authority and subject within a corporate body like a large church, a large firm, a large army, or the state, and in which the interaction or perception is initiated by an agent of authority with the intention of intruding on the privacy of the subject.

What is privacy about? It is, for one thing, about information concerning the one person, the two persons, the three persons, etc. But what is the question concerning this information about which privacy might or might not exist? It is a matter of the possession and flow of information. We say that privacy exists where the persons whose actions engender or become the objects of information retain possession of that information, and any flow outward of that information from the persons to whom it refers (and who share it where more than one person is involved) occurs on the initiative of its possessors. This means that other persons do not come into possession of the information, they do not observe the actions that are the objects from which such information is generated, nor do they receive it from records (photographs, documents, or recordings) or from other persons who have observed the actions in question. Privacy in one of its aspects may therefore be defined as the existence of a boundary through which information does not flow from the persons who possess it to others. The actions of the former are not reported to, or observed or recorded or otherwise perceived by, the latter.

What is the decisive element in a breach of the boundary that defines the area of privacy? It is the acquisition or transmission of information without the voluntary consent or initiative of those whose actions and words generate the information. Where the latter disclose the information entirely voluntarily and on their own initiative, we speak of a sharing of privacy. Where the information is acquired by manipulation, deception, coercion, or through a market mechanism, we speak of a disruption of or intrusion into privacy. Voluntariness on the part of the person or persons whose privacy is in question is an essential component.

The information which is in question here refers to any events that occur in the private sphere. There are past and present relationships of personal affinity and hostility, of friendship and love and hatred, erotic relationships or practices, the primordial relationships of spouses, of parents and children, of siblings, of kinsmen, and of neighbours. The information might be about the internal affairs of private corporate bodies, the achievements, failures, and rewards of individuals in such bodies.

Let us now consider the position of privacy in modern urban societies. We will begin with European and North American societies in about the third quarter of the nineteenth century.

It has often been said by sociologists who have studied urban society that it freed men and women from the oppressive moral opinion of village and rural society. It increased indifference to most aspects of the behaviour of most of one's fellow citizens; in so doing, it increased the amount of privacy that they enjoyed – by 'amount', meaning the proportion of their total range of activity and thought that was disclosed only to those to whom the actor chose to disclose it. Indifference was, of course, fostered by large numbers and by residential and occupational mobility, which habituated human beings to a condition in which they could live in relative freedom from the scrutiny of others and could control the flow of information about themselves largely at their own discretion.

Why did indifference increase? It was not a function of a dulling of sensibility and sympathy; it was, rather, a consequence of the expansion and diversification of sensibility. The urban environment was more stimulating. Politics, culture, individual careers and ambitions, all drew attention out of the narrow primordial sphere and turned it outward, toward public things.

The deflection of attention was helped by a number of ecological changes which were associated with urbanisation and industrialisation. The diminishing significance of handicrafts and of agriculture, and the increasing proportion of the population employed in factories and offices, meant also an increasing proportion whose place of work and place of residence were made more distant from each other. The separation of place of residence from place of work, and the occasional change of place of residence, permitted and sometimes enforced by the rapid growth of cities and by the change in the character of districts within cities, meant that many persons lived only segmentally and for relatively short periods within the range of scrutiny of a given group of neighbours. There was too much else to do and too little time for the focusing and penetration of curiosity into the lives of neighbouring families hidden behind thick walls, behind thick curtains and closed doors. Contacts between human beings became more segmented.

A greater element of voluntariness, arising out of personal affinity or affection, entered into life. Friendship and love took a somewhat larger place in the economy of human life and primordial compulsion a smaller place. Hence personal private matters came with greater frequency to be voluntarily shared, while indifference to those with whom such bonds did not exist resulted in a diminished curiosity and intrusiveness in the affairs of other families and individuals. Thus the privacy of personal and primordial relationships was furthered and sustained by the urban environment.

Alongside the basic ecological and economic changes, several other factors contributed to this efflorescence of privacy in the third quarter of the nineteenth century. One of these was the emergence of a conception of 'respectability' among the urban working classes of the industrial countries. Ambition, frugality, sexual propriety, an orderly familial life, became ideals that were manifested in well-conducted households with sharply defined boundaries vis-à-vis neighbouring families. 'Scandalous' behaviour was to be avoided; where it could not be avoided, it was regarded as imperative that it be 'hushed up' so that neighbours would not learn about it. The demand for and the practice of familial privacy were a common occurrence in the respectable working (and lower-middle) classes. 'Nosiness' was abhorred; the 'nosy Parker' became the object of revulsion.

A puritanical ethos gave another impetus to privacy. It not only emphasised each man's responsibility for his own soul and the well-being and propriety of his own family but also encouraged him to be ambitious. In doing so, it focused his attention on a remote goal and thereby diverted his attention from his neighbours. The womenfolk, who might not have been so ambitious and who were more domestically confined, were, however eager they might have been to penetrate into the affairs of their neighbours, correspondingly eager to seal off their families, to draw a boundary about their household, and to avoid the disclosure of domestic affairs. Ready though one might be to find out about one's neighbours, the unwillingness to allow one's neighbours to know about oneself made for discretion in informing neighbours and for care to prevent anything that might conceivably be derogatory from emerging beyond the walls of one's residence and garden. There was not just a preoccupation with the improvement of the status of one's family but an equal desire to avoid any action that might be injurious to the estimation in which the family held itself and wished to be held by others. There grew up, alongside and underlying these concerns, a sense of the inviolateness of what went on within the family.

The growth of individuality, the sense of one's identity as an individual, likewise supported the belief that one's actions and their history 'belonged' to the self which generated them and were to be shared only with those with whom one wished to share them.

The situation had not always been like this. When men lived in villages over periods of many years they inevitably became well known to their fellow villagers. Small variations in public conduct could easily be interpreted as expressive of changes in that sphere of life which was not directly visible. Each man in a sense was the possession of his neighbours. It was difficult to escape the scrutiny and the imagination of others. Urbanisation and industrialisation changed this to a considerable degree – but, of course, not completely.

The growth of literacy and increased education, and the gradual involvement of larger and larger sections of the adult population in education and politics, extended the radius of attention. People did not cease to be interested in their neighbours; but they had to contend with the increased resistance of their neighbours to being known and with increased difficulties in knowing about them. Many more persons became interested in affairs more remote than the affairs of their neighbours. The intense desire to penetrate into the affairs of one's neighbours was probably attenuated by the increased interestingness of the affairs of the larger world. This made for a greater ease in the maintenance of privacy.

The growth of religious sects in Protestant countries also fostered privacy because it added another element of heterogeneity to any given district. The attendance of the population of a particular district at a greater diversity of churches within that district further complicated the criss-crossing of lines of separation beyond what was necessarily entailed in the separation of place of residence from place of work.

On top of all this, governments became increasingly liberal and constitutional. The 'night-watchman' state set as its goal the prevention of collisions among its citizens. The respect for private property that the state was concerned to enforce helped to stiffen a general regard for privacy, and the ethos of economic individualism worked in the same direction. The result of all these developments was a great increase in the amount of privacy.

Of course, privacy was not a totally new phenomenon in the history of human society, but the growth to predominance of the northwestern European Protestant culture and its diffusion to the North American hemisphere and Australia meant also that civilisation had shifted its centre from Mediterranean and tropical climes, where much of life was lived out of doors. In societies in which heat, populousness, and poverty cause much of daily life to be lived out of doors and much of indoor domestic life to be lived in conditions of severe overcrowding of numerous persons into small spaces – into one or a few rooms – much more of life is visible than in colder climates and more prosperous countries. It is not that there is no sense of individual or familial privacy in these societies – there is in practically all societies – but rather that the limited physical or ecological opportunities for privacy are small, the culture prizes it less, and human beings do not demand it so much as they did in Western societies in the third quarter of the nineteenth century. In those latter societies, the ecological supports of privacy were stronger than they had ever been before, the economic and political systems favoured it, the culture was congenial to it, and it became integral to the prevailing moral outlook. No class of persons except scattered and unorganised gossips had an interest in breaching the barriers which defined the privacy of individuals and groups.

What we have said above applies largely to the upper sections of the working classes, the middle classes, and the elites of the period in question. There was also a large unskilled working class, immigrant and native. Among these, families lived under very crowded conditions; many persons shared one room, many families shared common facilities such as water taps, toilets, and baths. There was little opportunity for individual or familial privacy. Much of their nonworking time, especially in summer, was spent on the streets. Local gin mills, saloons, cafes were the scenes of their leisure time. Most of their members probably regarded this as a normal condition, and only the most sensitive found it painful to bear. Awareness about the doings of one's neighbours, the gratification of impulses of curiosity about and malice toward them, were perhaps among the main pleasures available to the more respectable who did not go in for brawling and drunkenness.

But if the poorer sections of the working class had little privacy with respect to their neighbours, they were pretty well left alone by the public authorities. They had to divulge a little bit of information about their numbers, occupations, ages, and so forth, to the census. Except for very occasional interventions by the police in the event of a serious brawl or a murder, they were left alone by the government. Such limited social legislation as there was did not entail the collection of much information from them. In America, the immigrant quarters and the local professional politician were still only emerging; there was little of the 'poor basket' charity which was later developed by philanthropists and ward politicians and which opened the private affairs of a family to outsiders. The mania of governments for information was still in a nascent state.

Finally, it should be pointed out that, even in the most industrialised and urbanised countries at this time, a great part of the population still lived from agriculture, either in villages or in the open country. In the latter, as throughout much of human history, corporate familial privacy was high, individual privacy was probably slight. In villages, there was much mutual scrutiny; tale-bearers, scandalmongers, and chroniclers of disgrace and misfortune were well established. On the other hand, the isolation of villages from each other meant that if anyone did come into one from the outside, his past remained his own possession. Government was as uninquisitive in the countryside as it was in the great cities.

* * *

Many changes took place in the half century that succeeded the 'golden age of privacy'. The trend toward industrialisation and urbanisation continued. Increasing prosperity and a higher standard of living afforded somewhat better housing conditions and therewith more individual privacy and more familial privacy as well. Occupational and residential mobility permitted and fostered escape from watchful eyes. The decreasing proportion of unskilled labour in the industrial working class meant an extension of the culture of 'respectability'. Thus, as far as the infringements of privacy by equals were concerned, the situation was rather like it was in the earlier age.

But it is not only the practice of privacy by equals within a narrow radius that interests us here. Privacy is also affected by the activities of those who stand at the centre of society, in positions of authority in political, administrative, and cultural institutions. Here a very considerable change in the situation of privacy occurred.

One of the ways of estimating the changed position of privacy since the golden age is to examine the development of those institutions at the centre of society which regard it as their task to intrude on privacy. The main intruders from the centre were popular journalism, private police and investigators, the specialists of personnel recruitment in large-scale private business, and the practitioners of psychological and, to a much smaller extent, sociological research.

The fact that the popular press was able to consolidate its position among the large new literate public was evidence enough that the previous expansion of privacy did not represent a unilinear trend in the course of which the human race would divest itself more and more of its concern to intrude into the privacy of others. The very lengthening of the radius of attention made possible by literacy and education gave a new instrument to the desire to penetrate into the privacy of others. Frustrated as it was locally by the barriers of walls and doors and the very deeply-rooted barrier thrown up by 'respectability', the hunger to subject others who were more remote to one's own scrutiny found new stimulus and sustenance through the popular press.

This early stage of the development of mass society was also a period of exfoliation of revolutionary movements on the Continent of Europe. This had numerous repercussions in the United States and Great Britain as well as on the Continent, although neither of the former had a revolutionary movement of any consequence. Vague apprehensions and acute fears of bomb-throwing anarchists were a major feature of the upper and upper-middle class culture of the 1890s and the first decade of the present century. In the United States this was aggravated by the violence of the conflicts between industrialists and their employees. Industrial police, 'coal and iron police', 'railway police', and private operatives came into existence on behalf of private property. They were the private property owners' means of self-help. Whereas in continental Europe such police were part of the state apparatus, in the United States they were to a substantial extent private enterprises. They were often established by former governmental police officials, and, once the pattern became established, their numbers multiplied. In Europe a police official could cease being an official only if he ceased being a policeman; in the United States this was not so. They performed not only the ordinary police functions of guarding property and supervising public places within and around industrial plants; they also performed 'undercover operations', penetrating into organisations by pretending to be sympathetic devotees of the cause of the organisation.

The changes in the mores of Western Europe and America which made divorce more permissible, while the legal obstacles to it still remained, also contributed to the growth of the investigative profession.

The establishment of a professional interest in the breaching of the boundaries of personal privacy was furthered by the simultaneous growth of mass-production industry based on semi-skilled labour and the growth of scientific academic psychology in the second and third decades of the present century. Employers, distrustful of their actual and potential employees, in whose capacity, loyalty, and honesty they had little confidence, were greatly attracted by the claims of psychology. The use of intelligence and vocational aptitude tests, which were first applied on a large scale for military purposes, helped to set the stage for the acceptance of 'personality inventories'.

Psychology as a subject of research and teaching in American universities did not owe its intellectual origin to these developments in American economic and social structure. It was one of the numerous interests imported from Germany when American universities drew their inspiration from the universities of that country. But once it became established, it responded to the American situation. Aptitude and intelligence testing, the psychology of personnel or industrial psychology, soon found a place in the American psychology syllabus and assumed a prominent position in the agenda of psychological research. (It was, in the 1930s and 1940s, joined by clinical psychology and the academic adaptations of psychoanalysis.)

The professional personnel manager and the university-trained psychologist naturally had a vested interest in the cultivation of these practices, and the apparent success of the Taylor movement on the physical side of the management of industrial labour power also produced a conviction in the employer that it was in every respect to his advantage. It was efficient and therefore profitable; it was scientific and therefore modish; and it appeared also by its reliability to divest him of weighty moral responsibilities.

Such was the situation as it developed in the United States from the last decade of the nineteenth century. Class antagonism, increased disrespect for authority, the growing sophistication of academic psychology, and the growth of literacy throughout the population had resulted in the creation of a number of occupations which specialised in intrusion into personal privacy, and which – as practitioners of any occupation usually do – regarded their activities as morally proper and socially useful. They were, moreover, numerous enough, and they served rich enough and powerful enough interests, for them to impose themselves at the margins of public consciousness as pillars of society.

*   *   *

The period since the end of the Second World War has witnessed a powerful reinforcement of those hitherto well accepted and generally uncriticised intruders. The war itself, and the Cold War which followed it, created new organisations of specialists in intrusions and new arguments for their indispensability. Espionage and counter-espionage flourished on public funds as never before. The preoccupation with 'security' provided another motive for intrusion into personal private affairs and the occasion for the formation of another vested institutional interest in the penetration of the private sphere of numerous individuals. The 'security programme' – governmental and private – gave a further impetus to the development of the occupations concerned to intrude into personal privacy. Familial relationships, friendships, personality qualities, sexual practices, relations with neighbours, recreational preferences – all extending far into the past – became objects of detailed scrutiny.

On top of all this comes the factual hunger of all government bodies. As the range of government activities widens, and as they reach more deeply into the structure of society, government departments gather more and more information about the persons for whom they provide services or whom they seek to control. There is nothing new in these information-gathering activities as such. Governments have always sought to obtain information about their subjects – the Roman census, the Anglo-Norman Domesday Book, and the Nuremberg and Swiss cantonal censuses of the fifteenth century are illustrative of the antiquity of governmental information-gathering. When the modern liberal order was envisaged by the Benthamite radicals in Great Britain early in the nineteenth century, inspection and reporting were the devices they foresaw to discover the effectiveness of reformative legislation. The interest of a government in examining its society in a matter-of-fact way and in publishing reports of what is observed testified merely to its interest in framing its policies in an enlightened way and in enlightening public opinion regarding the grounds and the efficacy of its decisions.

These considerations are still of great influence in the government's information-gathering. Two developments have intervened since the early nineteenth century. The first is the wealth of governments, coupled with the present-day belief in the central importance of social-science research. Governments can now employ many persons with social-science training and interests. For these persons, gathering information is a legitimation of their existence. With the mighty resources of the government at their disposal, it is only natural for them to collect all the information they can, particularly since it can be justified by the needs of rational administration, control, and service.

From this assembly of facts by various government departments, it is only a step, which some have already proposed, to the collation of all the information gathered about each individual into a computer-equivalent of a dossier. It is all conceived with innocent intentions, as if it were both necessary and just that each individual member of society should be exhaustively known by the government. They have in mind no particular or immediate use for these computer 'dossiers'. They just think that it is a 'good idea' to have them – so far have they strayed from respect for privacy.

Another factor in making it appear normal and necessary to collect, both openly and clandestinely, personal private information is the 'dishonesty crisis' in industry. Thefts by employees have been regarded as on the increase, as has the divulgence of industrial secrets. Since ordinary police practices were inadequate, the testing of prospective and present employees was adduced as a supplement. In addition, other methods of gathering information were applied in an effort, which has not been notably successful, to halt the ravages of the 'dishonesty crisis'. The very persistence of the crisis is deemed a justification for further intrusions into privacy.

The development of empirical social research in the period since the Second World War is relevant to our consideration of the vicissitudes of privacy in contemporary society. Ever since sociology became an empirical subject, it has lived in the presence of the privacy of the persons it studied. The technique of participant-observation involved the possibility of intrusions into personal privacy by direct interrogation – as does the contemporary survey technique. It also permitted, through long dwelling in the community studied, considerable observation of personal private actions which the person observed did not intend to disclose. As far as I can recall, until about 1955 there was never any question of the ethical status of this sort of research. It was generally understood that the anonymity of particular informants was to be observed, but nothing more was required.

The shift away from participant-observation toward sample surveys as the main mode of sociological fieldwork has been attended by a much more penetrating inquisitiveness into the personal private sphere. This is partly the result of psychoanalysis, which commended to the attention of sociologists phases of conduct with which they had not previously dealt. The progress and enlarged self-confidence of sociologists have also encouraged this, as well as the greater impersonality of the new techniques. The new techniques of sociological research, by restricting the tie between the investigator and the person investigated, have reduced inhibitions against intrusion into personal privacy. The absence of a personal relationship between investigator and the investigated weakened the barriers to penetration and intrusion which the quasi-personal ties in some way supported. The partial dissolution of traditional inhibitions regarding discussion of sexual practices opened a whole new front of intrusion into the personal private sphere. What was once prurience and voyeurism has now become 'scientific curiosity'. What was once 'exhibitionism' is now co-operation in 'scientific research'. What was once regarded as the subject of 'blue films' and 'circuses' is now called a 'research situation'. The result is the same – an invasion of personal privacy of an extreme character, more elaborate and naturally better documented than its pre-'scientific' predecessors.

*   *   *

In the course of the past quarter-century, certain trends in intrusion into personal privacy that date back to the last part of the nineteenth century have been accentuated. The increase that we have noted has been the accomplishment mainly of certain sectors of the elite of our society among the highly educated and literate and those who occupy authoritative roles. Intrusions into privacy have been so intertwined with the pursuit of objectives that are unimpugnable in our society, such as freedom of the press, the protection of public order, the prevention of subversion, the protection of private property, and industrial and administrative efficiency, that each extension of the front has been accepted as reasonable and useful. Each objective has appeared, to large sectors of the elites at the centre of society, to be well served by the particular form of intrusion into personal privacy that their agents have chosen for the purpose.

The movement has not been all in one direction. Certain sections of the legal profession, the judiciary, and legislative bodies have repeatedly attempted, since the end of the Second World War, to restrict and diminish the amount of intrusion into personal privacy. In the past few years, the enormities of intrusion have activated a quite new concern to protect personal privacy. But the resistance thus far is largely an elite resistance.

Intrusions into personal privacy are part of the currency of present-day society. Even though the government's intrusions, because they are usually held secret or confidential by their official custodians, do not give the pleasure that is given by those in the media of the press, daily and periodical, and the television, they are accepted as having the same legitimacy as laws, taxes, and trade-union fees. They are regarded as not necessarily agreeable but probably right and in any case inevitable.

The present concern for privacy does not rest on the belief that every individual or that every primary group must be a windowless monad. Communion is a good as much as individual autonomy. Self-transcendence is as essential to man's existence as the dignity of self-hood or individuality. The present concern for privacy does not absolutise privacy.

It is also to be recognised that the personal privacy of individuals and groups among their peers and intrusions into personal privacy among peers are not a great issue. Personal privacy among peers is as strongly entrenched as most individuals who possess it wish to make it. And in so far as it is not, most of the intrusions, which do not involve the new technology of intrusion, are beyond the bounds of control. At least they cannot be controlled by anyone except the persons or groups whose personal privacy is intruded upon.

Privacy has become a problem in the past few decades not because the human race has gone mad and wishes to renounce a valuable feature of existence. On the contrary, there is still a great deal of attachment, both in daily practice and in principle, to privacy, and that attachment is perhaps not less, and is perhaps even more, than in previous times.

Privacy has become a problem because it has become engulfed in the expansion of the powers and ambitions of elites and in the difficulties that they encounter in attempting to govern and protect and please vast collectivities.

It is not that some of these intrusions into personal privacy are not necessary and justified. The tasks which the electorate wishes modern governments to perform do require much information; industrial enterprises must seek to be efficient; the mass media must entertain as well as enlighten; public order must be established and maintained and subversion prevented; systematic empirical study of human society must be cultivated. Nonetheless, even though one grants that the common good cannot be realised in a society consisting only of private entities and that the common good requires some restrictions on the right of privacy, one is also impressed that many justifications in terms of the common good in very many of the instances of intrusion into privacy are mendacious in the extreme. A great deal of the intrusion into personal privacy is not only an immoral affront to human dignity, it is also quite useless and unnecessary from any serious standpoint. Much of it is unnecessary to effective government, efficient administration, national security, the progress of knowledge, or industrial productivity. Much of it is the frivolous self-indulgence of the professionals of intrusion.

When we contend for privacy in contemporary society, it is not that we are anxious lest *all* privacy be obliterated. That is not the problem. Obviously, each individual will always be private to most other people in his society; and even when his personal private affairs are penetrated, the knowledge so gathered will not be universally diffused. Such extreme possibilities are of no relevance to our discussion because they are so improbable.

The significant intrusions either affect small numbers of individuals whose personal privacy is intruded upon because they are allegedly of 'public interest', or because an ill-wisher seeks to 'get something on' them. Or else they affect large numbers, although segmentally; some authorities wish to be assured of their capacity for acting efficiently and loyally on behalf of the interests of those authorities.

Sometimes harm is done by these intrusions. Individuals are made unhappy and occupational opportunities are denied them. Sometimes it can be argued that they are injured financially by such intrusions. But these considerations appear to be of secondary importance. Intrusions on privacy are baneful because they interfere with an individual in his disposition of what belongs to him. The 'social space' around an individual, the recollection of his past, his conversation, his body and its image, all *belong* to him. He does not acquire them through purchase or inheritance. He possesses them and is entitled to possess them by virtue of the charisma which is inherent in his existence as an individual soul — as we say nowadays, in his individuality — and which is inherent in his membership in the civil community. They belong to him by virtue of his humanity and civility. A society that claims to be both humane and civil is committed to their respect. When its practice departs from that respect, it also departs to that degree from humanity and civility.

3 Does Research Threaten Privacy or Does Privacy Threaten Research?*

British Association Study Group

The sharp increase in the collection of personal information, combined with the development of advanced computers that can store and process this information in previously unimagined ways, has caused a steadily growing concern. Responding to public and professional concern, the British Association for the Advancement of Science set up a study group on privacy. It became clear that the general problem had been discussed in some detail over the past few years. There are a number of books on the subject and many countries have had one or more government committees. In the United Kingdom, the Rt Hon Kenneth Younger's Committee on Privacy issued its report (Cmnd 5012) in 1972. But one important component of the data profile has not been given full consideration, data compiled by researchers.

Most of the data on file – and traditionally the cause for greatest concern – is in normal administrative records: school, military, employment, bank, credit, police, etc. But researchers are collecting ever larger amounts of personal information as well, aided, as are the ad-

* Report of a British Association Study Group under the chairmanship of Lord Ritchie-Calder. First published as a pamphlet, 1974. Reprinted with the permission of the British Association for the Advancement of Science. ©1974 British Association for the Advancement of Science.

ministrators, by ever larger computers. This was brought home to many people when some 1971 British Census questions were justified primarily on research grounds.

Although research data can give a far more detailed and intimate picture of a person than the information normally data-banked, few people have really been concerned. This study group was composed of researchers who actually use this data and writers and civil liberties advocates who had a special concern for the problem. The group decided that its job was to shed light on this ignored corner of the data-bank problem, to look ahead as best it could to the implications for the future, and to attempt concrete suggestions.

This study group did not ignore the general problems of data banks and privacy. Rather, it assumed that the general problems will require an overall solution that takes into account many special problem areas. Thus, it chose to look at the area where it had knowledge. It also assumed that some sort of privacy or data-bank legislation is inevitable and necessary, and hoped through this report to encourage the inclusion of research uses of data in that legislation.

In the short term, however, it concluded that there were actions which researchers and administrators could take without legislation. Thus, this report is also aimed at those who conduct and administer research using personal information.

Whose Hand is in the File Drawer?

As modern science tackles increasingly complex human problems, its demands for personal information grow inexorably. Patterns of disease and social relations often lie buried in masses of apparently irrelevant details of people's lives and the way they go about their business. Solving these problems often means permitting the scientist to violate our privacy to a considerable degree.

The scientist is in a unique position because he or she has both the time and the training to study the world around us. Traditionally, society has recognised this position by giving the scientist a remarkable freedom of access to information. In exchange, society has tacitly expected three things:

  (1) in the long term the results will be beneficial;
  (2) in the conduct of the study, the subject will not be harmed;

(3) the scientist will respect the privacy of the subjects and not reveal personal information to third parties.

Despite some serious erosions, this relationship remains intact. But scientists can no longer take the relationship for granted, because they appear increasingly unable to keep their half of the bargain because of the vulnerability of the data they collect. It seems clear that the subjects of research need more power to protect themselves, and scientists need more power to protect their subjects. If they do not get this power, we could reach the stage where people simply refuse to co-operate with scientists. At present, there are only a few rumblings in limited areas, such as people refusing to co-operate with the census or refusals to permit some researchers into few United States ghetto areas. In practice, most people seem likely to co-operate come what may. But the situation could become bad enough to distort results, and prevent research that would be clearly beneficial.

There is reason to be concerned both about the invasion of privacy and about the impact of research. Although they are intertwined, one can look at them separately.

Public fears of privacy have been linked, in part, to the rapid rise in data collection and filing. Although the primary worry has been in the area of administrative data, the rise there has been paralleled by a rise in the collection of research data. Indeed, some of the data collection, processing and storage techniques developed for administrative files will be invaluable for researchers, especially when linked with modern statistical and research techniques.

There seem to be five areas of concern directly linking privacy and research:

(1) the increasing compulsory collection of research data, particularly the census;

(2) the use by researchers of files in schools, hospitals and elsewhere which were collected for other purposes;

(3) the building up of large stores of personal information which might be tapped by the police, employers, or others to whom research subjects would not give this information voluntarily;

(4) the use of research data for the study of topics very different from the one the subject had in mind when he gave the data;

(5) the fear that as more data are collected about groups, policy decisions will be increasingly based on the data picture of the group

rather than on contact with real people.

The growing sophistication of scientists about themselves and the public about scientists is bound to raise new questions about the impact of research, and particularly about the traditional belief that it will ultimately be beneficial and not be immediately harmful. This will be emphasised by awareness in three areas:

(1) scientists have prejudices and biases like anyone else, and thus are not neutral or infallible;
(2) research often involves conflicting interests, and thus the results are sometimes harmful to what one or more groups sees as its own interest;
(3) the sources of funds and peer pressure as to what is 'good science' sometimes combine to lead to fashions in research and choices that benefit some groups and not others.

In some cases it is simply a problem that the 'truth' hurts, sometimes it is that scientists failed to get at the heart of the matter. But in extreme cases, it can mean that research aids the government or an employer to control groups in certain ways rather than meeting what members of the groups see as their real need.

Fears about privacy and the impact of research about people are not significant yet – but they will be. Not all of them will be rational or valid, but they will be founded on real basic difficulties that need correcting.

What is Research Data?

Perhaps the biggest and most clearly defined fear is that data will leak from researchers' files and find its way into the hands of people who will use it to harm the original subjects, or it may be added to the dossiers that many people feel sure are already being compiled about them.

The problem can be made clearer by looking at a politically and socially sensitive area of current interest, women who have had more than one abortion. This group is important for research in three ways. First, the percentage of abortions being performed on women who have already had one reflects to some measure the extent to which abortion is used as a conscious form of contraception, and thus is important in determining official policy and legislation on abortion. This statistic, for example, was one of the more important ones in the recent Report of the Committee on the Working of the Abortion Act. Second, medical researchers would like to follow-up women with more than one abortion to find out what special problems or complications occur in order to provide proper care for this group. Third, social scientists would like to look at this group to see what action, such as providing free contraceptives, might reduce the incidence of multiple abortions.

On the other hand, women in this group could justifiably fear that having more than one abortion will attach a social stigma to them. It could be particularly difficult if a husband or boyfriend were to learn from such a file of a previous unknown pregnancy. Many women might fear that social-welfare benefits would be affected if a social worker knew about multiple abortions. And this could be taken as evidence of immorality or irresponsibility and used to deny a woman a job or promotion – possibly without her being told because the prospective employer might not want to raise a sensitive issue.

The problem arises because researchers need to collect precisely the information that, if it leaks out, could cause trouble. And this fear would surely be enough to cause some women to withhold such information from a researcher.

In practice, however, the most likely source of such information would not be from the women themselves, but from data collected for administrative purposes by a doctor, hospital, or clinic. Collected into the files of a GP, most people (correctly or incorrectly) would consider the information safe. Even in the typically voluminous files of a hospital, most people would not be too worried. But if the records of a large number of GPs or hospitals were stored in a computer, or if a special file were created on women with more than one abortion, then people would begin to worry. But that is precisely what researchers do – collect data taken for administrative purposes and put it into a special research file which is potentially much more powerful and dangerous.

This new file need not be large or computerised. It could be kept in notebooks by a sociologist doing an in-depth study of a dozen women with their knowledge and consent. But it could also be a regional computer data bank containing hundreds of thousands of records, which few of the subjects even know exists.

From this example, two points can be made:

(1) the same basic data can be used for a variety of purposes, but it is generally possible to distinguish clearly between administrative uses and research uses;

(2) researchers can make data potentially more dangerous by pulling together information on a large number of people or by compiling a lot of information on a few people.

The distinction between research uses can be spelled out in terms of purpose: administrators want to know about named individuals in order to make decisions about them, while researchers want to draw conclusions about groups. (In this sense, 'administrator' includes the family doctor who looks in his file to see what medication he gave a patient months ago.) Researchers, however, also use records of named individuals when they wish to follow them through time. But the important distinction is that the researcher uses names only for purposes of linking files, and when the day is done can discard the names and work with an anonymous record.

Unfortunately, the distinction is often only between research and administrative *uses*, rather than between research and administrative *data*. The same files and the same computers are often used for both, and data is sometimes put into administrative files for purely research purposes. The Working Party concluded that this practice is often unnecessary and must be considered unacceptable: the anonymity and security of research data will be protected only by drawing a sharp line between research and administrative data, both in collection and in use. Once that separation has been made, it is then possible to look at the two halves separately.

For administrative data, where the impact on the individual can be extremely important, the Study Group noted that all of the widely advocated rules were clearly necessary, particularly the right to know of the existence of a file, and to see and correct it. But the Study Group also felt that this topic had been well covered elsewhere, and that its job was to look at research data. Research data is clearly different in the respect that its accuracy is relatively unimportant to the subject. Its accuracy is important to the researcher, but he can accept a certain percentage error, and thus a few erroneous records. Accuracy in research data becomes important to the subject if the data leaks from the file. It has already been noted that this is the real fear, and thus the major problem is how to prevent leakage.

In light of this, it is worth distinguishing between identifiable and anonymous data. In the abortion example, little harm would be done if someone saw a medical record of a woman with two abortions if they could not find out who the woman was. Thus, the fear is only of identifiable records leaking. Two points should be made about the word 'identifiable': first, it can apply to groups as well as individuals (for example, it could be quite harmful to make public the information that a particular housing estate had a high rate of multiple abortions), and second, it refers to any record in which by some means the subject can be identified – it is not restricted to a record with a name attached.

If the researcher is to earn the continued co-operation of the general public, he or she must respect the basic right of privacy by keeping identifiable personal information confidential. The Study Group concluded that the overriding rule must be that

> The researcher must never collect identifiable information without the explicit informed consent of the subject, and that he or she must never pass that information to anyone else in identifiable form without explicit informed consent.

Although this rule is already often acknowledged, in a large number of cases it is not followed.

The converse of this rule is that if the researcher is to give or receive personal information without consent of the subject, then it must be in anonymous form, stripped of all identification. In most cases this is clearly adequate; records can just as well be identified by arbitrarily assigned numbers as by names. The only need for names is if some sort of follow-up is required, in which case the person will probably need to be informed.

This rule has two aspects: the protection of information and the obtaining of consent. Both clearly need new procedures if they are to be carried out. In the next section, a proposal for a research data bank offers a radically new way to protect information; in the following section a Code to protect research subjects lays down rules for obtaining informed consent.

Locking the Data Bank

The greatest threat to the traditional relationship between researchers and the general public would appear to be the danger of leakage of identifiable data from research files. It would be possible to apply many of the same rules which are suggested to protect administrative data banks, but it is clear that they are neither strong enough nor totally relevant. Instead, the Working Party proposed a much simpler and radically different concept: the creation of a special form of *research data bank* which would house research data separate from all administrative data, and which would have distinct and, eventually, legally enforceable rules.

The research data bank would have four properties:

(1) Data would be for research purposes only – it could not be used for any administrative purpose. The data could never be used to the personal detriment of the subject, and under no circumstance would information about named or identified individuals be available to any private or government agency.

(2) The data bank would be licensed by the government.

(3) Data would be separated from names and other identifying information in such a way that it is easy to update a file but difficult to find out who was associated with the file.

(4) Use of information from such a data bank would imply a special obligation to publish the results of the research and to permit others to check the work.

All four of these properties need additional explanation, which follows later in this section. In general, however, one would expect a research data bank to be large and computer-based – medical records and census data are examples. Researchers with smaller and non-computerised files would be encouraged to follow these procedures where suitable. Because the licence for a research data bank would offer certain protections, however, it is expected that some researchers would wish to follow all of the procedures and obtain a licence even for quite small non-computerised data banks.

The concept of a research data bank is based on the proposal for a statistical data bank made by the US Department of Health, Education, and Welfare Secretary's Advisory Committee on Automated Personal Records Systems in the 1973 report, *Records, Computers and the Rights of Citizens*.

Research only

The research subject will surely feel the most secure, and thus be the most open with the researcher, if he or she can be assured that research data will be used for no other purpose. The Study Group decided that this must be the guiding principle, but it recognised that this will present two kinds of problems: administrative and political.

This requirement would clearly demand that research data be kept separate from administrative data, at additional cost and operating difficulty. Although it would still be permissible for the same computer and the same data-handling programmes to be used for administrative and research data, it would be necessary for the research data to be kept in separate and well-defined sections of the computer memory with different and well-defined access controls.

The political problems are much more severe. Information in a data bank may provide a vital clue to a police investigation or provide important evidence that a person being considered for a post requiring a security clearance should not be permitted in that job. Some people would argue that the past evidence of mental illness or crime contained in a data bank should be used to screen people for sensitive jobs.

Indeed, it is already the case that the police, the Ministry of Defence, and even some employers can get personal information informally simply by pleading the 'national interest', the 'public good', or even friendship and school connections. When this does not work, the police can resort to subpoena and court order to get personal information from data banks.

The Study Group saw situations in which it would *seem* clearly to be in the public interest to release information from a data bank. The difficulty is that once access to research files is granted for extreme cases and certain principles established, the floodgates are opened and it will be virtually impossible to refuse requests for causes which seem almost as good. This must inevitably lead to a situation worse than the present one, and to the research subject would seem equivalent to no security at all.

This was clearly the most difficult problem for the Study Group. After much heart searching, it concluded that all such access must be banned, and that

No government or private agency, including the police and

Ministry of Defence, should be permitted access to research data under any circumstances.

It is inevitable that in drawing such a harsh and rigid line, some harm will be done to some people which might be otherwise prevented. But this short-term sacrifice must be made for the longer-term benefit. More people will benefit in the long term from full and open co-operation with research scientists than would benefit if data banks were made more open and people were less open with researchers. In any case, the benefit of opening the data banks must only be short term because precisely those people who one would wish to catch will be the first to refuse to co-operate in providing the necessary data.

On the other hand, many medical researchers mix research with therapy and would rightly object to any rule which prevented them from helping the subjects of their research. Therefore, the Study Group also proposed the rule that

No personal information may ever be used to the detriment of the subject, as he or she would define it.

Licensing

Regulation of data banks is both necessary and inevitable, and one purpose of this report is to see that research data banks are covered intelligently by such legislation. Licensing seems the best way to bring data banks under public control.

The licence for a research data bank would set as rules the three properties listed at the beginning of this section. In order to enforce the requirement that research data are used for research purposes only, the law setting up the licensing procedure would

Exempt licensed research data banks from all subpoenas, court orders, directives from secretaries of state, and all other demands for identified personal information.

The Tribunal should also expand its interest to the collection as well as storage of data, and would make a requirement of a licence that data collection follow a code of practice similar to the one proposed in the next section.

Finally, the licence should specify two operating details:

(1) A single publicly named individual is to be legally responsible for the data bank.

(2) The organisation, the named individual, and the person who actually committed the violation would be liable to criminal penalties for violating the terms of the licence, and to civil action by any injured party.

The Study Group realised that it would be some time before research data banks were given legal status. Therefore it proposed that

Even before research data banks are given legal status, scientists should establish such data banks themselves. Despite the lack of legal protection, operators of such data banks should commit themselves to refusing all improper demands for data.

Linkage

It is not sufficient simply to have rules, or even laws, preventing disclosure of personal information. People will break rules for friends or money, and laws can be changed. Therefore, it must be made difficult to get named records out of research data banks. Nevertheless, it is clearly necessary to have a way of identifying a file by name so that new material can be added to it. To accomplish both of these things, the Study Group proposed that

Research data banks would have three separate and distinct files, one containing data, one containing personal identification, and a third which links the other two in such a way that it is impossible to remove identified personal information without explicit approval of the person responsible for the data bank . . . The link file should be maintained by a different organisation from the one which maintains the data bank . . . A researcher could not use a research data bank to compile a list of people to be contacted for further study, unless that researcher had contacted the people in the first instance and had obtained at that time permission to contact them for follow-up studies.

Before research data banks have any legal status, however, there will be the problem that the link file as well as other files is subject to subpoena. Therefore,

> Whenever possible, and especially where the data is highly sensi-
> tive, the link file should be kept outside the United Kingdom in a
> country where it would not be subject to a United Kingdom sub-
> poena.

In any case, the most important aspect of this extremely complex
procedure is that it is very difficult for anyone with access to the data
files to associate the data with an individual. This provides a vital protection against accidental or intentional leakage which does not at
present exist. [These issues are discussed further in Chapters 17 and
18.]

Publication

The tradition of science is that all research should be published and
be checkable by other scientists. Although this has nothing to do with
privacy, it is a clear part of the relationship between the scientist and
the subject. The Study Group decided that where it was asking for
special protection for the scientist and his data to reinforce part of this
relationship, that 'part of the deal' should be to agree to uphold the
other part of the relationship, and that this should be enforced as part
of the licence.

This has two aspects. First, the researcher has the responsibility to
publish the results of his research unless there is a clear and compel-
ling reason not to. Second, the Study Group accepts the suggestion in
the US Department of Health, Education, and Welfare report that
operators of research data banks should be required to 'make fully
documented data readily available for independent analysis' so that
'data whose use helps an organisation to influence social policy and
behaviour [is] readily available' for independent study.

Secrecy in research is ultimately harmful to science and to the general public and must be discouraged. The Study Group saw only two
categories of research which should not be published: that which is
simply bad science, and that which would clearly be of immediate
harm to the subjects. It is not sufficient to stop publications just because the sponsoring organisation or other interested party does not
like the outcome of the work. The subjects of research must have the
opportunity to see what use was made of their contribution. This

means, whenever possible, that the subjects should be notified, either in person or through a local newspaper or noticeboard, of the availability of the published work.

The second aspect is more complex. The privacy rules proposed here will make it more difficult for other researchers to use the same data, and any loosening of the rules would permit the commercial exploitation of the data. There are, however, two ways in which data can be made available: either in anonymous form, or by going back to the original subjects to ask for permission to pass the data on to a new researcher. In any case,

> privacy must never be used as a smokescreen to prevent others from checking research.

Unfortunately, this is done. The Study Group noted one example where a local authority used a study of housing conditions to justify the choice of a road route, but refused to let others check the original data on grounds of privacy. A researcher who was able to get the help of the subjects claimed that in fact the local authority had distorted the data to justify a selection already made, and was refusing to release the data for fear that this would be discovered.

And well intentioned honest researchers sometimes simply draw wrong conclusions from their data and the errors are not clear in the published work.

The Study Group also sought to extend this right to check research from the limited realm of other scientists to the subjects of the research themselves. Although community groups can often get help from interested scientists, they often come from fields not directly related to the one in question. Thus, the researcher must be prepared to explain his work and make data available in a usable form to people outside his own research field. Anyone who did not get full cooperation from a researcher would have the right to appeal to the Data Bank Tribunal.

Collecting Data

The researcher's primary contact with the public occurs when he collects his data, and it is at this point that he must convince the subject that he is upholding the traditional relationship. Thus the Study

Group proposed a Code to Protect Research Subjects. It is merely a codification of what is already recognised as good practice in this area, but it should be written out and issued to anyone who provides data for research purposes.

Code to Protect Research Subjects
The researcher will:
(1) Explain the purpose of the study, name the sponsor, and say if the results will be published.
(2) Leave a card giving his or her name and address, a summary of this code, and answers to the questions in the code.
(3) Specify how the data is to be kept and what will be done with it after the project.
(4) Not give identified data to any other person for any purpose.
(5) Not give the name and address of the subject to anyone else for any purpose without first obtaining explicit permission.
(6) Ensure, if the subject is a member of a captive population such as a school or hospital, that this Code still applies and that this is made clear to the subjects; also, that the institution is not putting pressure on subjects to participate, that no sanction of any kind will be applied to anyone who refuses, and that this too will be made clear to the subjects.

The subject should be told that he or she may:

(1) Refuse to participate.
(2) Terminate participation at any time, even after the interview has begun.
(3) Refuse at the outset to permit the data to be used, even in anonymous form, for a purpose other than the one specified by the researcher. If this stipulation is not made, however, the researcher is free to use depersonalised data for other research, pass it on to other researchers, or put it into a data archive.

The Study Group was conscious that any code is merely an empty set of words without some enforcement procedure, and that it will be difficult to find ways to enforce this code. In the long term, it is hoped that the code would be part of the data bank licence. In the medium term, it would be hoped that grant-giving bodies such as the Social Science and Medical Research Councils would make adoption of the code a condition of any grant, and that government departments would adopt it for their own research. In the short term, however, the best that could be realistically hoped would be that a few researchers, social-science departments, foundations and concerned local authorities would adopt the code voluntarily, and give it publicity in the very act of implementing it by giving copies to research subjects.

Implicit in the code is that participation in research is voluntary and requires informed consent. This is often not the case now, when research questions are often scattered among administrative ones. Therefore,

> Any questionnaire which combines research questions with administrative questions that the respondent must answer should clearly separate the two and state in bold type that the research questions are optional.

Census forms and job applications are typical examples.

Most research does not, in fact, require elaborate follow-ups. Often, one simple set of questions asked on the doorstep is all that will ever be required. In these cases, there is no need to put identifying information on the questionnaire at all. The Study Group accepted that it is necessary to take names and addresses to be able to check that fieldworkers have in fact visited the person in question. But there is no reason why this information should be on the questionnaire. Therefore,

> When no follow-up is required, the data should be kept anonymous from the time it is first collected. If it is necessary to collect names and addresses for check-up purposes, this should be done separately.

This would offer an additional level of confidence and protection to the subjects, and would encourage participation by stressing the lengths to which the researcher is going to ensure confidentiality.

Secrecy and the Government

Any attempt to regulate the use of research data must grapple with the problem of the government, one of the largest users and collectors of such data. At present, government policy does not come up to any of our standards. Administrative and research data are often mixed, and are collected and transferred without the knowledge of the subject. In particular, as the census showed, the individual does not have the right to refuse to participate in government research. An even worse example is the requirement that employers provide identified personal information about employees for research purposes, but with no requirement that the employees even be told. Although the government has a basically good record on confidentiality, it has been breached – as with the use of census data to find nurses who had retired. And other government research files can be breached on order of a secretary of state.

The biggest problem, however, is lack of publication. Far too many government research projects never see the light of day, and it is often impossible to check the original data. Although the Official Secrets Act is often cited, we suspect that the real reason is more often an attempt to avoid criticism. But the result of hiding from peer review is more likely to be bad research.

The rules for research data banks must apply to the government as well as to private researchers. The biggest fears centre on the census, medical records and other government data collections.

More Power to the People?

The increase in public understanding of science in the past few years has led, among other things, to the realisation that scientific research is not always beneficial.

For the most part, it is probably best to let scientists get on with their work, shortcomings and biases notwithstanding, and hope that the normal process of constant review which is part of science will eventually squeeze out the bad work and lead to benefits that will balance the harm.

But the Study Group agreed that there were some areas of research where the results could not be intelligently used by the community, and where the results of the research might lead to social tensions or unwise government policies which would cause unnecessary harm. Therefore, the Study Group agreed that

> Some research is best postponed until a future time when society is able to cope with the results.

The Study Group was particularly concerned about the problem of the harm that research might do to the people who co-operated with the study, and it discussed the matter at some length. Implicit in the Code to Protect Research Subjects is the right of the subject to refuse to participate in research, and that if enough subjects refuse to participate, the project will be effectively vetoed.

But is this sufficient? The Study Group disagreed on this point, with one half arguing that subjects and affected groups needed more power, and the other arguing that it provided sufficient protection. The latter group argued that giving the subjects any additional power would hamper scientific inquiry, and that the general good was best served by letting research continue as unhampered as possible. It was further argued that there is a serious danger of politically motivated attacks on researchers by self-appointed group of spokesmen, that giving affected groups more power would only increase the number of attacks, and that this danger is at least as great as the danger of misuse of research data.

The others, however, felt that even with the Code the power situation remained unbalanced. They argued that research was often done on disadvantaged groups because they could not object, and that if one were to ask a board chairman what one asked the poor, he would either throw out the researcher or send for his solicitor. In practical terms, it was noted that some race-relations studies, if done now, would be used by the Home Office to the disadvantage of immigrant groups.

The entire Study Group agreed, however, that once research had begun, it should not be censored. Even the members who wanted some sort of subject-group-veto believed that the veto must come before the project begins.

Data Archives

One of the most important powers that the computer has given to modern scientists is the ability to store data after it has been used for a research project and draw on it later for totally different purposes that may never have been considered when the data was first collected.

There have been many successes in this area. The first evidence of a link between lung cancer and smoking was found because doctors in twenty-five British hospitals were willing to make the medical records of lung-cancer patients available to researchers. Similarly, the knowledge that an early version of the contraceptive pill caused blood clotting in a tiny fraction of women emerged from the scrutiny of records of death throughout Britain and of hospital admission records for an entire hospital region.

Increasingly, research-data archives are being set up by organisations such as the Social Science Research Council. This is an exciting prospect. For any library, the more material that is available, the more can be learned from it. The existence of archives also makes it easier to check past research. Naturally,

Archives should contain only anonymous data, stripped of all identification.

Conclusion

All research on individuals and groups threatens their privacy. This report is intended, in part, as a warning that people's jealousy for their privacy will come to be a threat to research if researchers cannot guarantee to defend that privacy. The greatest danger is not from conspiracy, but absent-mindedness and public apathy. The possibility of leakage from an ever-increasing aggregation of data will sooner or later cause a public reaction with serious consequences for scientific research. Debate and responsible action are essential now so that research in the future can continue without harm being inflicted on an unsuspecting public.

Part Two

Social Survey Research and Privacy

4 Introduction

Martin Bulmer

The opening chapters have considered general issues concerning privacy and quantitative social research. The core of the book will now examine two specific types of social research – social surveys and population censuses. Privacy in social research poses problems which cannot be resolved in the abstract. They need to be considered in the context of particular types of data and specific methods of social research. This section considers social survey research.

What sorts of issues are we concerned with? G. T. Marx and M. Useem, discussing ethical issues in social research, highlight one aspect:

Most people's lives are visible to only a very limited community of associates. This is partly because of the conscious design of many people to restrict the spread of knowledge about their own lives, motives and inner feelings. People harbour much secret and sensitive information about themselves and the complex social webbings in which they are embedded. Many lead active and busy lives; spare time is at a premium. Bidding for these extra moments is the stranger who wanders in one day describing himself as a 'social scientist' engaged in a study of 'personal wealth and income'. The ensuing request for an in-depth interview may be charitably characterised as an opportunity for the approached person to express himself on an issue of burning public importance. Less generally, the request for co-operation may be viewed as a direct invasion of privacy.[1]

One hundred years ago this intrusion would have been unlikely to happen. Social survey research as we know it today is a modern twentieth-century phenomenon; a century ago it was virtually unknown. Such social-scientific research as was undertaken treated the direct questioning of individuals about aspects of their background and experience as either totally inappropriate or purely secondary to other sources of data. It was widely believed that members of lower social classes were incapable of giving accurate responses to questions put to them directly. Considerations of privacy were not an issue. Rather, poorly-educated lower-class respondents were often considered an unreliable source of data.

Social changes altered this situation. The extension of political rights, the growth of universal education and the development of popular journalism for a mass market led to a greater interest in the experience and viewpoint of the individual citizen. Pioneering social investigators such as Charles Booth and Seebohm Rowntree in Britain and Paul Kellog in the United States showed that it was possible, using embryo survey methods, to gather social data relevant to policy issues, which could indeed act as an engine of social reform.[2] Technical innovations, most notably the introduction of probability sampling by A. L. Bowley of the LSE in 1912, paved the way for the development of survey methods on a more scientific basis.[3]

After the First World War, survey methods were widely adopted by consumer research organisations in the United States, and then for political polling. The 1936 presidential election saw the triumph of the Gallup poll prediction based on systematic interviews with 3000 people selected randomly over the 2.4 million replies received by the *Literary Digest* to their non-randomly distributed unsystematic questionnaire.[4] Since that time, the use of social survey techniques has continued to grow both for market research and public-opinion polling, until there are today sizeable social research industries, carrying out millions of interviews a year, on both sides of the Atlantic.

Parallel to these developments in market research has been the refinement and widespread adoption of sample survey techniques by both academic researchers and governments. In Britain, the social survey movement flourished between the wars. It was in the United

States, however, that the more notable methodological advances, particularly associated with the name of Paul Lazarsfeld, were made. Post-war there have developed in the United States in particular a large number of academic centres of social survey research, of which the Columbia Bureau of Applied Social Research, the Michigan Institute of Social Research and the Chicago National Opinion Research Centre are the most important. These are today worldrenowned centres of expertise in social survey research.

Governments, too, have enormously increased the scale of survey research. In Britain, the establishment of the Government Social Survey (now the Social Survey Division of OPCS) dates from 1941. It now carries out annually a very wide range of both continuous and *ad hoc* surveys on subjects of interest and relevance to government departments. In the United States, the Bureau of the Census conducts much survey research in addition to undertaking the census. In both countries, more recently, there has also developed an independent research sector that is neither governmental, nor academic, nor commercial in the sense that market research is commercial. It undertakes much social survey work on a contract basis.

There is thus in contemporary society a very large amount indeed of social survey work being done, with obvious implications for the privacy of the individual. This section of the book considers some of the issues raised. The social survey is a scientific technique for eliciting factual or attitudinal data from respondents who form part of a small sample drawn from the whole population.[5] (Spurious and bogus uses of surveys – for example, asking questions as a prelude to salesmanship – are not considered here. This is frequently an invasion of privacy, but one based on deceit.) Though other techniques are sometimes used – notably mail surveys and telephone interviews – the majority of such encounters are face-to-face interviews between the representative of the social research organisation (the interviewer) and the member of the public (the respondent or interviewee). The respondent's participation in this is entirely voluntary. No reliable estimates are available, but millions of such interviews are conducted in countries such as the United States and Britain each year.

An initial important, if somewhat metaphysical question is: why do people consent to be interviewed at all when faced with a request for a social-research interview? What is in it for them? Social research involves interaction between those who collect social data and members of the public. It involves social researchers asking members of the

public, usually through interview or questionnaire, for information
about themselves, some of which at least is of personal and more or
less private nature. To a very considerable extent, those who conduct
social surveys rely on the goodwill of respondents to give information
for nothing more than the fact that it is requested of them.

Most people are co-operative, some no doubt because they are intimidated by the data collectors, but most because they feel that they
have nothing to hide or consider that in order to get essential social
services they must provide the information requested of them. This,
it has often been said, is part of the 'price' we pay for such services.
Indeed, the willingness and sometimes the eagerness of many
people voluntarily to provide information about themselves, even
when no tangible reward is offered them – as in the case of the
United States Census or public-opinion surveys – is a far greater
asset to data collectors than their computers. The fact that census
enumerators and household interviewers are almost always strangers to their respondents is still another asset to the data collectors,
perhaps particularly when it comes to sensitive areas of questioning.[6]

How far, in the last quarter of the twentieth century, can social
scientists continue to rely simply on the goodwill on the part of
respondents for successful data collection? Shils argues in an earlier
chapter that survey research represents 'a much more penetrating inquisitiveness into the personal private sphere'. What are the conditions under which this intrusiveness on the part of social researchers
will be accepted? It is clear that the general public has a very high degree of tolerance. A majority of respondents, when approached, are
either eager or willing, or not unwilling, to be interviewed on a range
of subjects. Experience demonstrates that complex and sensitive
questions can be asked successfully and without giving offence, on factual subjects such as income and on attitudinal ones such as married
women's intentions about future fertility and family size.[7] In an Australian study of confidentiality, privacy and sensitivity of questions for
the World Fertility Survey, for example, only 0.007 per cent of 2600
respondents refused to say whether they had ever used any form of
contraception and a similar tiny proportion refused to answer a question on abortion. (Reasons for refusal to participate at all in this
survey will be considered shortly.)[8]

Nevertheless, despite the continuing high level of co-operation from the public, professionals in the social survey field are increasingly concerned about the social acceptability of their research. This concern is actively shown in each of the four chapters which follow. One basic problem stems from the growing scale of survey research. Sir Claus Moser, until 1978 head of British government statistical service, has suggested that the British population may be over-surveyed.[9] Academic researchers in both Britain and America have made the same point. The SCPR group in the next chapter note that: 'the sheer volume of surveys is, of course, still growing rapidly, and we are sporadically warned that sooner or later saturation point will be reached, public co-operation will dry up and we will have to think of new ways of obtaining data'. Already this appears to be happening with certain sub-groups of the population. In Chapter 8, the American Statistical Association group refer to the problems of over-sampled groups such as American Indians and certain metropolitan inner-city areas conveniently accessible to down-town researchers.

There is no doubt, too, that survey research suffers both from its improper commercial imitators, who use questioning as a 'front' for selling, and from over-zealous social scientists who have intruded into private areas or taken advantage of their superior social position. The use of questionnaires and interviews can indeed be sometimes improper.

> The questioning can be intrusive and bruising; the information gained can be misused and exploited. Political surveys, questions asked of the vulnerable and the powerless; these can turn inquiries into inquisitions. School children, for instance, are currently subjected to research on sexuality, that can only be described as inexcusable prying. It is no accident that much research of a questionable nature has been conducted on the most vulnerable and helpless; on children, the institutionalised, the sick and the poor.[10]

One recent phenomenon of interest is *collective* resistance to survey research of a more or less organised kind, partly prompted by abuses such as those referred to, but drawing greater strength from 'anti-establishment' political movements among the poor and deprived. Eric Josephson in Chapter 7 provides a most instructive case study of local responses in Harlem to a particular Columbia University survey. It is not suggested that this is typical of survey research in general. However, this is not an isolated instance of resistance by Black Americans to social science over the last ten to fifteen years. Tension between members of minority groups, particularly as they gain in political consciousness, and the established society, may take the form of resistance to attempts to do research involving the minority. Writing in 1973 about Detroit, D. Warren has claimed that

> researchers with credentials derived solely from the academic world are increasingly distrusted by black communities. Access to black neighbourhoods without establishing legitimacy with specific community elements can no longer be considered automatic.[11]

M. Useem and G. T. Marx argue that in recent years various domestic United States groups have become sensitised to perceived abuses by American social researchers. This is especially the case in several urban black communities.

> In 1970 Boston's Black United Front, representing a variety of concerned groups in the metropolitan region, established a 'Community Research Review Committee' for evaluating all social science investigations targeted for the black community. Approval is required, as is a ten per cent levy on the project's funds to keep the board operational, before research can be undertaken. A number of investigators have been barred from the area, including some black researchers.[12]

Such group resistance to social research is relatively unusual, but is in future as likely to increase as to diminish. As H. Kelman has observed,[13] research may compare a minority with the majority population on a number of social and psychological dimensions to the disadvantage of the minority. Publication of such results (often derived from biases in measurement, interpretation and evaluation) may have damaging consequences for the minority in reinforcing negative stereotypes and giving support to social policies detrimental to their interests.

Survey research into minorities does differ in significant respects from cross-sectional surveys of national samples drawn from the whole population. As Josephson notes in the case of the latter, such research has a relatively brief impact upon particular localities, which does not allow time for organised opposition to develop. What other evidence is there of resistance to survey research in national samples?

The decision of the individual respondent to participate or not in a survey is reflected, in part, in the response rate. Where probability sampling is used in a survey, the response rate is the number of completed interviews expressed as a proportion of total numbers of persons originally drawn in the sample. Non-completion may occur for two broad kinds of reason, not-at-homes and refusals. The contribution of refusals to trends in non-response rates may throw light on public concern about privacy issues.

American evidence on this is summarised in Chapter 8, reporting experience of falling response rates in the 1970s as compared to the 1960s. Part of this is accounted for by social changes: urbanisation, population mobility, more women working, and by current fieldwork standards of survey organisations.

Part of the increase in non-response rates, however, is apparently due to refusals or resistance to social surveys. In part, this may be due to concern about urban crime. To safeguard middle-class Americans against crime,

> engineers and architects have devised ingenious barriers and surveillance techniques for transforming middle-class urban homes and apartments into veritable fortresses, again emulating the rich. In this respect, privacy is sought to ensure that there is no sharing of our wealth with burglars or with travelling salesmen, or our opinions with public-opinion survey interviewers.[14]

British evidence is provided by a working party of the Market Research Society, which reported in 1976, and which found some evidence of an increasing reluctance on the part of the general public to co-operate in market research and continuous social surveys.[15] It is thought to be harder to obtain co-operation from the general public than it had been ten years previously. The evidence is by no means as clear cut as the American, but is nevertheless suggestive. There was less evidence of increasing numbers of not-at-homes than of increasing refusal rates or increasing inability to conduct the interview (because of age, language etc.). Again, social changes are identified as responsible in part: increasing urbanisation; the increasing proportion of married women working, which increased by over 50 per cent between 1961 and 1971; and increasing concern with personal security and crime. Some parts of London, Liverpool, Glasgow and Birmingham, they note, are 'no-go' areas for interviews. Once again, however, privacy concerns are identified by the MRS group as important. A number of the market-research organisations which the working party visited

> mentioned increasing concern about privacy as one of the factors that had made the field managers' and interviewers' task more difficult over recent years. We think that it is likely that the general heightening of public consciousness that privacy and confidentiality should be matters of concern to the individual may make potential respondents more suspicious and reluctant. The researcher, therefore, is under greater pressure to demonstrate both that the data collected will be kept confidential and that there is a real need for the data.[16]

An example of how public attitudes towards privacy may affect response is provided by surveys of individual wealth. Economists in particular have made various attempts to study the distribution of personal wealth in Britain (which is very unequal, with a very large proportion of personal wealth concentrated in the hands of a small section of the population). Sample surveys of wealth, however, have tended to achieve fairly low response rates, with non-completion accounted for by a high proportion of direct refusals. In the Oxford Savings Surveys of 1953 and 1954, the most thorough attempts of this kind, response rates of around 66 per cent were achieved, but with systematic bias in the non-response. Lowest response rates were from the self-employed (for example, businessmen and farmers). It was also low from the professional and executive classes, and among the retired, especially the more wealthy. In addition, among those who responded, there appeared to be systematic under-reporting of wealth-holdings. The net effect is a systematic under-representation of large wealth-holders, which render sample surveys alone unsatisfactory for the purpose of determining the distribution of personal wealth.[17] Admittedly this example is an extreme one, relating to a highly personal and private matter. It may also be that wealth data are regarded as potentially more damaging than other sorts of personal data. However, with increasing public interest in and concern about privacy matters, the sorts of issues which are regarded as sensitive may well change in the future.

Illuminating evidence about non-response and survey sensitivity is available from the Australian trial for the World Fertility Survey quoted earlier.[18] Out of 3067 women who were eligible and accessible in this survey, completed interviews were obtained from 87 per cent, while 13 per cent refused. (Not-at-homes are excluded from the 3067.) Reasons for refusal on which data was available were classified as follows:

2.4 per cent too busy due to multiple jobs, sickness in house or other genuine reasons

2.2 per cent would not co-operate with any private inquiry irrespective of subject; mostly people who never co-operated with anyone who came to door

3.5 per cent objected to the focus of this particular survey on sex and fertility

0.6 per cent objected to the suspected inclusion in the survey of an income question

1.8 per cent objected on the grounds of privacy and confidentiality in general

This suggests that refusals were a mixture of people who are genuinely too busy; people who either do not co-operate with doorstep callers or object on general grounds of privacy; and those who objected to the particular content of this survey. While one would expect the latter proportion to vary according to the sensitivity of the survey, it indicates a core of respondents (4 per cent in this case) who would not co-operate on principle.

Definitive evidence about whether such principled objections are on the increase is lacking. Those who conduct surveys, however, are well aware that they are increasingly called upon to explain, justify and rationalise the purpose of the survey which is being undertaken. There are still many people who for one reason or another are willing or even eager to participate in a survey. But, increasingly, the survey practitioner is called upon to demonstrate that there is a need for the data he or she seeks, and that the data once collected will be kept confidential.

There is no obvious answer to the general problem of how to gain and maintain the goodwill and co-operation of respondents in social survey research. It can be argued that to some extent social survey research is self-regulating in this respect. The close dependence of survey researchers on public co-operation acts as a natural brake on intrusiveness in the nature of the questions asked of respondents. Survey practitioners know that if they become too demanding, they threaten the public goodwill on which they depend. Against this, it can be argued that the increasing scale of survey research undermines this safeguard. If saturation is approaching, it is small comfort to know that the content of questions is being closely monitored. Another counter-trend, not directly within the control of social survey researchers, is the misuse of surveys by salesmen or journalists, giving the activity a bad name by association.

The general problem can only be tackled by social research workers collectively examining the problem and making recommendations for action. The next chapter (continued in Chapter 16) is a notable example of this concern. It reviews the problem of privacy in survey research and draws attention to a number of issues earning attention. Chapter 6, too, reflects a similar, if more generalised, concern on the part of a leading representative of American public-opinion research. Survey researchers know that privacy cannot be ignored.

The seriousness with which the issue is treated is shown by the making of more explicit attempts to gain the co-operation of respondents. It is often argued that the research 'bargain' is unequal and needs to be more fully spelled out. There is a fundamental asymmetry in the relationship between the researcher (who gains a lot of personal [and sometimes private] information) and the respondent (who gives up this information in return for slight and rather intangible rewards). The doctrine of 'informed consent', discussed in the next chapter, is an attempt to make clear the nature of the research bargain, to ensure that the respondent realises not only that co-operation in the survey is entirely voluntary, but also for what purpose and under whose sponsorship it is being undertaken. Such concerns have received a powerful impetus from moves to protect the rights of the individual against institutional encroachment and abuse, first an issue in the biomedical field. As these concerns extend to social survey research, there has been argument between those who favour new rules on ethical grounds and those who believe that more information given in advance to respondents and stronger prior assurances about confidentiality will lower response rates and threaten social research. A recent American study by E. Singer showed that in a carefully designed experiment, response rates to a survey on a number of highly sensitive issues (drinking, drug use, sexual behaviour and mental

health) were not affected significantly by informed consent procedures.[19]

Other techniques for assuring respondent privacy are discussed in
Chapter 18 by R. Boruch, and means of ensuring the confidentiality
of data have been discussed in Chapter 1 and are further considered in
Part 4. All these are relevant to the public acceptability of survey research.

Further questions relate to control over survey activities. In Part 4,
the question of the professionalisation of survey research, and the
sanction of ethical codes, is further considered. This is one means of
providing safeguards to the public about the good faith and high standards of survey research workers. The SCPR group concluded, in the
section of their report reproduced in Chapter 16, in favour of a regulating commission to oversee the collection and custody of social data.

One limited instance of attempts to institute such a system is provided by the control exercised by ethical committees in biomedical research and by human subjects committees in the behavioural sciences
in the United States. At the University of Delaware (to quote an
example given in a recent textbook),[20] social researchers are required
to satisfy both a departmental review board and a University Human
Subjects Committee in respect of the research objectives of a particular study; the involvement of human subjects; the content of interview
schedules etc; what the subjects will be told about their involvement in
the study; how informed consent will be obtained and recorded;
whether there will be any potential risks to the subject (including discomfort, irritation or harassment); what inducements they will be
offered; and what measures will be taken to safeguard the welfare of
the subjects, their rights of privacy and the confidentiality of information being handled.

The social responsibilities of survey researchers are thus very much a
live issue and one about which various steps are being taken. They
will be further considered in Part 4. Privacy raises problems and poses
dilemmas which the four following chapters demonstrate but do not
entirely resolve. The most illuminating social issues, however, are
often those which are most difficult or intractable.

5 Survey Research and Privacy*

SCPR Working Party

Data Needs and the Role of Surveys

The need for information

The requirement of societies for data about themselves, about their social relationships and about their constituent individuals is not new. As societies have become more complex, the need for data has grown. Similarly, the ability to use data has been given a sharp additional impetus in the present century by the development of techniques of data processing which far exceed the capacity of their predecessors.

In parallel with the technical ability to handle and analyse large quantities of data, there has been over the past few decades a rapid growth of what we may call 'data-need'. Decision-makers both in government and in business have become increasingly conscious of the complexity of their roles. They have seen that their actions have sometimes failed to produce the intended result and that many unexpected consequences have followed. Their task has become more difficult as the societies on whose behalf they act have become more

* ©1974 Social and Community Planning Research, London. Report of a Working Party established by Social and Community Planning Research, London (an independent social research institute), first published as a pamphlet, 1974. Reproduced by permission of SCPR.

politically conscious and articulate. Although there has always been a feedback from governed to government, at no time before the present century have the repercussions of government action on all sections of society been so rapidly reported back, and even anticipated, by those affected. Under these conditions, governments can no longer rely on the inertia and inarticulateness of the masses. They need constantly to remain sensitive to the need for a nicely calculated balance between the sometimes opposing needs of different parts of the social system.

In business, too, boards and their managers have been made more conscious of the effects of their decisions. In an era of mergers, conglomerates and international corporations, vast sums of money (and often long spans of time) are involved in decisions. There is increasing interaction between business and other parts of the social system so that, unlike the convention of nineteenth-century capitalism, businesses have begun to develop what the Americans refer to as 'corporate social responsibilities'. But the concentration of economic power into larger corporations has also meant that decisions about new products (or new markets) involve far greater resources than ever before. Hence the growing need for reliable and detailed knowledge about consumer behaviour, preferences and demand. Theoretically, at least, this kind of information should lead to products or services being better adapted to consumer preferences.

So, in order to find a more secure basis for taking decisions, governments and businesses have come to rely inescapably on better sources of information – a reliance which has arisen both because of the greater efficiency which accurate information can provide and because it enables resources to be more effectively (and possibly more equitably) allocated. Attention has thus relatively recently turned to survey research as a means of data collection. In Britain, it became prevalent only after the Second World War, and even in the United States (where it developed more rapidly) survey research has been conceived and organised on a large scale only during the past thirty years.

This growth on both sides of the Atlantic has meant that the type of 'inspired' decision-taking which characterised nineteenth-century management techniques has slowly given way to (or at least had added to it) a more information-based and rational process. To do their jobs economically and effectively, governments and industries must have feedback; they have to monitor changes in public attitudes and behaviour and to be responsive to them; and they have, therefore, to collect increasingly complex statistics to supplement their obligatory administrative records. Much of this additional information has been compiled from data which members of the public have been asked to provide on a voluntary basis. And it has grown in scale and scope alongside the increasing acceptance (in some areas of government and industry) that small samples can provide remarkably accurate information about very large aggregates of people.

And it is not only government and industry which have come to rely on better sources of information for their respective roles. In the academic world also, surveys are making increasingly important contributions to academic theory and scholarship.

The need for survey research

The Working Party's starting point was that democratic societies have the need to know only a *limited* range of things about their individual members, but a very *wide* range of things about their collective characteristics. In the latter case, however, they must not take into account (or, if they do, must immediately forget) the identities of individuals who voluntarily supply the information from which a wider and better understanding of our society can be created. We attempted therefore to work out how we could diminish the areas of conflict between our need as a society to know more and our entitlement as individuals to be protected from the threats inherent in the disaggregation of that knowledge.

Hence the peculiar functional advantage of sample surveys over the more elaborate means of data collection by means of individual records. In the first place, the use of sampling automatically implies a lack of concern with individual identities: sample surveys always seek aggregated rather than individual data. And in the second place, there is no other readily available means which can equal the sample survey as a tool for collecting data that are objective, varied in scope, flexible, economical and sufficiently accurate for the purposes they are normally intended to serve. These attributes are obviously relative: a survey may well take several years to complete and its cost might run into five or even six figures (though many surveys, particularly in business, demand much shorter time spans and considerably smaller budgets). But they remain a unique means of getting systematic and anonymous information of considerable complexity. Again it is the use of sampling – the central feature of surveys – which reduces costs and time to a fraction of what is required by full census.

It is impossible to impose a tidy structure on survey applications. Most surveys simultaneously serve rather different aims. Moreover, in addition to their overt content they frequently have a catalytic effect on current modes of thinking which transcends the direct value of their findings.

Perhaps the most common function of surveys is that of *description*. At their most generalised, public-sector surveys are designed on a regular basis to collect a range of basic data which it is felt will contribute to better-informed government by the identification of trends. But descriptive surveys are also undertaken as 'once-off' studies of particular topics, or as the basis for a review of future policy and management: a local authority may initiate a sample survey of housing needs and of the housing stock available in order to equip itself to meet future requirements.

There are, of course, countless functions and uses of survey research in addition to the descriptive role we have mentioned. Survey research is used for a great variety of purposes by a great variety of different people and organisations. In some cases it is used as a means of empirical testing of theories, products or policies; in others it is to evaluate current demand for goods, services or policies; sometimes survey data are used as a basis for model-building or forecasting; and so on. Whether or not all aspects of survey research are thought to be valuable or even desirable, the survey has undoubtedly become part and parcel of the democratic process. This is not to say, however, that the Census of Population or survey research can ever replace the ballot box as a means of democratic control. It is simply to emphasise that the survey has an increasingly common role in a participatory democracy.

Probably the greatest value of survey research is the opportunity it offers to all people to have their views expressed in a way that can be understood by policy-makers, without necessarily mechanically binding the policy-makers to those views as is usually the case with referenda. Moreover, the information provided by surveys is usually a great deal more profound than the extreme over-simplification of a referendum's 'yes' or 'no'. Public opinion is almost invariably composed of a very complicated mixture of conflicting and contradictory attitudes and is far from being the simple entity so often declared categorically to favour this course or to be outraged by that.

Neither survey research nor any other panacea will ever make us become fully rational, detached analysts of our own condition. The Working Party's view is simply that the ability to gain insights by objective, systematic and anonymous observation of the dynamics of our social system is a great advance on the unsystematic messages that in the past used to reach us from self-selected elements in the structure.

Individual and statistical data

For the most part, the collection of data on a systematic basis has in the past been concerned with individuals per se. It was found at a very early date that in order to collect taxes it was convenient to have a list of individuals liable to tax, compiled either centrally or on a district basis. Similarly, elections demanded lists. It was also found to be useful to record individual births, marriages and deaths, because these events obviously had a bearing on the status of an individual with respect to tax, eligibility to vote or to marry, military service or welfare benefits. This type of information, which we refer to as *individual data*, is concerned to distinguish between one person and another. It is almost universally collected for administrative purposes by governments, but in the private sector it has other applications, for example in credit rating. Leaving aside the private sector, it is axiomatic that a democratic society must have certain centralised pieces of information about its constituent members: the only dispute can be about the precise nature and extent of this information.

It is extremely important that we should distinguish between individual data of the type described and *statistical data*, which should be essentially indifferent to the identity of the individual: trying only to answer questions such as 'how many?' or 'what proportion?', not 'who?'. Unfortunately, the distinction often becomes blurred in practice for two reasons. In the first place, much statistical analysis is based on data initially and primarily collected for their value as individual records. And in the second place, although statistical data are unconcerned with individual identities, the individual is usually the necessary starting-point. In sample surveys, for example, selection of individuals by name can be a necessary part of the sampling process, even though there is usually no need to *retain* the identity link once the interview has been achieved or the questionnaire returned.

Within the general category of *individual* data, much of it is already publicly available. For example: the Electoral Register;

births, marriages, deaths; wills; Armed and Civil Services List (status and salaries); company accounts (salaries of certain directors); share registers (shareholdings); valuation lists (rateable values); telephone, street and other directories; membership lists, professional and trade registers; court proceedings; *Who's Who.*

In other cases, access is limited, even though the limitation may not be stringent. Credit ratings, bank references and employment references are cases where information may be supplied to anyone who has apparently 'bona fide' grounds for requesting it. Personnel files are another example, since there are no uniform safeguards and the standard of confidentiality is at the discretion of the employer.

But there are also cases where it is generally accepted that there should be no public access, for example: tax records; police records; medical files; bank accounts (except for references); post office and other savings accounts; census records; parts of the vital registration records.

In the case of *statistical* data, it has already been emphasised that the name of the individual is of no interest, but it frequently has to be recorded at some point in the process. In most interview surveys, for example (including of course the census), this is the case. So, too, is it the case in surveys of administrative records which do not involve fresh data collection at all: for example, a sample of filed tax returns might be analysed for purely statistical purposes by the tax authorities, and – although the individual returns are retained within the Inland Revenue – they are identified by name.

There are, however, various types of survey (some sample-based, some not) where the contributing individuals are not specifically identified at all. Traffic counts, museum entrance counts, ticket sales, secret ballots and most surveys based on observation techniques are of this kind, as are a minority of interview surveys (for example, when someone is briefly interviewed in the street or at a transport terminal).

There are also surveys and statistical analyses based on measurements which do not directly involve the individual *at all*. Some examples are sales per head of certain goods, per capita consumption of gas or electricity, environmental noise levels, atmospheric pollution indices, population density, and so on.

It is usually the method of obtaining the sample rather than the content of surveys which determines the extent to which individual identities are at risk, although sufficiently detailed content can also create some risk even when individuals are not named.

The focus of our attention

The Working Party has concentrated largely on *statistical data* in its consideration of privacy issues, as a result partly of its origins in the disciplines of survey research but also because it was in this area that there was the greatest scope for a fresh contribution shortly after the publication of the Younger Committee's very thorough general review of privacy (Cmnd. 5012, 1972).

The Younger Committee's report was not published until about halfway through the Working Party's life, but its comparative lack of emphasis on social and business survey research reinforced our belief that there was room for an independent review of this area. Moreover, the Younger Committee's terms of reference excluded the public sector where much survey research and other statistical research is undertaken. The Working Party has, of course, been able to take account of all activities of this kind, whatever their origin.

Our emphasis has therefore fallen on what we have described as statistical data, and in particular on those situations where individuals are named or identified as part of the process of data collection. But we were concerned only with voluntarily provided data, the compulsory census falling outside the scope of our attention as part of a separate debate. Similarly, the specific problems of industrial research are largely excluded.

There are two strands of our argument which underlie the rest of this report: in the first place, it was the Working Party's unanimous view that as a society we have a right and a need to know more and more about our collective characteristics and behaviour. In any urban industrial society, there is a need for 'look-out stations' which enable us to see in what direction we are moving; a need for 'seers' – but accurately-informed seers – who can comment wisely and warn us about changing characteristics and behaviour. Those who choose to withhold information on which this collective knowledge can be built have a right to do so and may have good reasons, as may those who withhold publication of results and therefore restrict our ability to become wiser analysts of our own condition. But, in our view, both these groups are wrong, provided that we can ensure that the benefits of greater knowledge do not carry with them inherent threats to individuals.

So the second strand of our argument is that we must scrutinise the methods we use to collect information to ensure the anonymity of the sources of that information. Unless this can be done effectively (and unless it is seen to be done) the case for refusing to take part in surveys etc. is understandable and possibly unanswerable. We must close the loopholes in present research methods; we must publicise abuses; and we must act quickly to establish (or reinforce) widely accepted norms for data collection which are communicated both to researchers and to their potential sources of information, the public.

The Risks Attached to Surveys

Characteristics of a survey

Before describing the potential hazards of survey research, it must be stressed that there are very few reported cases of these risks having materialised with any ill effects. We were dealing here with potential hazards rather than responding to an already grave situation. Nevertheless, the considerable risks of abuse do, in our view, need attention and action.

In order to highlight these risks, it would probably be helpful to abstract and describe the essential characteristics of a 'typical' survey, bearing in mind that any such description is bound to be a caricature. In fact, the 'typical' survey described below (a pre-selected sample survey) is only one of many types of survey. Although other types – involving quota samples or purposive samples or observation techniques – require different methods, they still raise almost identical potential problems for the individual respondent. So to describe one type cursorily is probably sufficient.

After completing the design and planning stages of a survey, the first step is usually to draw a sample from a source such as the Electoral Register. The selection may be of individuals or addresses (or if other sources are used, of doctors or hospitals or schools or universities or businesses, or indeed of any other definable group).

Once the sample has been selected, each member of it is then called upon (by an interviewer) or written to in an attempt to gain co-operation. Those who agree to co-operate are then questioned as to their behaviour, knowledge or attitudes in relation to the subject under study, usually by means of a set questionnaire designed for the purpose. Since co-operation is voluntarily given, the respondent may, of course, withhold any information, withdraw at any stage of the interview, or refuse to be interviewed at all.

The respondent's name and address is known both to the interviewer and the office staff who issued it. But there is no need to record it on the questionnaire itself. (Current practice varies in this respect.) As part of the interviewing process, field supervision checks are also carried out, sometimes involving a second visit to the respondent's home.

After the interview, the questionnaire is returned to the office, along with many others, and is subjected to checking (for completeness, consistency and, as far as can be determined, accuracy); coding (the classification of responses into a limited number of categories); and transfer to punched cards or other computer input. Finally, statistical tables are produced by computer, normally dealing with analyses of fairly large groups (of, say, fifty or more) and not with individual records.

At each stage in this process, issues of privacy or intrusion can arise:

The use of a particular source list for sampling purposes may itself constitute an intrusion into privacy.

The interviewer's visit to the sampled person at home may constitute an intrusion, particularly if the interviewer is unduly persistent.

The sampled person may be misled as to the purposes or sponsorship of the interview, or may wrongly be led to believe that co-operation is obligatory (though this is perhaps an issue of deception rather than intrusion).

Questions may be asked which cause the respondent embarrassment or offence.

Information given about an individual or family may be disclosed to third parties during the course of a survey (either by the interviewer or by office staff).

Subsequent disclosure of personal information may occur through the medium of the stored computer tapes or other stored documents and records.

Before dealing individually with each of these issues, it is worth noting that many of them are by no means exclusive to survey research. The last two issues, in particular – which relate to misuse and disclosure of personal data and which are the most common causes for anxiety about surveys – are relevant to *all* personal data however it is collected. The *main* cause for concern is the treatment of personal data, regardless of its source; but there are also other issues of importance, relating mainly to the methods employed in data collection, which have so far generated much less public interest or anxiety. For all that, they remain important and are likely to become more so.

The use of records for sampling purposes

It is evident that the use of records for sampling purposes must be governed initially by the character of those records. If they are publicly available there is usually no objection, but it is generally accepted that records to which there is normally no public access (such as tax records) should not be available for sampling purposes to anyone outside those to whom access is normally permitted. Some argue that such confidential records should not be used at all for sampling purposes, since this use was neither explicit nor implied in the original collection of information. However, this objection can be made equally to publicly available lists such as the Electoral Register, and there seems no reason to institute a different rule for private lists: the cardinal point of the argument is that the normal access to any list should not be extended for sampling purposes without the express permission of those affected. And this applies even where only the name and address, with no other data, are concerned.

A situation that is not uncommon relates to the possible use of survey records themselves for sampling purposes. It is often advantageous to make a second interview, after a lapse of time, with someone who has been interviewed before. But the same considerations would seem to apply: the names and addresses of people interviewed constitute a confidential record to which access should not be extended to anyone outside the original limits. It is worth noting perhaps that repeated interviews with the same individuals (even by the same organisation) could constitute an undue intrusion, unless respondents had given explicit approval to be re-interviewed at a later date (or at least been written to for approval before each subsequent round of interviewing). This problem is exacerbated by a growing demand – particularly in the commercial sector – for 'address banks', whereby the names and addresses of various minorities are accumulated over time for subsequent re-interview on other topics and by different organisations.

A further point to be made about the use of sampling lists is based on the doctrine of 'informed consent' which is extensively adopted as a standard in American codes of research practice. Its premise, broadly, is that a potential respondent should be told truthfully why, and for whom, the research is being undertaken and how the results will be used. Similarly, he should be disabused of any impression he may have that his co-operation is obligatory. We shall need to return to this concept in the next section, but its implication for the use of sampling lists is that the respondent should always be told the source from which his name or address has been obtained, even though in some situations (and with the respondent's consent) it may need to be disclosed only after the interview has been completed. In these cases the respondent should be given the right to insist that the record of his answers be destroyed.

Intrusion into the home

One of the objections that has sometimes been made to surveys is that – quite simply – people have a 'right to be left alone' and that survey research, by its very nature, violates this right.

The acts of telephoning people, of writing to them, of calling upon them and generally communicating with them are so basic a part of life in an organised society that no serious objection to them can be sustained unless – and it is an important proviso – they are performed in an unreasonable way or to an excessive extent. It is only against abuses that safeguards are needed, and a blanket 'right to be left alone' clearly goes too far, failing to discriminate between use and abuse. The Younger Committee concluded that the normal activity of an interviewer, or a salesman for that matter, was sufficiently restricted by the right of the person interviewed to terminate the interview at any stage, or to refuse to give it. Moreover, the Committee felt that the act of calling to request an interview could not be objected to except in certain additional circumstances which might bring it under the scope of other specific laws, such as trespass or nuisance (Younger Committee report, p. 124, s. 417).

While accepting these views as a general statement, the Working

Party did not feel that the ability to refuse an interview was of itself a sufficient safeguard, particularly for certain groups such as the very old and very young. We agree, however, that further *legal* safeguards would almost certainly be impracticable.

Informed consent

Almost anyone is able to gain co-operation from the majority of households in Britain on the pretext of carrying out a survey. The public appears to enjoy participating in surveys and to remain co-operative and unsuspicious. It is *because* of this, perhaps, that its interests should be safeguarded. The ability to refuse an interview is hardly protection if it is only a notional option because there is seen to be an implicit obligation to participate. We believe it to be important that the interviewer should avoid exerting undue pressure to obtain an interview. Quite simply, if consent is not freely given, the interview should not take place.

The doctrine of 'informed consent' requires that the respondent should be told at the outset not only that co-operation is entirely voluntary, but also for what purpose and under whose sponsorship the research is being undertaken. There is an undoubted difficulty about both these points. Since the success of surveys depends to a large extent upon the level of response, it seems naive to require that interviewers should go out of their way to invite a refusal from someone who *might* be under the impression that he was obliged to participate. And as far as announcing the purpose of the survey is concerned, a 'response set' or bias may immediately be created which could invalidate the results. For example, it is often found that respondents may make concessions to what they think the interviewer would like to hear; so, in order to obtain valid responses, it is sometimes necessary to play down an interest in a particular topic by a general explanation which – though accurate – is sufficiently broad to overcome the problem.

In practice, it is only the public who would be able to ensure the practice of 'informed consent'. The 'foot in the door' is one of the less reputable tools of the interviewer's trade and although we are convinced of the value of survey research, it is still incumbent on us to ensure that consent, when it comes, should be informed and unambiguous. If it is not, or if the particular survey had to depend on subterfuge in order to gain co-operation, then the survey is probably the wrong method of obtaining the information required. Survey research depends essentially on information being freely given without duress, obligation or deception.

This doctrine becomes even more important when interviewing is being carried out within an institutional setting, like a school or factory or prison. In these cases a feeling of obligation is often created simply by the fact that an authority figure has agreed *on the respondent's behalf* to an interview. In all such cases, the absolute right to refuse should be asserted.

The interview content

Even if an interview has been freely given on the basis of full information as to the sponsor and purpose of the study, the questions asked can themselves cause distress or offence. And there is, of course, no real safeguard against this: an apparently innocuous question may touch on a particular personal circumstance unknown to the interviewer. Moreover, there can be no uniform criteria for the evaluation of questions or indeed subject matter for research.

These risks of interview surveys are essentially related to the professional conscience and sensitivity of researchers and will have to remain so. The British Market Research Society's Code of Ethics contains the following general clause to urge caution:

> In the conduct and control of interviews, members are required to exercise all reasonable precautions to ensure that informants will in no way be adversely affected as a result of the questions administered.

Similarly, the British Sociological Association Code has this to say on the subject of 'observation techniques', a form of enquiry which does not depend on the prior consent of the subject and which is a considerable potential intrusion on the privacy of the individual:

> The professional sociologist should be aware of the ethical issues involved in observation . . . of subjects without their knowledge, a form of research enquiry which should be resorted to only where it is not possible to use other methods to obtain essential data. These methods should only be used when it is possible to safeguard completely the interests and anonymity of the subjects.

These two extracts from professional codes, admirable as they both are, raise some unanswerable questions about the ethics of survey research. In the first place, the phrase 'to ensure that informants will *in no way* be adversely affected' by the questions asked is to ask that survey research can rarely if ever be carried out. At the individual level, it is possibly attainable. But at a general level it is not. Surveys are usually administered for the purpose of providing information and knowledge, so that decisions may be better informed. It is rare for a researcher to know in advance whether or not the decision taken as a result of that information will necessarily be of benefit to all his respondents. It might, for example, result in a price rise, or a policy of redistribution, or the pruning of a service, which would not have a universally popular appeal. Our own view is that survey research, like any other form of knowledge, often involves threats to certain interest groups. Its overall effect is, however, to minimise prejudice by aiding understanding. It is undoubtedly true that for those whose interest will be jeopardised by a clearer understanding of the *status quo*, survey research is certainly no ally. And in any case, no researcher could ever undertake to be responsible for all the consequences, direct and indirect, foreseeable and otherwise, which might flow from a particular survey.

The code of the British Sociological Association raises a quite different issue, concerning the question of 'essential data'. It argues that observation techniques may be used if, and only if, the data are 'essential'. From a consumer viewpoint, however, there may be no data so essential that this kind of intrusion (observation methods) would be justified. The problem is, of course, that professional codes of ethics are generally written by professionals for professionals. They take commendable steps to safeguard consumer interests, but only perhaps insofar as they do not conflict with professional interests.

Confidentiality

There can be no absolute safeguards against disclosures of information at some stage of the survey process, or subsequently, once the respondent has been identified by the interviewer. Yet the use of reasonable precautions, linked with the existence of codes of ethical behaviour for survey research, can reduce this risk to very small proportions indeed. It is striking that in spite of less rigorous confidentiality procedures than those we believe should be applied in the future, past survey research in the United Kingdom has given rise to hardly any known cases of abuses of confidence. In general, survey researchers have subscribed to one or other of various codes of practice; and ethical standards regarding confidentiality have been maintained at a high level. There is, of course, a vital element of enlightened self-interest, as well as professional conscience, involved: survey research depends on the willing co-operation of the public, and to forfeit this through improper or even merely slovenly behaviour towards confidential records would be self-destructive.

A further point is that deliberate disclosure of individual records, or even of those of an entire survey, would often have little practical point. The great majority of surveys contain information of what to the outsider would seem an anecdotal kind – a melange of items related to some particular topic (such as attitudes to the environment, or leisure habits) but not a concise encapsulation of the life-style and circumstances of the respondent. It is rare, for example, for enough financial information to be included to be of more than marginal value to a credit-rating agency; yet we accept that credit-rating agencies appear to thrive on marginal snippets of information which can be built up and used too easily to the detriment of the individual to whom they relate. On the other hand, the difficulty of linking this financial information to life-style information and individual identities would be formidable unless the survey organisation deliberately re-organised itself to facilitate the retrieval of identified data. And even if it did so, the fact that it deals only with limited samples of people would mean that the chance of its having information about any particular individual for whom a credit rating is sought would be very small indeed.

Nevertheless, however unlikely it is that disclosure would take place even without stringent precautions, these precautions must be taken. There are essentially two: one is the maintenance and enforcement of codes of standards and the other is the adoption of practical safeguards.

The most powerful safeguard is the separation of identifying material from the questionnaire replies. The interviewer needs to be supplied with a name and address, serially numbered. But once the questionnaire has been completed, only the serial number, not the name, need appear on it while it goes through the necessary checking procedures to ensure, for example, that everyone on the sampling list is accounted for. The questionnaire can then be identified only by consulting the sampling list in order to 'decode' the serial number. When punched cards are prepared from the questionnaire, it is customary to employ a fresh serial number, both on the questionnaires and the cards, because the original serial number may be complex in form and will in any case not run consecutively (because not all the original sample listings will have produced a completed questionnaire).

The purpose of this fresh number is simply that when the computer tape is edited for accuracy, each query can be referred back to the relevant questionnaire. It will be evident that once the tape has been edited, the only link between it and the identity of respondents is via the questionnaires: if these are destroyed, no subsequent linkage is possible.

In the absence of some external key to identity, it is only very seldom that identification is possible from internal evidence alone. Such instances occur mainly with firms and other organisations. It is obvious that in a sample of major British manufacturers, data on tape about numbers of employees, turnover, geographical location and nature of product might be sufficient to identify individual manufacturers. But in a normal population, survey identification by such means would be impractical, since although the data might be as unique to an individual as his fingerprint, how is the possessor of this particular set of attributes to be found? Even so, however unlikely it is that an individual will be identified, in some cases it is worth excluding even the most remote possibility. In the release of census data, for example, there is a minimum cell size for identified locations, below which the data will not be published.

But there is a further danger to confidentiality. By the nature of the survey process, the co-operation of several different organisations is frequently involved. Here again, a practical safeguard is that questionnaires should not contain identifying material. The research organisation alone should retain the identity key; punching and computing sub-contractors should have no means of identification. The sponsoring body might receive no direct output at all from the survey, but if it does, the same principle of anonymity must be maintained.

Finally, it should be noted that, contrary to popular belief, the use of computers and other sophisticated techniques of processing data enables a greater degree of confidentiality to be maintained. When all data are stored in a machine-readable form, quite simply they cannot be understood by most individuals. Before identities can be discovered, they need to be decoded by programs written by highly trained personnel. Manual systems of the past enabled much greater access to individual identities.

Manipulation of the public

The Working Party has been mainly concerned with potential dangers to privacy along the lines of the foregoing paragraphs, but others have argued that there is a much more potent threat to society from social research itself. The Sociology Liberation Movement in the United States maintains that:

> (Social scientists) have provided their sponsors with the knowledge needed for controlling modern society.

The context of this comment makes it clear that surveys are regarded as a weapon of authority in the power struggle with emergent classes of society. The argument, which was also in evidence in Britain at the time of the census in relation to immigrants, runs approximately like this:

> by agreeing to disclose their private attitudes and behaviour patterns to social scientists, and by confiding in them, the public is providing the establishment with the tools it needs to maintain the *status quo* and to strengthen its own position; these disclosures enable the manipulation of the public by the establishment, based on the fears, grievances, aspirations and weaknesses they have discovered.

The Working Party dissents from this view: it does not believe that information of the kind afforded by surveys does offer this manipulatory facility. On the contrary, as we have argued, surveys enable minorities to have a voice which they would otherwise lack. The obtaining *and dissemination* of objective information must be conducive to liberty rather than repression: totalitarian governments suppress it. But dissemination is vital. The Sociology Liberation Movement advocated that:

> Sociologists should regularly communicate their findings to those who are affected by them in a language in a medium and at a price accessible to those affected.

A large proportion of publicly-sponsored research in Britain is already published, as is academic work, but most business and market research is not, partly because of competitive considerations and partly from lack of any positive incentive to publish.

The quotation above seems to call for a more direct dissemination of information to those who were actually interviewed on the project. An extremely interesting example of this was the National Child Development Study in Britain. The survey results were published in the *Sunday Times*, and the fee for publication was used to purchase and post a copy of the magazine to every child in the sample.

Few would argue the *desirability* of informing respondents of the results of research in which they were interviewed, but many would question its feasibility. There are problems of interpretation, since most research reports are written for peer group rather than public consumption; and the financial problems cannot always be as neatly solved as in the example quoted.

Although the Working Party was by no means unanimous on this point, there was a very strong case made for the results and inferences drawn from government survey research (at least) to be published. It was felt that there had to be an overwhelming case for information collected on behalf of the public, using public resources, to be suppressed from public scrutiny unless such publication would lead to individual identification. There appeared to be few other circumstances in which publication would be against the public interest. In any case, wide dissemination of survey results (regardless of sponsor) was felt to be desirable in itself. In the first place it contributes to a better understanding of society; and in the second place, the wider the publication, the less would be the proliferation and duplication of surveys which occurs through lack of knowledge of what has already been studied. And this applies as much to foundation-sponsored research as to the public sector.

It should also be stressed that in publishing survey findings, it is extremely important that full details of the methods used, sample size etc. are included so that proper critical assessments may be made of the findings.

Interpretation

Although it takes us outside the strict terms of reference we set ourselves, we would like to add that in our view a further danger of surveys lies not in privacy aspects, and still less in the notion that they
may be a repressive tool of authority, but in simple misuse of the findings through faulty conception, execution or interpretation – most frequently perhaps, the first of these. It is all too easy to ask questions
and get answers without regard to the conceptual framework within
which the respondent operates, which may be totally different from
that of those whose needs initiated the survey.

It sometimes seems to be implicitly assumed that if the
decision-maker can formulate his problem in the form of a question,
its incorporation in a survey is likely to give him the answer. Nothing
could be further from the truth. Often we find that the decision-maker
and the respondent have widely different terms of reference, and that
the job of translating the decision-maker's questions into a totally different set which can be put to respondents (whose replies must then
be re-interpreted in terms of the original questions) becomes the most
taxing that the survey researcher has to face. The rapid growth of
survey research has tended towards a situation where experienced
people are comparatively thinly spread, and the superficial but misleading simplicity of some aspects of surveys, notably questionnaire
design, allows many projects to be conducted and interpreted on the
basis of misleading concepts and unreliable information.

Equally important, however, is the misuse of survey results by
means of distortion or crude misrepresentation by others outside the
survey field. If survey research is to occupy an increasingly important
role in the process of policy formulation and decision-making, its
practitioners may have to take more positive steps to counter the kinds
of misinterpretation to which survey results can be subjected. The responsibility of the researcher may increasingly have to extend not
only to specifying the limits within which his data may legitimately be
interpreted, but also to correcting and disowning the illegitimate interpretations which – on some subjects – are a frequent occupational
hazard.

[The remainder of the SCPR report is continued in Chapter 16 in this
volume, discussing policy issues.]

6 The Issue of Privacy in Public-opinion Research *

Robert O. Carlson

In this chapter I shall view with some alarm the short-term prospects of public-opinion research as it relates to the issue of privacy. I believe it is a real issue and that, by the very nature of public-opinion work, we must invade the privacy of our respondents in some measure. I feel this invasion can be justified, but unfortunately we have done a poor job up to now of explaining ourselves and our work to our publics.

Things have been going along rather too well for us as a profession, and except for an occasional effort to legislate against door-to-door interviewing on a municipal or state level, as well as some scattered instances of pseudo-surveys being used for selling merchandise, the Executive Council of the American Association for Public Opinion Research (AAPOR) and its Standards Committee have lived relatively trouble-free lives in recent years. Certainly AAPOR experience compares favourably with the harassment and the investigations which those in the field of psychological testing have undergone. I am concerned that we in the survey research field underestimate the likelihood of our activities facing similar scrutiny and public controversy.

* Presidential address to AAPOR conference, reprinted from *Public Opinion Quarterly*, **31**, 1967, pp. 1–8 with the permission of Elsevier North-Holland Inc.

As a thriving new profession, exercising considerable power in government, academic and business circles, it is unrealistic to expect that we can escape the searching eye of critics and the general public with respect to the issue of privacy and the work we do.

Some of us seem to operate on the bland assumption that the issue of privacy has little or no relevance for the field of public-opinion research. In its most extreme form, this view is reflected in the philosophy that we as researchers have the right to ask people their opinions on a broad range of questions and they, in turn, have the right to answer or to refuse to answer our questions. Let us pause at this juncture and give a little more thought to this beguiling and comforting proposition. However, let us view it from the point of view of a potential critic who turns the tables on us and begins to ask us some questions about the basic tool of our trade – the interview.

For example, what is our answer to the critic who may say, 'The people you interview in your surveys are not all alike. Some are well educated, have a high socio-economic status, are intellectually and psychologically secure and sophisticated, and these, of course, can be expected to know that they do not have to answer the questions your interviewers bring to their homes. But,' continues our critic, 'what of the others in the population who are old, poor, badly-educated members of ethnic groups who harbour fear of authority figures from the outside world and a host of similar categories – are these people equally aware of their right not to answer your questions and are they equally prepared psychologically to exercise this right?' I do not think we have adequate answers to this question, and yet answers would be of considerable interest to us from a purely research standpoint, quite apart from the light such data might shed on the privacy question itself. Why should not the appendix of each opinion survey give the available characteristics of the people who refused to be interviewed as well as those who participated in a survey?

Clearly, the interview situation in a typical public-opinion survey is the point at which the privacy issue takes on its greatest meaning. It dramatises the dilemma of where the rights of the individual leave off and the needs of our society for better scientific information on human behaviour take over. It would be naïve and even amusing for me to suggest that interviewers should preface their questions with a reminder to a potential respondent that he has a right not to be interviewed. However amusing and ingenuous this idea may seem, I remind you that our psychological colleagues are very much concerned about it. Many of their leading spokesmen have stated that every individual should be informed that he is free to participate or not in any particular psychological test before it is administered to him.

But there are still other aspects of the interview situation that our critics might insist represent an invasion of the privacy of respondents, and we do well to consider these matters. For example, an interviewer may gain access to a home by indicating in vague terms the nature of the survey he is conducting. Once having been admitted and having established rapport with his informant, the interviewer is free to move from his relatively innocuous initial questions into subject areas of a highly personal nature – posing questions having to do with the political, religious, economic, and moral beliefs and practices of the respondent. Such questions no doubt are essential for many of the surveys we conduct, but they also are capable of generating resistance and resentment. In such instances, does the average respondent realise that he has the right to break off the questioning any time he may wish, even though he has given his earlier agreement to participate in the survey? This rhetorical question merely illustrates one of the many aspects about the interview situation on which we have far too little data. True, there are countless articles on how to win rapport, how to phrase questions, how to probe for more complete answers, how to assess interviewer bias, and so forth – but we have uncommonly few descriptions of the interview as a real-life power situation in which both the respondent and the interviewer play out their separate and often conflicting roles. Central to any such discussion of the interview as a social phenomenon would be a consideration of how much the respondent knows about his rights vis-à-vis the interviewer. Such a study would be a splendid addition to the standard textbook, *Interviewing in Social Research*, by Hyman and his associates at NORC.

Still another related aspect of the privacy issue in survey research work arises when the respondent is asked to report on the actions, attitudes, beliefs and behaviour of his family, his neighbours, his fellow-workers, and others who are in close association with him. To what extent do we in the research fraternity run the risk of being seen as professional snoopers and private CIA agents when we employ such questions? Once again, one can see the potential conflict between our valid need for this kind of information in understanding aspects of human behaviour and the equally salient concern which the public has that the research process may be abused or misused.

On another score we face a similar moral dilemma. Today there is widespread concern over the extensive use of electronic devices to spy on the most private aspects of our lives. Whether the gadgets are hidden cameras or microphones or tape recorders, they have in common the aim of causing people to reveal things about their lives that they would be most reluctant to reveal of their own free will. With this widespread concern being expressed in the press and in legislative halls, is it possible that we will be criticised for planting projective questions in our interview schedules and thereby psychologically bugging the minds of our respondents and causing them to reveal information about themselves that they otherwise would not? Far-fetched and ludicrous, you say? Perhaps, but it can be argued that when we use projective questions in a general opinion survey, we are employing the tools of the clinical psychologist without always ensuring that the same controls are imposed on the use and analysis of these projective questions that the psychologist imposes with his clients.

Of course, one of the most common means of gaining electronic entry to a home is the telephone. Because it is a relatively quick, inexpensive and convenient research tool (particularly when we are trying to locate certain kinds of respondents from a much larger universe), we all have a stake in encouraging a responsible use of the telephone in survey research. The several telephone companies, interestingly enough, do not feel that this is part of their responsibility. At any rate, it is safe to assume the average telephone subscriber does not see himself as just another potential sampling point in one of our surveys. He pays a monthly rental for his phone and usually has a proprietary feeling about it. The day may come when he reacts to increasing sales solicitations and public-opinion surveys by asking why he should help subsidise the research and sales activities of others. There is agitation in some sectors of our country to have phone books indicate by a symbol whether or not the subscriber is willing to co-operate in surveys and sales pitches, and this movement could profoundly affect us.

Still another aspect of the privacy issue is raised when we find it necessary to ask respondents questions about topics that may induce considerable stress and anxiety in their minds – questions having to do with their health or their level of information on diseases such as cancer, or questions on the likelihood of an atomic war or the possibility of a depression. Once these issues have been raised to the surface of a respondent's mind, they may cause him worry and upset long after the interviewer has said goodbye. In most test situations set up by psychologists, provisions are made for some form of psychic support and therapeutic reassurance to be given to respondents after they have been exposed to anxiety-producing questions. Is it totally unrealistic to have our interviewers give some written or oral reassurance to a respondent at the end of an interview when the subject matter of the survey has dealt with an anxiety-provoking issue?

Finally, on the matter of privacy, there are those standard questions one finds at the end of most surveys dealing with the age, sex, socio-economic status, education, race, and often the political and religious affiliation of the respondent. It is ironic that we have come to refer to these as census-type questions, inasmuch as the Bureau of the Census has the greatest difficulty in getting approval for collecting data on some of these attributes, even when it can prove that it has an elaborate mechanism for protecting the confidential nature of its data.

The issue in this case is not only our right as researchers to collect such data but, more important, our discretion and maturity of judgment in using them in reporting on the attitudes and the behaviour of subgroups in our samples which might be identified and damaged by such revelations. Frankly, I am surprised that we have not felt greater pressure from the various action groups organised to protect the rights of minority groups, regarding our practice of categorising and reporting on subgroups in our samples. In theory, it can be argued that any subgroup that can be identified by data in a survey report has had its privacy invaded. While I personally would be inclined to reject such reasoning as specious and misguided, I feel we cannot dismiss the possibility of this developing into an important issue at some future date.

In summary, then, the first part of this chapter has belaboured the proposition that the issue of privacy in public-opinion research is a very real one, and that it manifests itself in a wide variety of ways, but most particularly in the interview situation. It may also obtain when we use sloppy procedures in screening, hiring and supervising coders, typists, clerical personnel and all other employees who have access to personal data collected in our opinion surveys.

* * *

If you grant that we do indeed invade the privacy of our respondents in some measure in the work we do, then I think you might also agree that it becomes important for us to ensure that the public understands why we need this kind of information and why we can be trusted with it. Stated bluntly, the issue of privacy then is linked to the question: What does the public get for permitting us to enter their homes, use up their leisure time, and often explore very private nooks and crannies of their lives? The psychological tester in industry or government can point to a number of direct benefits to the individual, his family and his society from the various psychological tests he administers. What gratifications and rewards do we offer respondents who take part in our public-opinion surveys?

The first and most obvious is that we provide a sympathetic ear to them and offer them a way of getting problems and opinions off their chests. Moreover, respondents probably have their self-esteem enhanced when they are asked opinions on important problems of the day. But, alas, there are also many instances in which the subject matter of a survey is pretty dull and trivial and of interest only to the sponsoring client. What do the respondent and his society get from co-operating with such data-gathering efforts?

Analogies may be misleading and misplaced, and yet I feel it is appropriate to use one in discussing this question and its broader implications. Let's face it, we are able to collect our research data only because the general public continues to be willing to submit to our interviews. This acceptance of us by the public is the basic natural resource on which our industry is built. Without it, we would be out of business tomorrow. Other industries also have been built on the exploitation of other kinds of natural resources – our forests, farmlands and mines – and it is instructive to remember that during the nineteenth century in this country many of these industries made two errors that in time caused public outcry and pressure on government to regulate them. First, they assumed that the public was not interested in what they were doing and so made no serious effort to explain the contributions they were making to society. Second, they failed to find a mechanism to police a certain few of their members who did not serve the public well.

To date, we in the opinion research business have done a poor job of informing the public about the work we do and the benefits it brings to them. On the other hand, we have formulated a sound code of ethics. Unfortunately, we have only informal means by which to enforce these standards and it may be unrealistic to expect that we will ever be able to do more. Those in our business who most frequently do violence to our standards usually do not belong to associations such as AAPOR and do not respond readily to informal pressures.

What is the story we should be telling about public-opinion research and the benefits the public derives from it? The substance of this message will obviously vary, depending on the type of organisation that sponsors public-opinion research. Broadly speaking, there are three kinds of clients who commission most public-opinion research studies. They are (1) the government, (2) academic and quasi-academic research institutes, usually operating on a non-profit basis, and (3) commercial research firms, usually trying to operate on a profit basis and fortunately succeeding.

I suspect that each of these three groups has a different degree of acceptance from the public. In the case of government-sponsored research, a certain amount is actually required by law, the best example being the census. But even when not required by law, studies sponsored by government agencies, both federal and state, seem to have general acceptance – particularly those dealing with problems in the field of agriculture, health, education and public welfare. The research work done by these government bureaux has earned high recognition from scholars as well as the general public. In speculating on the degree of acceptance by the public of government-sponsored research, it should be noted that the public ultimately exercises control over these studies through their elected officials, who can authorise greater or less government research effort. Yet, ironically enough, it is in government today that the use of psychological tests is most widely being called into question by congressional critics and others. Is our turn next? Perhaps now is the time for an educational effort to be undertaken with key members of Congress to explain the role public-opinion surveys can play in ensuring better planning by government agencies.

It is difficult to speculate on how much the public is aware of the research being carried out by academic and non-profit research institutes. I suspect there may be times when the recondite nature of their studies may puzzle the public, but I find no evidence that any appreciable number of people question either the motives or the integrity of these research organisations. I assume most of you would agree that a persuasive case can be made for the benefits that the general public derives from these studies. Once more, however, I find myself generally unimpressed by the quality of the reporting these groups do in telling their story to the non-research-oriented world. Their annual reports, when they elect to publish them, are often pedestrian and dull, apparently assigned to a staff writer, and failing altogether to catch the excitement and significance of the problems on which these institutes are working.

Finally, there is the vast field of commercial research, which is designed to help a client improve his market position or his corporate acceptance. These projects are sometimes treated in a pejorative and patronising way by those who do not know the rigorous technical standards and the imaginative research designs employed in many of these studies. One frequent justification for the social utility of commercial research is that it permits the public to communicate its likes and dislikes to the companies that manufacture our consumer products; produce our newspapers, television programmes, and magazines; and provide a host of other consumer services. We in the research business generally assume this function is perfectly obvious to the general public, but I doubt this.

But telling the story of the contributions public-opinion research makes to improving the consumer's products must be done with skill. It would be unwise, for example, to use the old cliché that the public is the real boss of the marketplace and that by asking for its opinion about various consumer products we bring democracy to the councils of the business world. One example of where this theme could come back to haunt us is the automotive industry, which has carried out countless consumer surveys. These surveys may or may not have been a factor in causing manufacturers to put chrome and tailfins on their cars instead of building greater safety into them. But the auto industry, and every other industrial consumer of opinion-research data, should make it clear that they employ survey-research data merely as one among several sources of information that influence their decisions on product design and changes. Thus, opinion surveys provide the consumer with a forum from which he may speak to management, but they do not guarantee him a seat in the board of directors' room.

Candour requires that we also admit that not all commercial surveys have direct social value to our society. Putting aside the question of whether or not cigarette smoking is harmful to health, it just is plain difficult to see how the public benefits when a client commissions a survey designed to learn why the public prefers Brand X to Brand Y. In such cases, the argument I would offer on behalf of the social value of commercial research is that it frequently helps perfect research techniques that can be applied to problems of greater social import- ance, provided these new research techniques are made available to the world of research scholars. The Roper Public Opinion Research Centre at Williams College represented a pioneer effort in the direc- tion of making such data available, and the Council of Social Science Data Archives consolidates the resources of the Roper Centre with those of seven other libraries of public-opinion research data. Even so, only a small fraction of the research carried out for private industry ever finds its way into those archives or the public domain.

The time has come, in my opinion, for those of us who earn a liveli- hood from public-opinion research to consider how we might make a more concrete contribution to our society. As a very tentative and in- adequate first step in this direction, I suggest that individual firms (or a consortium of some of our larger commercial and academic research groups) donate several public-service surveys each year on subjects of importance to the people of the United States. There are endless topics crying out for such study, and some do not have sponsors with money enough to commission such research.

I have spoken at length about our less than excellent public re- lations position because I think our profession has the resources and reasons to improve it. This job should be undertaken at once, not alone to forestall government interference and regulation of our work, and not alone to protect the dollar investment and the professional commitment that we have in the field of public-opinion surveys, but also because a better understanding of our work could very conceiv- ably improve the quality of the data we get from the public. Once we accept the fact that the question of 'privacy' is relevant for us in the public-opinion research field, I am convinced we can justify our ac- tivities and demonstrate their social worth.

7 Resistance to Community Surveys*

Eric Josephson

The Problem

The co-operation – passive or active – of respondents and the communities in which they live is the *sine qua non* of survey research. Carlson comments in the previous chapter that: 'We are able to collect our research data only because the general public continues to be willing to submit to our interviews. This acceptance of us by the public is the basic natural resource on which our industry is built. Without it, we would be out of business tomorrow.' So far, those engaged in surveys which are relatively innocuous as regards purpose, content and populations being studied, have been able to take that co-operation – or inertia – for granted.

However, judging by the experience which my colleagues and I at the Columbia University School of Public Health have had with protests against a study of adolescents in a well-known ghetto, research projects dealing with the 'pathologies' of slums or with deviant behaviour should be prepared for trouble.[1] The situation is by no means desperate, but it is serious and worthy of serious consideration. Ironically, at a time when there are greater demands on survey research

* Reprinted from *Social Problems*, the journal of the Society for the Study of Social Problems, **18**, 1970, pp. 117–29, with the permission of the publishers and the author.

than ever before to deal with problems of demonstrable public concern, such as poverty, ill-health or youthful drug use, resistance to surveys threatens to make such research increasingly difficult and sometimes impossible.

Before describing the opposition which confronted me and my colleagues, I want to distinguish between studies or projects which are national in their scope or in the interest they arouse, and those which are essentially local in their focus and significance.

At the national level there have been controversies over Project Camelot and the Moynihan Report, debates inside and outside Congress about psychological testing and data banks, and most recently, the campaign to try to get the Census Bureau to eliminate questions about flush toilets and other embarrassing matters. In the controversies which these and other such *causes celebres* have aroused at home and abroad, attacks have been made against the sponsorship of research projects (especially when it is concealed or Establishmentarian), their alleged uselessness, the failure of investigators to consult with the communities or populations being studied, the threat to individual privacy (as in reporting deviant behaviour), and the invidiousness of research findings. These are charges which have been made against social research by intellectuals, politicians of left and right, and spokesmen for the black community.

Nationwide survey organisations have, so far as I know, continued to conduct studies on a variety of controversial topics – for example, the urban riot studies. What explains this success is that the investigators and interviewers are rarely in evidence long enough to become conspicuous targets for attack. In other words, such studies have relatively limited and brief impact on the communities being sampled.

But studies, such as ours, which focus on a single community for a fairly extended period of time lack this advantage of low visibility. The investigators become part of the local landscape, so to speak, thereby increasing the chance that they will become embroiled in local controversy. Among the relatively few published reports of such cases are those by Rainwater and Pittman regarding their problems in studying deviant behaviour in a St Louis housing project[2] and Moore's description of the difficulties which she and her colleagues encountered in a study of Mexican Americans in the south-west.[3] What these and other such reports add up to is a picture of lower-class sensitivity about being studied, suspicion of outside investigators and their motives, scepticism about the benefits of research – in short, disenchantment with the nature and conduct of social research – especially among local community leaders. This is not new. What is new, as some of these reports suggest, is that community leaders, demanding a voice in the research enterprise, are in a position to exact a price for their co-operation. As a consequence, research may at times be diverted from its original, 'purer' purpose.

Aims of the Project

Our original objective was to produce data on the relationship between poverty and adolescent health. At the beginning we found that despite the almost inordinate attention which has been paid by social scientists to adolescents, rich and poor, relatively little was known about their health. We know a great deal about the health status and medical care needs of the very young and the very old; but very little about those between childhood and adulthood. This neglect has been due partly to the assumption that at least the physical, if not the emotional, health of adolescents can be taken for granted. And to be sure, in terms of morbidity, adolescents are in an advantageous position as compared with their juniors and seniors. But evidence from studies of draft rejects, the National Health Survey, job-training programmes, accident, suicide and homicide statistics, suggested to us that this neglect was unjustified and that adolescents living in slums were in a particularly disadvantageous position.

As social scientists, we approached the problem by taking a broad view of 'health', that is not only concerning ourselves with traditional measures of health status and medical care needs, but also with self-perceptions regarding health practices, moods, aspirations and expectations, sexual behaviour, the use of drugs, violence, thoughts about death etc. Our aim from the beginning was to collect two kinds of data about adolescent health: one based on what youngsters themselves might report in interviews and the other based on examinations of them by medical teams. The result, we hoped, would be a comprehensive picture of the health status and medical care needs of adolescents which would contribute to planning for improved delivery of medical care in disadvantaged communities. I must add that since we were planning to deal with minors in the eyes of the law, we recognised from the start that we would have to obtain some form of parental consent both for interviews with and medical examinations of adolescents.[4]

In 1967, we obtained funds from the Children's Bureau to undertake a pilot study of adolescent health in the Washington Heights health district of New York City. The opportunity to do so was presented to us by the work done earlier on a comprehensive family health survey of the community conducted by Elinson, referred to as the Master Sample Survey.[5] Our technique was to go back to adolescents, here defined as between twelve and seventeen years of age, in households which had previously been approached in the most recent Master Sample Survey. This we did in the summer of 1967, completing 122 interviews with youngsters and arranging for medical examinations of half of them at the nearby Washington Heights Health Centre. From a methodological point of view, it was successful; that is, it gave us an opportunity to produce and test instruments for a larger study. Although the average length of the interview was two and a half hours, adolescents and their families were extremely cooperative. There was no controversy about the project.

But Washington Heights, although diverse in its ethnic and income characteristics, is not exactly a slum; and, as noted earlier, our intention was to study the poor. Once again, an unusual opportunity presented itself given the new role which Columbia University began to play in Harlem's medical affairs. As part of the affiliation contract between the University and the City of New York with regard to Harlem Hospital (a municipal institution), plans had been laid for a comprehensive evaluation of the health status and medical care utilisation patterns of the community being served by Harlem Hospital, including a sample survey of households in the community. Directing the overall evaluation was Elinson.

As previously in Washington Heights, our plan was to go back to households which had been approached in the larger survey and, with parental consent, interview adolescents about their health and offer them free medical examinations at Harlem Hospital. Starting at the end of 1967, we intended to interview as many as 1000 adolescents twelve to seventeen years of age. Since the larger community survey had been under way for six months and had been proceeding without any unusual difficulties, we anticipated none with regard to our project. Once again, funds for the study were made available by the Children's Bureau.

While ours was to be the first large-scale study of adolescent health in Harlem, it was not the first study of adolescents in that community.

Several years earlier, Haryou-Act, the major local anti-poverty agency, had conducted a survey of adolescents in Harlem which, so far as I know, produced no controversy. But in 1967, we at Columbia represented a university with which Harlem was beginning to have increasingly strained relations. For example, the charge had already been made that Columbia was exploiting Harlem Hospital for its own purposes and ignoring the wishes of the community with regard to health matters.

The Protest

Late in 1967, we made the necessary arrangements with our colleagues in charge of the larger community health survey and with the staff at Harlem Hospital. Our own team of interviewers would go to households already visited in the other survey; with parental consent, adolescents would be interviewed and offered a medical examination at the hospital. Before starting fieldwork, however, it seemed necessary and desirable to determine whether the questionnaire we had used successfully in ethnically mixed Washington Heights would be appropriate for a survey in which most of the respondents would be black residents of Central Harlem.

Therefore, we decided to conduct a small number of (approximately thirty) unstructured interviews with adolescents in households previously contacted by the larger community health survey. The chief purpose of these interviews was to provide information about the salience of 'health' and medical care for adolescents in these households and about ways of questioning them about such matters – in short, to help us revise the questionnaire which we had used previously in Washington Heights.

Since the new questionnaire became controversial, a brief description of it is in order. It contained such innocuous items as 'When, roughly, was the last time you saw a doctor – for any reason at all?' But the questionnaire also sought to elicit from youngsters suggestions as to how we might best interview their contemporaries about health matters. Thus, we asked: 'The word "health" – what does it mean to you? (Probe: How would you describe a healthy person?)' We also asked: 'What do you think we should ask young people about sex? (Probe: What should we ask about their sexual relations and sexual experiences?)' Regarding drugs, we did not ask adolescents whether they themselves were taking drugs but rather what they knew about drug use among others their age. Regarding 'trouble with the police', we asked them whether they had ever had such trouble and also what kind of trouble their neighbours had had. Regarding riots, we did not ask whether they themselves had participated but merely what they thought about riots. Perhaps the most sensitive questions were, 'Have you ever thought about killing yourself?', 'When was the last time you beat somebody?' and 'Do you ever carry a knife?' In somewhat different form, all of these questions had been tested successfully in our Washington Heights pilot study and in other surveys. Also, the Central Harlem Adolescent Study, conducted earlier by Haryou-Act and to which I referred above, included such questions as 'When was the last time you carried a knife, gun or some other weapon?', 'When was the last time you tried reefers or another drug?', 'When was the last time you had been in any kind of a fist fight?' and 'When was the last time you had been in gang fights?' Our plan was to conduct these unstructured interviews early in December 1967.

Precisely because of the nature of these exploratory interviews – requiring a considerable amount of probing – we hoped to recruit field-workers with some experience in social surveys as well as the ability to improvise variations in the wording and sequence of questions. Friends at the Bureau of Applied Social Research and at the National Opinion Research Centre referred a number of interviewers to us who worked out well; others (about whom we knew little) were recommended to us by members of our own staff. Of a total of seven interviewers who were finally recruited for the exploratory study and asked to come to a training session, three (all graduate students in the social sciences) at the very outset began to raise serious questions about Columbia's 'image' in Harlem and about the propriety of the study. Although our staff began to have misgivings about letting them undertake interviews, we did nothing at first, permitting them to leave with their assignments. However, the day after the training session, we decided that the three interviewers who had expressed such strong doubts about the project should not be permitted to proceed with their assignments. Our fear was that they might antagonise respondents and thereby jeopardise further contacts by other investigators with these households; this was a risk we did not want to take. They were, therefore, called back before doing any interviews, asked to return all study materials, and offered another, more consultative role on the project. This offer they declined. Meanwhile, the other four interviewers completed their assignments, reporting no difficulties in obtaining parental consent for the interviews or in conducting the interviews with adolescents. Altogether, eight interviews were completed.

So far, this had been a fairly ordinary situation in which a few interviewers felt uncomfortable about a project and then withdrew from it. However, the three discharged interviewers had managed to make copies of our questionnaire before returning their assignments kits and began to circulate copies of the questionnaire in Harlem, thereby setting in motion a protest against the project and against the university under whose auspices it was being conducted.

Within two weeks of our initial training session and the departure of the three hostile interviewers, a story appeared in *The Amsterdam News* announcing the formation of an 'Ad Hoc Citizens Committee Against Columbia University . . . to protest a health survey being conducted among Harlem adolescents'. Spokesmen for the committee were reported as having taken this action 'after seeing samples of the survey questionnaire which, they claim, contains "derogatory and prejudicial" questions'. More specifically, we were attacked for asking questions about narcotics, beatings, knives, and street fights and riots. At approximately the same time, under the aegis of a 'Harlem Committee for Self-Defence' (another name for the Ad Hoc Committee) leaflets regarding the project began to circulate in Harlem. One of them charged that Columbia 'was doing a study under the guise of health' and attacked us for asking twelve year olds about their sex lives, their use of drugs and alcohol, their friends, the last time they beat someone or were beaten, their militancy, the weapons they carried, whether they had ever thought of killing themselves, and their participation in riots. 'If the Man was interested in your health,' this leaflet continued, 'he would send a doctor, not an interviewer. They are using black interviewers to fool you. They know white cops can't do it. So now they're sending black ones. There will be other studies and other disguises. Don't tell anyone anything about your business!!! Protect yourself and your black brothers and sisters. Join with the Harlem Committee for Self-Defence to stop this study before this study stops you!!!!' Still another leaflet referred to our project as a 'Trick Health Survey'.

What followed was a meeting devoted to our project held at the Abyssinian Baptist Church; approximately seventy-five people attended. Chaired by one of the interviewers we had discharged, the meeting heard him say (according to a published report) that our survey was intended 'to determine just how far (Columbia) can go before people rebel and resist'. Also aired at the meeting were charges that the results of the survey would 'wind up in police precincts, not in the halls of the University' and that the survey was a 'fraud'. After the chairman asked, 'What can we do to stop Columbia?' one suggestion from the floor was to 'give the interviewer a good head whipping'. To which another participant added: 'You will have to spill your own blood to fight Columbia.' In addition, a woman described as an 'indignant mother' took the floor to say that 'I would not allow anyone to come into my house and ask my children anything.' A young man on our staff who attempted to defend and justify the project was shouted down, accused of 'selling his people down the river for a few pieces of silver', and ordered out of the church.

How much interest the protest was beginning to generate is hard to determine. A few radio broadcasts mentioned it, as did local and student newspapers. In a story about Columbia's relations with Harlem, *The New York Times* quoted one of the leaflets but did not mention the project. The radical organ, *Challenge*, devoted a full page to our survey under the headline, 'Harlem Hits Columbia Snoopers'. According to the story in *Challenge*, 'the project and the interview form have just enough questions dealing with health to make it look good, but in reality it has nothing to do with improving anyone's health. It's just one more method used by the ruling class to determine how best to suppress the Black people with the least amount of trouble.' But 'some of the people who were supposed to be interviewers, after reading the letter, the "interviewer's guide" and the questions they were supposed to ask, saw how Columbia and its masters, the U.S. Government, had something besides "health" in mind.' *Challenge* went on to describe how the three interviewers had 'called a meeting of people from Harlem to discuss this situation and map out a plan of action to combat this and every other attempt to use Harlem as a laboratory to experiment on our people like the Nazis did in Germany'.

As the protest continued, our project was linked by militant blacks with a number of other activities in which Columbia was engaged. So far as I and my colleagues were concerned, however, the climax of the protest against our survey was reached late in January 1968 when a demonstration by black militants and their supporters took place at Columbia University's main campus. Perhaps as many as fifty demonstrators marched along Broadway for half an hour, some of them carrying placards which said 'Don't let Columbia interview Blacks' and others with signs saying 'We need hospitals, not surveys'. Our project was not the only target at this time, Columbia was also being attacked for its plans to build a gymnasium and for evicting some of the tenants in University-owned apartment buildings. The spirit of the occasion was summed up by the placard with the phrase, 'Columbia get the hell out and stay out'.

More recently, there has been further agitation in Harlem regarding the Hospital; but so far as we know the controversy over our project either died a natural death or was displaced by other, more pressing concerns.

Aftermath

Such, in brief, is the history of the protest against our project in Harlem. Before discussing some of the more general implications of the attack, let me describe what we tried to do about it.

First of all, it was important to evaluate the extent to which the attack against the project reflected community sentiment. Our judgment was that a small group of people in Harlem were exploiting our survey for their own political purposes and that they had little community support; most people in Harlem, we assumed, knew little about our survey, or if they did, were indifferent. Indirect support for this assumption has been provided by the telephone survey which Nash and Epstein of the Bureau of Applied Social Research conducted in Central Harlem soon after the disturbances at the lower campus; they found that relatively few people had strong feelings about Columbia and that most were either favourably disposed towards the planned gymnasium or neutral on the subject.[6] To the best of my knowledge, nobody mentioned our study.

But even if most residents of Harlem were neutral towards our survey, the fact that agitation against it had become linked with a much broader attack against Columbia University and its role in the surrounding community meant that more was at stake than the survival of the adolescent health survey.

In view of all that was involved, we faced the following alternatives: to abandon the project, to continue as if nothing had happened, or to modify our plans. The first of these alternatives was not entirely unthinkable: one of the deans on the main campus (no longer at Columbia) strongly urged us to delay the start of the project and even to consider abandoning it. To their great credit, this suggestion was rejected by our colleagues at the School of Public Health. The second alternative was obviously unthinkable. Therefore, if we were to continue, certain changes in objectives and procedure would have to be made.

These changes consisted chiefly of taking out of the questionnaire almost all items dealing with deviant behaviour, meeting with spokesmen for some of the protesting groups in an attempt to have some dialogue with them about the project and their feelings about it, and discussing the project at meetings of the Harlem Health Council – a voluntary body of individuals and agency representatives with an interest in the health of the community. In March 1968 the Health Council agreed to form an *ad hoc* advisory committee in order to facilitate community participation in the project.

As conceived by the Harlem Health Council, the advisory committee was not expected to have veto power over the project or its staff. Rather, in establishing the committee, the aim was to alert project staff members to health problems of particular interest to the community and to provide a means of getting reactions to our objectives and methods, particularly our interviewing procedures. Committee members, in turn, could help explain our project in the community. Since its formation, the advisory committee has held about half a dozen meetings and has been supportive in many ways, as in strongly backing our requests to the federal government for continued funding. Suggestions by committee members have been incorporated in revisions of our interviewing procedures; indeed, it was at the instigation of the committee that we restored the controversial question on adolescent drinking behaviour to the household interview schedule. It is fair to say that the committee is less interested in the research than in the service aspects of the project – that is, the direct benefit to the adolescents who would be provided with free, comprehensive medical examinations at Harlem Hospital and in the more indirect benefits to the community in having available information which may be useful in planning for improvements in the delivery of health care to youth in Harlem. But this would be expected, since the committee may be involved in the implementation of findings from our survey.

Another consequence of the protest was that we were forced to delay the start of fieldwork approximately six months. This period of time was used in revising our questionnaire and in seeking some measure of community support. But it was a costly delay, for the Children's Bureau, dissatisfied with the progress we were making, sharply reduced the size of our grant. This in turn compelled us to limit the scope of the project and the size of the sample to be studied.

However, by mid-1968 we were back in the field and have since completed approximately 700 interviews with adolescents twelve to seventeen years of age – achieving a respectable completion rate of approximately 80 per cent of those assigned to interviewers; co-operation in the medical examination phase of the project has been equally high. So far as we know, none of the relatively few refusals to co-operate with either interviewer or medical examination team can be attributed to the controversy. Most non-interviews have been due to our dependence on a list which is at least six months old. Furthermore, the much larger community health survey (never a source of controversy) has been continuing without prolonged interruption and is now approaching a total of 9000 completed interviews in Harlem.

But if the protest failed to prevent us from resuming our work, it succeeded in forcing us to narrow the scope of the project. To be sure, we are collecting data on the physical health status of adolescents in Harlem; but we have been unable to pursue certain related areas of interest to us such as drug use. What makes this particularly ironic is that if there is any single health problem about which there is widespread concern in Harlem, it is adolescent drug use. Indeed, one of the leading political figures in the community, consulted about the project, told us that he regarded the youthful drug problem as *the* most important of all social questions facing Harlem. And yet we have been unable to interview youngsters about drugs. This has been part of the cost of continuing the project.

Implications

Two kinds of lessons can be drawn from the protest against this project. One has to do with the practical problems of doing research under such circumstances; the other has to do with the more basic questions which such attacks raise about social research.

At the practical level, one obvious lesson is to screen prospective interviewers more carefully than we did, since in this case (as in several other surveys about which reports are circulating) they started the controversy. But under the circumstances of rising tensions between Harlem and Columbia, we could hardly have given them a test of loyalty to Columbia. Besides, who is going to screen the investigators themselves?

Another lesson is that there are times when and places where it is difficult, if not impossible, to collect data on deviant behaviour; in our case I suppose we should have been more cautious about the content of the questionnaire which got us in trouble. But again, experience elsewhere has demonstrated that even the most innocuous questions can be upsetting to some respondents or to the communities in which they live. In other words, while the content of questionnaires may have something to do with the fate of a survey, many other factors are involved. How else explain why some surveys of ghetto life have been attacked, while others have been spared?

Perhaps our greatest error was that we failed to obtain some degree of community participation in planning the project. Once again, however, the problem was how and at what points to make contact with the community. Actually, we had considered forming an advisory committee earlier but were uncertain about how to proceed. Who represented 'the community' in such matters? And obviously, there was far less community interest in our project at the beginning than after the controversy had started. Nevertheless, if there is anything practical to be learned from our experience, I think it is here: investigators of ghetto life should make a serious effort to obtain some degree of community support and involvement before starting their research. This may create problems for researchers, as I shall suggest later; but the alternatives are even less attractive.

But even the most loyal interviewers, the most innocuous questionnaire, and a sympathetic advisory committee are no guarantee that a project will remain uncontroversial. While the community as a whole and most prospective respondents may be neutral or even indifferent to such research, the fact remains that a handful of people can disrupt it. We can speculate about their motives or draw up elaborate plans for coping with such controversies after they begin; more important, however, are the implications of such attacks for social research in times like these.

In turning to the broader significance of the protest against our project, I want to make it clear that I do not regard such resistance as necessarily unhealthy. On the contrary, I feel that such episodes have something positive to teach us – if we are prepared to listen.

One issue has to do with the perception of studies, such as ours, as threatening; this was illustrated in the charge that we were planning to turn information over to the police, or that what we were doing was part of a genocidal plot against Harlem. I am not suggesting that fear of research is widespread; indeed, our subsequent experience and that of most research teams suggest that it is not. What is significant, however, is that research can be perceived as a mechanism of control. Nor is this completely farfetched; much of social-science research *is* manipulative in its intent or purpose. It is awareness of this purpose which underlies fear of the invasion of privacy and scepticism regarding our ability to protect that privacy.

This is particularly the case when researchers deal with 'deviant' behaviour. Here the implication is that such research is invidious in its purpose – that is, that its intent is to show how much more 'deviant' or 'pathological' the ghetto is than other communities, or that findings regarding pathology will be misinterpreted by the investigators and misused by the institutions they serve. Sensitivity about these issues is one of the more serious obstacles to such research.

Fear of research is also related to awareness on the part of some ghetto residents that most studies of their communities are initiated on the outside. People in communities such as Harlem may wish for information about certain problems, such as drug use, but usually lack the resources and the expertise with which to study them. But those resources and expertise may be found on the outside. Hence the feeling that social surveys are a form of exploitation (by the investigators for their gain) of helpless or powerless communities which gain little or nothing from the research.

One reaction to this is the demand for participation in the research process, both in terms of planning surveys and in terms of jobs. Another response is the notion that communities like Harlem have been over-studied by outsiders. There is no evidence that this has in fact been the case; indeed, our impression is that there have been relatively few systematic surveys of Harlem (and until now none dealing with health) apart from national or citywide studies which merely include its population as part of a larger universe. Nevertheless, the idea of over-exposure to surveys prevails.

These are just some of the issues which such protests raise. Whether representative of community sentiment or merely the product of a few who seek political gain, negative or hostile feelings about the work we do confronts us with the problem of demonstrating more effectively than heretofore, first, precisely what safeguards we can offer our respondents in regard to the information they give us, and second, the utility – immediate or long-range – of our findings.

With regard to safeguards for informants, I feel that we need much more than elegantly phrased codes of ethical conduct which we are scarcely able to enforce among ourselves. Of course, investigators may deny that they will turn information over to the police; but if pressed, they have no legal grounds for not doing so. Or, if they have special 'understandings' with the police and other agencies of law enforcement so that self-informants of 'deviant' behaviour will not be prosecuted, investigators risk compromising themselves. Here is a dilemma. 'In situations of this type,' says the President's Panel on Privacy and Behavioural Research, 'investigators are well advised to seek expressions of confidence from the entire community about the importance of their studies and of the absolute necessity of maintaining the confidentiality of their data.'[7] But what is meant by 'the entire community' and how can researchers get expressions of confidence from it, particularly in a period of conflict? This needs much more attention; for as Wolfle has pointed out, if we as investigators fail to codify the relationship of researcher to subject, the courts will do it for us – and in ways that we may not like.[8]

With regard to the utility of research – which I personally consider the most important of all the issues raised by protests against surveys – a number of questions present themselves. First, utility for whom? For us, as social scientists, for the elite policy-makers we usually serve, or for the communities we are studying? The distinctions are important. Irving Louis Horowitz has asserted, 'There is a direct relationship between the ability to pay and belief in the utility of the social sciences. Who are the high users? The federal government, some state governments, basic industries, marketing industries. Who are the low users? Farmer-labour groups, the poor in general, minority groups (with the exception of highly sophisticated groups such as affluent religious organisations that spill over into the high-users category). In the main, racial and ethnic groups do not place much value on the uses of social science. Perhaps the use of social-science research is itself a suave reflection of wealth. Those who wish to use social-science agencies extensively are wealthy enough to afford them; those who disparage social-science groups are often rationalising their own lack of affluence.'[9]

Finally, there is the basic question as to the real importance of the research we do. If we as researchers cannot easily persuade ourselves of the utility of what we do, how can we hope to convince the communities and populations which we are studying? To be sure, there may be payoff from social surveys over the long run; but as Keynes said, in the long run we are all dead, and communities such as Harlem are impatient.

To recapitulate, while overt resistance to surveys is not as yet widespread and there is no reason to believe it will become so, I think it is necessary to recognise its significance when it occurs. In some communities and in some populations, there is apparently the feeling that survey research is useless, representing merely a form of exploitation by the investigators for their gain or for the gain of the institutions and powers they serve. What, if any, are the rights of communities and study populations to know about the aims and sponsorship of the research? How can communities participate more actively and constructively in the research enterprise? And if they are to become involved, how can social scientists preserve their autonomy with regard to the nature of the problems being studied, the findings produced and the implications drawn? Then, too, in an age of data banks there is some fear – not altogether unjustified – that information collected in surveys will be used for purposes of controlling the populations being studied. How can this fear be overcome? How can we demonstrate the utility of such research?

Moore has written of her experiences in studying the poor, 'The license we are given by our subjects to collect a great deal of information – much of it confidential – entails in our case an almost explicit bargain with them that this information will be used discreetly and presented expertly in such a way that they will collectively benefit. This bargain also implies that we may not be able to afford – either ethically or financially – the kind of theoretically-oriented research that runs the risk of accomplishing little more than the verification of null hypotheses.'[10]

In short, we face the problem of justifying ourselves and the work we do. Not only is our usefulness to communities and study populations uncertain, but we have yet systematically to codify our relationships with informants, as in medicine or law. Resistance to social research will be overcome when we have done far more than heretofore to win the confidence of the communities and populations we are studying by protecting their rights to privacy and by demonstrating that what we are doing can be of some value to them – in other words, by committing ourselves as social scientists to major social change. Whether we can achieve these objectives remains to be seen.

8 Is the Public Acceptability of Social Survey Research Declining?*

American Statistical Association

Introduction

The American Statistical Association, under a grant from the National Science Foundation, brought together in 1973 a diversified group of distinguished social scientists and survey methodologists to discuss the problems of present-day surveys of human populations. The primary purpose of the conference was to explore whether or not these problems may now have reached a level or are growing at a rate that pose a threat to the continued use of surveys as a basic tool of social-science research. The widespread use of survey research to try to understand human behaviour and as an aid to public and private policy-making has long been recognised. The possibility that these surveys might be in difficulty because of changes in society or public acceptance has only recently become a matter of concern.

It was not the purpose, nor did resources or time permit the confer-

* Report of the American Statistical Association Conference on Surveys of Human Populations. Reprinted from *The American Statistician*, **28**, 1974, pp. 30–3, with the permission of the American Statistical Association. ©1974 American Statistical Association.

ence to conduct a full-scale study. Rather, the goal was to try to quickly determine whether there are in fact problems of a scale that require immediate and detailed study and action. The discussion centred largely on surveys that involve the use of detailed questionnaires of varying complexity and length, usually administered in face-to-face interviews. Such surveys sometimes involve a complete census of a given population but more frequently the use of sampling techniques, most often a probability sample.

Conclusions

The conference arrived at five general conclusions about survey research in the United States:

(1) That survey research is in some difficulty.
(2) To an undetermined scale that difficulty is increasing.
(3) The problem varies in incidence between government, private and academic research.
(4) The grounds for concern are great enough to urge the prompt initiation of a more intensive examination of the problem and programmes to meet it.
(5) There are many potential areas for action, some of which could start now.

Findings

In support of these conclusions the conference made the following findings:

Finding No. 1 *Little hard data are available for evaluating changing acceptance by respondents or other survey difficulties.*
This finding, while not invalidating the general conference conclusions, does mean that identifying the exact characteristics of the survey problem or making comparisons over time and between different kinds of public and private survey activities is very difficult. Where attempted it may not be very precise. Data for some surveys are available from government agencies. These analyses have been very helpful to the conference. For private research organisations and

university-based groups, however, there is wide variation as to the amount of records kept and the availability of those records or any analyses made of them. The overall result is that the conference was able to find only very limited data for the private sector, on either a one-time or periodic basis.

Finding No. 2   *Even where hard data are available, comparisons are difficult because of lack of uniform definitions.*

One reason for the lack of comparative data for a broad spectrum of surveys of human populations may well be because of confusion in regard to what is meant by such measures as completion rates, non-response, refusals etc. Some professionals within the private public opinion and consumer research field who have become increasingly sensitive about changing completion and response rates in interview surveys may even have altered their definition of completion rates so that the drop would not seem as great as it may have been. If, for example, as some organisations have reportedly done, the completion rate is redefined as the number of completed interviews divided by the sum of completed interviews and refusals, leaving out entirely language barriers, ineligible respondents, and not-at-homes it yields a higher figure. Obviously this figure differs greatly from a completion rate which includes in the universe the non-response categories listed. Unfortunately there is no clear standard or practice universally used throughout the survey community.

Finding No. 3   *Regardless of the scarcity of hard data and the difficulties of making precise comparisons there are a significant number of reports of completion rates declining, or where achieving a satisfactory completion rate is becoming increasingly more difficult.*

The conference finds that where completion rates are available they reflect a considerable range of experiences in recent years. At one extreme is the case of the US Bureau of the Census where the problem has largely been finding people at home and not refusals to answer the questionnaire. Under these circumstances the Census Bureau has been able by extra effort in its Current Population Survey sample to hold the overall completion rate – by their definition the total to be interviewed less refusals, not-at-homes and other causes of non-interview – to between 95 and 96 per cent. A similar experience is reported for the Health Interview Survey by the National Centre for Health Statistics. In the study of consumer expenditures conducted by the Bureau of the Census for the Bureau of Labour Statistics where a much more complicated schedule is used the completion rate is much lower.

At the other extreme, spokesmen for a number of private survey organisations, large and small, who were queried by one of the conference participants, all report that their completion rates on general population samples now average approximately 60 to 65 per cent, in spite of three or four callbacks. This recent experience is in contrast to a completion figure of 80 to 85 per cent for the same firms in the decade of the 'sixties. The remaining 35 to 40 per cent non-response divides about equally between refusals and not-at-homes.

Virtually no meaningful hard data are available for the experiences of survey research organisations operating in university settings, but a canvass was made to obtain as much informed opinion as possible from persons operationally involved with such organisations in gathering field data. Almost all of the persons talked to are in agreement that assignment completion has become more problematic because of a sharp increase in not-at-homes. Some researchers, who seem to be a minority, do not believe refusals or terminations have changed significantly as factors affecting the overall completion rate. Others believe growth in refusals has been confined to special population subsets from such over-surveyed groups as American Indians, core city residents, etc. where completion poses a real problem but is not a general phenomenon.

Still others among the university survey people believe that, on the contrary, it is only among certain other population subsets that refusal rates have remained constant at a low level. Growth in refusals and the less tangible phenomenon, resistance, is in fact the more general case. In any event agreement is almost total that achievement of a given sample survey completion rate has become more difficult and, therefore, more costly; disagreement has to do mostly with what factors are responsible.

One survey director did express the thought that much of the discussion on response rates exaggerates the problem. In his view, difficulties, if any, are more likely to be a function of deterioration, or lowering of standards with respect to staffing and supervision rather than public receptivity. If this is true, it is not obvious why there has been such deterioration or lowering of standards. Other administrators argue that whatever trends exist in response rates exist in a context of greater not lesser emphasis on quality control. Indeed, it is sometimes asserted that tightened quality-control procedure and more complete record-keeping will reveal some of the problems which now may be alleged not to exist.

Finding No. 4   *Because of the difficulty of obtaining completion rates adequate for reliable data the dollar costs of surveying human populations have risen to a point where those costs may become the critical factor in whether some surveys can be done at all.*

As was noted in Finding No. 3, increasing difficulties in reaching a completion rate which will satisfactorily permit full confidence in the reliability of the data obtained often bring with them greatly rising dollar costs. The private organisation which reported that their completion rate in recent months had dropped to around 60–65 per cent said the rate could still possibly be raised to the former 80–85 per cent. To do so, however, would be at the prohibitive cost of seven times the original survey. The Health Interview Survey by NCHS reported that their costs have increased by 20 per cent in the last ten years. Not all of the rise in survey costs of course is due to the increasing difficulties of interviewing. Such operational costs as wage rates for supervisors and interviewers, cost of transportation, telephone calls and mailing charges have all risen too.

There may be circumstances where extremely high survey costs are still considered a relatively marginal expense for a project devoted to some special goal. Under these circumstances surveys go on regardless of rising costs. Key multiple-use projects, as are many of the government surveys, also may have some advantage as far as funding in the face of greatly increased costs. But for most social-research users these options will not be available and it is here that the problem becomes especially acute.

Finding No. 5   *Neither survey research nor its functions have been precisely defined.*

Almost every kind of information-gathering task has at one time or another been called survey research with the result that probably too much has been included under the rubric. Consequently it is difficult at times to determine important matters such as accepted practices and standards for a community whose dimensions are not clear. At the same time, the functions of survey research are necessarily as uncertain as its definition is imprecise. It is plain that data gathered by survey methods are used for a wide range of legitimate scientific, social policy and other purposes. It is also plain that much so-called survey research has addressed trivial problems of negligible importance either to society in the large or to the particular persons acting as respondents. Consequently, a view of survey research as an exploitative enterprise in practice may have a good measure of justification. Add to this the fact that unscrupulous individuals and organisations can under the guise of conducting a legitimate survey use the procedures for biased and even nefarious purposes, and the problem is doubly serious. Whatever may be the status of survey research in the mind of the American public, concern for its integrity is very much in order among its practitioners.

Finding No. 6 *Many of the important problems involving survey research today lie outside of survey research itself and are really part of the larger rapidly changing socio-economic climate.*

The conference found broad social changes taking place today that apparently are having some very important effects on the conduct of survey research. At the same time the conference makes clear that just because these factors lie outside of the survey research community's ability to do much about them directly, this does not absolve the community from recognising the impact of the changes or lift their obligation to try to adjust to them in the most valid way. In identifying those changes in society considered to have important effects on survey research the conference points out: the increasing urbanisation of the population and accompanying changes in the population life-style; the rising concern with the invasion of privacy and fear of lack of confidentiality; the refusal to answer questions as a form of protest against some part or all of established society; and the growing expectation that research can or must play some more definite role in meeting rising expectations and solving the problems of the day.

The impact of increased urbanisation on survey research takes several forms. The accelerating population movement off the farm and out of the small towns since the 'thirties has resulted in some special mechanical problems, problems which certainly bring increased costs if not ultimately an increase in non-response. When people lived on farms and in small towns they tended to stay put, could be more easily identified and reached and were more willing to talk with the interviewer. As the population has shifted to the cities and suburbs the respondents frequently cannot be found in the place the latest sample design might expect them to be, or are not as apt to be home for interviews either during the day or for callbacks at night.

The shifting of population to the cities has brought a greater proportion of working wives, which is another factor that contributes to making it harder to find someone at home to interview. Again, the increased number of callbacks and the odd hours required to get a completed schedule have meant higher costs per schedule and sometimes no schedule at all. With more urbanisation has come crowding and crime, with a growing suspicion of strangers and a need or desire to avoid any unusual involvement. For the survey researcher this has meant the need for better selected, more skilled and better trained interviewing personnel. Even then there still may be a rising non-response rate.

The privacy and confidentiality issue has a variety of impacts on survey research as it gets more attention from all sides. The simple heightening of consciousness that these should be matters of concern to the individual may make a respondent more suspicious and reluctant. More than ever before, too, the researcher is called upon to demonstrate the validity of any assertion that the data will be kept confidential – and sometimes to demonstrate that there is real need for the data. It is true, as the head of a large opinion research organisation has said, that there still are many people who for one reason or another are willing and even eager to participate in a survey. But apparently also there are an increasing number who now feel that it is an invasion of their privacy or an imposition on their time. Some surveys have attempted to meet the latter objection with cash or premium rewards to the respondent and with some success. The results of other experiments are inconclusive.

It is possible that there may be resistance and costs which simply cannot be compensated for. Some of these costs may be social as well as monetary. Participation in a survey may lead respondents to expect improvements in the conditions being studied – social services, housing, medical programming. If the purposes of survey research are not made clear or the results do not validate them, more often than not disappointment and disenchantment may ensue. When surveys encompass sensitive, emotion-arousing issues, such outcomes are the more deplorable as well as more likely. With no decision-making rights regarding research design, procedure or reporting, people are increasingly asked to provide data that form a basis for decisions about arrangements for their lives that may or may not be beneficial to them as individuals or representatives of social-interest groups. This emphasises the necessity for being aware of what might be called the morality of survey operations as well as the refinements and improvements of techniques.

Part Three

Population Censuses and Privacy

9 Introduction

Martin Bulmer

Censuses, unlike social surveys, have a much older history: they stretch back to Biblical times, with an ancient lineage. Modern censuses date from the late eighteenth and early nineteenth centuries. The first United States Census was held in 1790,[1] the first British Census in 1801.[2] The need for the state to conduct a complete count of its population was not easily established. In Britain, for example, a good deal of opposition to the introduction of the census was expressed, and attempts to start one in the mid-eighteenth century were defeated in Parliament.[3] The importance attached to the taking of the census in the United States is reflected in the fact that the requirement for a decennial enumeration is written into the first article of the American Constitution. Censuses are now conducted every ten years in almost all countries, following guidelines and standards laid down by United Nations demographers and statisticians.[4]

What is a census? A census is a method of collecting demographic and social data by means of individual enumeration. Within a given territory it is universal, simultaneous and carried out at fixed intervals. It is usually conducted by the government of the territory and is compulsory. It thus resembles a social survey in that it seeks to collect demographic and social data, but it differs in important respects. A census, unlike a sample survey, is an enumeration of the *total* population, producing 100 per cent data for that population. Its results therefore provide coverage down to very small geographical areas and very small sub-groups in the population. They are not subject to sampling error. Censuses are usually conducted simultaneously in all parts of a territory. This makes them a very much larger-scale operation than any social survey and requires the temporary employment of large numbers of part-time census enumerators. They are correspondingly much more expensive to conduct than sample surveys. The cost of the 1981 British Census was estimated in 1976 prices at £45 million.[5]

Censuses are traditionally carried out every ten years, as they have been in Britain and the United States since 1801 and 1790 respectively. Some countries have introduced five-year intervals for censuses. In Britain, a five-year census on a 10 per cent sample basis was held in 1966; a full census planned for 1976[6] was cancelled for reasons of economy. From the point of view of research policy, one of the most important features of the census is that it is compulsory and it has the force of law behind it.

Unlike the sample survey, the 100 per cent census eliminates sampling error. In theory a census also eliminates non-response due to not-at-homes or refusals, since enumerators are required to count everyone and completion of the form is compulsory. (Refusals to do so, as Dr Hakim notes in Chapter 10, are very, very few in number in recent British censuses.) This is not to say that census data are perfect by comparison with survey data. The coverage of censuses in practice is not quite complete; a small degree of under-enumeration occurs. Overall, it rarely exceeds a very small percentage, though it may be sizeable for sub-groups in the population, e.g. American blacks.[7] The scale of the census, too, means that the staff employed as enumerators are much less highly trained than survey interviewers and this, together with the use of a self-completion schedule, may produce data which in overall quality is somewhat inferior to that collected by a trained survey interviewer in a personal interview with a respondent. It is an important reason why census questions tend to be short, simple, factual and non-controversial.

As a census requires legal compliance, its content is scrutinised very much more closely than the average sample survey. The government department which conducts the census will consult other parts of central government, local (or state) governments and non-governmental census users. The content of a modern census is determined

by the amount of funds . . . available, historical precedent established in previous censuses, the existing technology for collecting
and processing data, the taste of census bureau officials for risk
under conditions of uncertainty, the imagination of Census Bureau
staff, the needs of the economy, the tenacity and ingenuity of those
who plead for special causes, and by the experience gained in the
pre-test.[8]

Generally speaking, the topics included in the census have
expanded over the years, from basic demographic data such as name
and address, sex, date of birth, marital status and position in the
household, to a range of social topics including migration history,
housing, employment, educational qualifications, workplace and
transport, language spoken and income.[9] Not all of these topics are
covered in every country's census. For example, as a whole the United
States and Canadian census questionnaires are longer than the
British and include questions on income which in Britain have been
judged too sensitive for inclusion.

In Britain, the content of each census requires approval by the
government and approval by a positive resolution of both Houses of
Parliament. One consequence of this is to confine census questions to
subjects of direct utility in public policy-making; a significant sociological variable like religion is not included, at least in part because it
lacks utility for policy. Each question requires careful justification,
particularly new questions on topics which can conceivably be controversial. As this is written (1978), the British OPCS has proposed
that the 1981 Census should include a direct question on race and
ethnic origin for the first time,[10] which has already led to lively newspaper correspondence on the appropriateness of such a question. William Petersen in Chapter 13 reviews the course of similar controversy
in the United States a few years earlier.

An important check on the length of the census schedule is the
census authority's judgement of what the public will take.

Many countries, including Britain, have asked more and more
questions in each successive census. This has tended to over-
burden the public and sometimes to arouse its hostility. Some of the
new questions have in fact been too far from the ideal of the factual,
simply-framed and non-controversial question which produces an

accurate answer from the great majority of respondents.[11]

Increasingly, census-takers have had to justify themselves to the public.

From the outset, however, census authorities have been clear about their responsibilities for safeguarding the information which they collect. Because governments collect personal and private information about the whole population by compulsion, census bureaux have a particular responsibility to ensure that this data is kept confidential. Concern for individual privacy, as already noted, influences the content of the census. But once this is determined, other safeguards operate to ensure that once the data are collected on the census schedule they are not improperly released. The safeguards are of several kinds.[12]

Enumerators, who are often other government employees of various kinds, are required to give a legally-binding assurance not to reveal information which they collect in the course of their work for the census. Since tens of thousands of enumerators are employed, there is particular need for vigilance here. Confidentiality issues form part of enumerator training and any breaches of duty are severely dealt with by legal penalty. Other aspects of enumeration raise privacy issues. Efforts are made to assign enumerators to areas in which they do not live, in order that they are not known personally to the citizens with whom they come into contact. In recent censuses in Britain, arrangements have been made for the return of census schedules by post, so that the enumerator (or in some cases his superior as well) does not see the form. (In the 1971 British Census, out of 18 million census forms issued, some 1 per cent were returned direct by post to the central census office, by-passing the local enumerators.)[13]

Confidentiality safeguards also apply to the custody of census records and their entry on the computer for data processing. Individual census returns are not available for a long period of time – 100 years in Britain – and individual names and addresses are not entered on the computer for the statistical analysis. In addition, important safeguards apply to the publication of data in statistical form, in order to prevent the identification of individuals from their social characteristics. In all British census tables, totals are rounded. In data from small geographical areas, where the possibility of identification is least inconceivable (though highly improbable), it is made impossible altogether by random error injection (adding +1, 0 or −1 at random to every cell in small area census tables) and by not publishing enumeration data for districts (mainly in rural areas) with a population below a certain figure.

There are thus strong safeguards for the confidentiality of census returns. These are absolutely necessary, despite the legal enforceability of completing the census schedule, because any census requires a high degree of co-operation from the public. It would clearly be impossible to carry out a successful census against the wishes of even a significant minority of the population.

> Most citizens are prepared to supply personal information to the authorities provided they are educated as to the purpose served by the census and provided they are assured that the information will be treated as strictly confidential. This assurance is greatly strengthened if the guarantee of confidentiality is given legal force.[14]

Conrad Taeuber in Chapter 12 describes the safeguards in the United States. These legal safeguards apply even where another part of the government attempts to obtain census data. A notorious case in which the census was asked, and refused, to release data on Japanese Americans during the Second World War is described below on page 206. Dr Hakim traces British policy in this respect, showing the very stringent concern with confidentiality.

Chapter 10 also traces how the assurances given to the public about the confidentiality of the information which they provide has been strengthened. In recent years, public concern about the conduct and outcome of censuses has undoubtedly increased.[15] In Chapter 11, an analysis of British parliamentary opinion on the census shows that, in the recent past, issues to do with census content, privacy, compulsion and data confidentiality have become much more salient. This has undoubtedly occurred for some of the reasons discussed in Chapter 1, but is given added sharpness by the particular characteristics of the census – it is universal, compulsory and conducted by the government. When a census is held, social-research procedures are subjected to particular close scrutiny, sharp questioning and (as William Petersen describes in Chapter 13), in cases, outright denunciation.

In Britain, civil liberties' lobbies and the Liberal Party have recently been particularly loud critics of the census. The National

Council of Civil Liberties has pointed to possible breaches of confidentiality by enumerators, from the commercial sale of small area
data and through the use of the census as a sampling frame for other
surveys.[16] It has been argued that compulsion should only be used to
require name, date of birth, sex and usual place of residence, and that
the remainder of the census questions should be asked by means of a
voluntary, anonymous questionnaire.[17] The General Secretary of
NCCL at the time of the 1971 Census later co-authored a book which
described the 1971 Census form as 'a document mined with hazards
to privacy', and the conduct of the census as an operation 'embarked
upon in an euphoric spirit of misplaced confidence. Not enough al-
lowance was made for public misgivings, which might have been fore-
seen but evidently were not.'[18]

The official response to criticism was quite rapid at the time. The
Registrar-General held press conferences and local visits during the
census period at which criticism of the census was aired. Within a
short time after the census, OPCS invited both the Royal Statistical
Society and the British Computer Society to appoint nominees to
examine statistical and computing aspects of census security and confidentiality. These reports were published as a White Paper in 1973,
with the government response to them.[19] The attack on the census
produced a prompt response.

In addition, a few people were prosecuted for refusal to complete
the census schedule, but still a very very tiny number by comparison
with the number who co-operated. It is probably reasonable to conclude that

> most of the objections to the census came from a small but vocal
> minority whose views made headlines in the press and provided
> the stuff of political controversy. The great bulk of the popula-
> tion, on the other hand, saw the need for the census and co-
> operated well, and the refusal rate was negligible as in the past.[20]

What was remarkable about many criticisms of the 1971 Census
was their strident tone and failure to appreciate the safeguards
which the census office itself had established. In press treatment of
the census, single incidents were exaggerated out of all proportion
and lapses and errors were described as if typical, whereas they
were highly atypical. As Petersen points out, census-takers have a
difficult job which is not helped by immoderate criticism. In seeking

to balance the need for adequate information for planning with the right of the individual to control personal information, critics of the census have sometimes inclined so far to the latter to lay themselves open to accusations of 'know-nothingism'. Certainly, the potentialities of the census for social research have been given very short shrift indeed by critics.

Public concern about the privacy implications of census-taking is justified and necessary. Perhaps because it is a case of 'bureaucracy in action', the census-takers have often been given less credit for their record than they deserve. Nevertheless, the climate of census-taking is nowadays a more stormy one. 'The experience of the 1970 round of censuses in various countries suggests that there can indeed be some political risk in taking a census without adequate assessment of, and preparation for, its public reception.'[21] The chapters which follow examine some aspects of the conditions under which censuses are conducted and the public reception which they receive, both in detail and in more general terms. One particularly important subject for further research is public perception of the census. If over one-third of respondents in a survey believe that one of the main purposes of the census is 'to provide a record of people's addresses for the government', or that over one-quarter believe that those allowed to see individual census forms were 'people working for government'[22] (neither of which is true: individual census returns are confidential to OPCS Census Division), then clearly there is a major task of public education to be undertaken by the census authorities.

Other developments affecting the conduct of censuses and their potentialities for social science are also taking place. One is the increasing pressure on governments to limit the scope of census inquiries. Additional questions are difficult to justify; the trend is to take questions out rather than to add new ones. Secondly, there is some evidence of a shift to follow-up, census-linked, surveys of a voluntary kind for questions not included in the census itself. Both these developments are illustrated by the fate of an income question in the 1971 British Census. In the House of Commons debate before the census, in 1970, the minister responsible revealed that a question on income had been tried in the pre-tests carried out by the census offices, but had been omitted from the final list of questions to be included, even though it had been 'strongly pressed by almost all users of census results'. Local authorities, regional planners and central government departments had all argued strongly for its inclusion in order to identify variations in income level between areas and to direct resources accordingly. Several had quoted in support the inclusion of this question in the United States and Canadian censuses. The strong case for including the income question gave way to two objections. The first was technical, the difficulty of wording a suitable question to deal adequately with the complexities of income; the second was the public response to the pre-test.

There was also some evidence of public opposition to the question . . . less than was expected, but still sufficient to be taken into account, because of our wish to avoid asking any questions which even a minority of the population might find objectionable.[23]

Public resistance to an income question in the census pre-test is unsurprising in the light of Table 1.4 on page 16. It is an important matter for social scientists, however, since it involves the exclusion of a key social variable and the rejection of an important question in the face of the near unanimous advice that it should be asked. The underlying reasons for excluding the question seem to have been of two kinds. The first was a political judgement about the possible effect of asking a relatively controversial question, and the sensitivity of politicians to accusations of encroachment on privacy. It may be that the question was excluded by political decision. Certainly Mr Crossman's *Diaries* suggest that leading members of the Cabinet at the time, including Mr Callaghan, were opposed to the inclusion of the question on political grounds.[24]

A second argument is technical. If you include controversial questions in the census, they are likely to be answered less fully and accurately than non-controversial questions. The effects of this on the rest of the census schedule are likely to be detrimental. The controversial question will lower overall co-operation and reduce the care with which other questions are answered. This point was made by the government spokesman at the end of the debate in 1970. The income questions were not included, he said,

because there is no guarantee that they would be as widely accepted by the public as is necessary if the results of the census are to be of the accuracy and completeness we must have, and if people are to be persuaded to co-operate.[25]

Income was judged too sensitive on this account. Privacy concerns thus placed a limit upon the scope of the 1971 Census, in a direction broadly inimical to social science.

However, the objective of gathering income data was achieved by means of a census-linked social survey, carried out one year after the census. This was a mail questionnaire sent to a 1 per cent sample of adults enumerated in the 1971 Census, seeking detailed information on their income in the year ended April 1972. The response rate varied with age, from 25 per cent among men aged twenty to twenty-four, to just over 50 per cent among the age group sixty-five to seventy-four. However, a check could be carried out of the representativeness of respondents since the survey data was merged for analysis with the corresponding census data for the members of the sample.[26] Such census-linked surveys may become more common in the future for subjects not deemed suitable for inclusion in the census itself.

A third development may, however, in the long run, be of greater significance. This is the tendency for the sharp distinction between censuses and social surveys to break down to some extent. In part, it is eroded by the greater use made in censuses themselves, as they become more complex, of sampling methods. Not all questions are asked of all members of the population. Whole censuses, as in Britain in 1966, may be conducted on a sample basis. The sharp distinction is also eroded by developments such as the Federal German Mikrozensus of 1 per cent of households in April and 0.1 per cent in each of the other three-quarters of the year, which is compulsory.[27]

Large-scale continuous social surveys such as the United States Current Population Survey, the British Family Expenditure Survey (FES) and General Household Survey (GHS) are comparatively recent developments. They are designed to provide data on a wider range of topics than the census, for example, income and expenditure (FES) and morbidity (GHS). Sampling fractions vary, but they are a good deal less than 1 per cent of the population (the GHS is about 0.1 per cent). Though very large by social survey standards, they are small-scale inquiries (and correspondingly more intensive) by comparison with a census. Their great advantage for policy-makers, of course, is that they provide data on a wider range of subjects than the census and on an annual, rather than a decennial, basis. The chapters which follow, however, discuss decennial population censuses.

10 Census Confidentiality in Britain*

C. Hakim

Introduction

The population census is the largest single survey of demographic and socio-economic conditions in any country; it is also usually the most visible. As such it occupies a special position both as a source of social and demographic data and as the most prominent example of social research more generally. In recent years, the population census has become the subject of public debate, not only in Britain, but also in most other countries in Europe and North America. To some extent it now carries the burden of justifying not only itself but social research more broadly. And as the most visible of official data collections, it must bear the brunt of the new concern with privacy and data confidentiality.

Our aim here is to review the policy and practice of census confidentiality in Britain as it has been developed by the Census Office[1] over a period of 170 years, a period which has seen the extension of the census from a basic head-count to a broader survey of the population, and the introduction of computer processing of census results.

* Original material © 1979 C. Hakim. Material from government publications quoted in this chapter is Crown Copyright. The author was previously on the staff of the Office of Population Censuses and Surveys, but the views expressed here are personal and do not necessarily reflect the views of that department.

It is important that the two concepts of privacy and confidentiality be distinguished, for we are concerned mainly with the latter. Privacy can be defined as the preservation of personal (or business) information from public knowledge or inspection. The right to privacy implies the ability to control the release of information about oneself, whether to give it free circulation, limited circulation or no circulation at all.[2] A broader definition of privacy was presented in a recent White Paper, *Computers and Privacy*. Privacy of the individual was seen to be at issue in respect of the accuracy, completeness and relevance of information held on a person, security measures and access to the data, and its confidentiality.[3] However, confidentiality is more commonly distinguished from privacy. Confidentiality involves the conditions of use and disclosure of information about individuals or businesses once it is collected. In terms of the census, privacy concerns the type of question that is to be included or excluded from the census form, while confidentiality concerns the limits on the release of data and the use that is made of the information once it is collected. The two are related in that public concern over confidentiality is likely to be greater where the information collected is considered to be private.

The public's perception of census confidentiality has important implications both for public co-operation with the census and for the quality of the data collected. The accuracy and completeness of the information collected in the census forms may be prejudiced if respondents are not fully reassured that the information is completely confidential, and this will affect the validity and reliability of the statistical data compiled from the census returns. As outlined in the White Paper on the 1981 Census, census statistics inform policy-making, planning and research in a wide range of government programmes.[4] A decline in the quality of the data can prejudice decisions taken within these programmes, particularly when these concern relatively small areas (such as inner urban areas) or relatively small sub-groups within the population (such as one-parent families). Census statistics can only contribute to the enhancement of our awareness and understanding of social issues and social change, given the willing co-operation of the public in providing a snapshot of the nation at regular intervals.

The census is currently carried out under the provisions of the Census Act 1920, which outlines its statistical purpose. Information is collected through heads of households, people in positions of responsibility in institutions, or directly from individuals in households and institutions, and is then held by the census office to produce statistical reports. It thus differs from administrative information, which is collected primarily to run the public agency in question (for example to administer a hospital or social security office), but can also be used to provide statistical data on the public agency and its activities. Administrative records will include names and addresses or other identifiers of the person, household or business concerned, to ensure that action is taken with respect to the correct individual or legal entity. Such identifiers are not directly required for statistical and research purposes and can be deleted before the information is processed for compiling statistical data. It is generally agreed that administrative records can be processed to produce anonymous statistical data without a breach of confidentiality. However, a breach of confidentiality would occur if information collected originally for statistical and research purposes was used for administrative purposes.

Although names and addresses are recorded on census forms, the information is not used for administrative purposes. The practice of recording them has been adopted for purely practical reasons, for use while the census is actually being carried out. They help the heads of households, who have the legal obligation to complete the census forms, to ensure that all members of their households have been included, and they show that the respondents' duty under the law has been fulfilled. The identifiers help enumerators to check that returns have been obtained from all addresses, and the census offices to check receipt of forms from those households that have arranged to send them in direct. When it is necessary for census staff to call back and verify the information on the form or obtain any missing answers, the names and addresses enable the right person to be approached.[5] As names and addresses are not needed for compiling statistics once the returns have been collected, they are not entered into the computer.

Census Confidentiality: Principles and Legislation

There is no single and comprehensive statement of the principle of confidentiality that has been applied to population censuses. Nor is there a particular point in time at which the principle of census confidentiality was formally adopted. The picture that emerges from Parliamentary debates, official assurances to the public, Census Acts, the White Paper on census security[6] and, most recently, the White Paper on the 1981 Census, is of a taken-for-granted assumption that has been progressively defined, refined and formally backed by legislation over the decades. A key point in this process has been the general recognition that the population census was carried out for statistical and research purposes – other uses of the information being considered unjustified. Nor has there been a comprehensive, formal and public statement of the working definitions of confidentiality and operational policies that apply to all stages of the census operation. These have always existed, however, and there have been periodic reviews and reformulations within the census office of the operational policies and practices applied to each stage of the census cycle to ensure the confidentiality of the information collected; however, it is not customary to release detailed accounts of these procedures to the public.

This is not altogether surprising. The privacy and confidentiality of personal information has only become the subject of public debate in recent years. It does not seem that official assurances of census confidentiality had ever been demanded in any detail, nor even that the principle was ever questioned.[7] It may be, however, that the absence of such official statements has contributed in part to public misgivings in recent years about the existence and stringency of any operational policies in force.

The earliest censuses (1801–31) took the form of simple head-counts, with the census enumerator responsible for recording the number of people at each address within specified categories, mainly age, sex and marital status. Householder returns were first used in 1841; and in 1851 the statistical and research purpose of the census was defined by the Registrar-General's statement on the front panel of the census form:

The Return is required to enable the Secretary of State to complete the Census; which is to show the number of the population – their arrangement by ages and families in different ranks, professions, employments and trades – their distribution over the country in villages, towns and cities – their increase and progress in the last ten years.

The first public statement of the principle of census confidentiality was made on the front panel of the 1861 Census Householder's form:

The facts will be published in General Abstracts only, and strict care will be taken that the returns are not used for the gratification of curiosity.

At succeeding censuses the assurances of confidentiality given on the census form were progressively refined,[8] as in other countries.[9] In 1891, the assurance was extended to say that census returns would not be used 'for the gratification of curiosity or for other purposes than those of the Census'. From 1901, the term 'confidential' or 'strictly confidential' was used. In 1911, a note inside the householder's census form stated that 'The returns are not to be used for proof of age, as in connection with Old Age Pensions, or for any other purposes than the preparation of Statistical Tables'. By 1971 the assurance read:

> The information you give on the form will be treated as CONFIDENTIAL and used only for compiling statistics. No information about named individuals will be passed by the Census Office to any other Government Department or any other authority or person. If anyone in the census organisation improperly discloses information you provide, he will be liable to prosecution. Similarly you must not disclose information which anyone (for example, a visitor or boarder) gives you to enable you to complete the form.

In addition, a slip-in leaflet to the census form described the planning uses of census statistics and stated:

> The facts are fed into a computer where they are added to millions of other facts contributed by other people. When published, they will be in tables of figures in which you are certainly not mentioned. You'll be there all right, somewhere among the statistics, but neither you nor any other member of your household will be identified.

Thus, by 1971 the assurances had been extended to exclude the release of information on both named persons and un-named but identifiable persons in census tables.

Although no references to confidentiality appear in records of Parliamentary debates, Census Acts or Schedules until 1861, it seems to have been assumed by Members of Parliament that the census returns were confidential; at least no one contested a remark by Mr Beresford Hope who, in the Second Reading debate on the 1871 Census Act, said: '. . . after all, the census papers were confidential; they are not published to the world. They must depend on the fidelity and secrecy of the collectors . . .'[10]

Penalties for infringements of the confidentiality rule were first included in the Census Act 1900, which made it an offence under the Official Secrets Act 1889 for any person employed in taking the 1901 Census to communicate, without lawful authority, any information acquired in the course of his employment. A similar provision was made for the 1911 Census. The Census Act 1920 laid upon the Registrar-General the duty to carry out future censuses; it also set out more fully the penalties to be imposed for unauthorised disclosure of census information. Section 8(2) states that:

If any person –

> (*a*) being a person employed in taking a census, without lawful authority publishes or communicates to any person otherwise than in the ordinary course of such employment any information acquired by him in the course of his employment; or
> (*b*) having knowledge of any information which to his knowledge has been disclosed in contravention of this Act, publishes or communicates that information to any other person;

he shall be guilty of a misdemeanour, and shall on conviction be liable to imprisonment with or without hard labour for a term not exceeding two years or to a fine, or to both such imprisonment or fine.

The Census Act 1920 does not of course preclude the release or publication of information with 'lawful authority', but does not attempt to define any such case. It is generally understood, however, that the release of information on a particular person (or household) is unjustified if it would *adversely* affect the person's rights, benefits or privileges.[11] Information about a person is most commonly perceived to have been misused if the use in question is damaging to the individual.

The uses to which census returns are to be put are specified very broadly in the Census Act 1920 (paras 4 and 5). The Registrar-General must prepare reports on each census to be laid before Parliament; he may, at the request and cost of any local authority or person, have additional abstracts prepared. In addition he should, between censuses, collect, co-ordinate and publish any available statistical information on the population. Thus the Act allows for a wide variety of statistical material and abstracts to be produced, not only for Parliament but also for any person or authority whose request for census data is considered reasonable.

Confidentiality: Working Definitions and Policies

Procedures to protect the confidentiality of census information must cover each of the three main phases of census-taking: enumeration (fieldwork), processing of the results, and publication or dissemination of census data. As with policy, the procedures and regulations adopted in practice have developed and changed over the decades to take account of developments in data-processing technology, public opinion on census matters, and developments within government statistics more generally.

Perhaps the most important single change has been the adoption of automated data processing for the analysis of 1961 and subsequent census results. The introduction of computers has contributed to some increase in the number of questions asked on census forms, although even now the amount of information collected in Britain is more restricted than in other countries such as Australia, Canada and the United States.[12] There has been a more significant increase in the amount of statistical data that can be produced from the census. Much of it is not now published in book form, although it is publicly available in other forms – this type of output is referred to as unpublished statistics in this chapter.[13] More generally, the use of computers extends the range and type of statistical work that can be done with the census and other sources, work that remains invisible in large part unless the final report on the study in question provides a good deal of methodological detail. These interrelated developments have contributed to heightened public interest in the confidentiality of census and other official data. The census probably receives more than its fair share of concern, because it is the most publicly visible of all such data collections, and can be used as a case in point by those whose concern is more general.

Public disquiet about various potential threats to the privacy of the individual had led the government in May 1970 to appoint the Committee on Privacy under the Chairmanship of Sir Kenneth Younger to conduct an inquiry into the private sector. When public concern over privacy focused on the 1971 Census, the government accepted an offer by the British Computer Society (BCS) to review the census security arrangements. In response to an invitation from the census offices, the Royal Statistical Society (RSS) nominated three of its members to make an independent study. The White Paper *Security of the Census of Population* presents the reports of the BCS and RSS, together with government response to them, and some information on public attitude to the census. It provides much detailed information on the procedures adopted to implement the principle of census confidentiality.

Census enumeration

There is little information on the training given to enumerators for the early censuses. It is likely, however, that some were known to many of the households they visited, as enumerators were often recruited among the clergy or local officials. Since the turn of the century, enumerators have been informed that the Official Secrets Act or, more recently, the Census Act 1920, impose penalties for the misuse or unauthorised disclosure of information, and required to sign an undertaking to perform their duties in accordance with the Acts. So far as is known, past security measures have protected all the census data collected. The White Paper notes that there are no records of census enumerators ever being prosecuted for a failure to protect confidentiality, with a single exception after the 1971 Census.[14]

Press reports on the 1971 Census suggest, however, that enumeration procedures attracted more attention than in the past. In many cases, the concern arose from the fact that the enumerator was known to the householder, who objected to handing over the completed census form to a known person, irrespective of whether the information was treated as confidential. Census officers are instructed, in recruiting enumerators, to avoid as far as possible placing them in an area where there are people known to them, but this is not always practicable. Problems arise particularly in rural areas with a relatively small and scattered population, where enumerators sometimes have to be local residents in order to carry out their duties within the specified period of time. In urban areas, the large number of enumerators required must be of an adequate calibre to deal effectively with the special problems of enumeration that may arise, for example with multi-occupancy dwellings and language difficulties. The very magnitude of the time-specific census operation imposes problems that do not arise with sample surveys. The 1971 Census employed some 104,000 fieldworkers, who were specially recruited and trained within a limited period of time: 8200 supervisors, census officers and assistant census officers, and 96,700 enumerators. Many of the field staff are recruited among local officials: in 1971, 28 per cent of census officers were recruited from the locally-based registration service; 44 per cent of census officers and 29 per cent of enumerators were local government officers.[15]

Census enumeration procedures are discussed in some detail in the White Paper on census security. The report of the Royal Statistical Society nominees commented on the 1971 Census fieldwork arrangements and made a number of recommendations. The government considered the implications of these recommendations, accepting the majority for implementation in future censuses.[16] The RSS nominees recommended that enumerators should operate at least five miles away from either their home address or their place of work and, more generally, as far away as local transport circumstances allowed. They further recommended that local government officers, if recruited as enumerators, should not operate within the area of their own authority. It was considered that census confidentiality was at risk if enumerators could potentially use for other purposes information gathered whilst taking the census.

There are two main objections to implementing the distance and exclusion rules recommended for field staff: cost and data quality. It has been estimated that the increased travelling costs resulting from a 'five-mile rule' would add some 10 per cent to the field cost of a full census. More important, however, is the likely reduction in the efficiency and quality of the census fieldwork and, hence, a reduction in the quality of the data collected if the two rules were implemented. The recruitment of sufficient enumerators of the required calibre would be hindered; there is a greater risk of under-coverage and poor rapport when enumerators work in unfamiliar physical and social surroundings. The government decided, therefore, that the distance and exclusion rules could not be implemented in future censuses, although extra care would be taken to reduce the chance of overlap between an enumerator's personal or business contacts and his enumeration area.

Another solution to the problem is to increase the use of sealed envelopes for returning census forms either to the local census officials or directly to the census office. The RSS nominees' report recommended greater provision for postal returns and, more generally, a reduction of the enumerator's involvement in checking completed census forms. Here, again, there are problems of efficiency and cost and the risk of a reduction in data quality. The collection visit allows the enumerator to assist the householder in filling in any parts of the form that were not understood, and to point out any inadvertent omissions that can be rectified on the spot. An opinion survey after the 1971 Census found that 82 per cent of adults thought it helpful to have the enumerator call to collect the form. More complicated (and costly) arrangements for checking inadvertent omissions or possible errors would be required to replace the enumerators' function and also to check that a complete set of forms had been collected for each enumeration district. Nonetheless, the government accepted that the option of returning forms unseen by the local enumerator should be offered more extensively in future censuses. Facilities for making postal returns will be made clear to householders in the 1981 Census; if the enumerator should be known to the householder, an envelope will be offered to allow the census form to be returned unseen by the enumerator.[17]

Census forms and the Public Record Office

Census forms are held centrally by the census office before and after the processing cycle is completed. They are not destroyed – as in some countries – nor are they returned to the relevant local authority – as in France. Policies governing the preservation of census returns, and access to them, have been developed over the years.

Enumeration books for the 1801–31 Censuses were all destroyed – the only surviving information being contained in the *Census Abstracts* for those years.[18] Enumeration books for the 1841 and 1851 Censuses were preserved and released to the Public Record Office in 1912, for the primary purpose of enabling those who were then (or about to be) eligible for an old-age pension to adduce some evidence of age – compulsory registration of births which began in 1837 not being fully effective until 1875. With this exception, census returns were treated as confidential for a period of 100 years, a policy that was formalised only in 1966 in an Instrument of the Lord Chancellor stating that decennial census records were selected for permanent preservation and would not be available for public inspection for 100 years. The aim of the 100-years rule was to ensure that census forms would relate to only minimal numbers of living people when released. But the period chosen is a good deal longer than in the United States and Canada, for example, where the same principle led to a confidential period of seventy-two years only – the approximate life-span of an individual.[19] In Scotland, a forty-years rule was adopted in 1923, but this is now being extended to a 100-years rule.[20]

The Public Record Office is thus responsible for the surviving census records for 1841–71 for England and Wales, and the census office currently is responsible for the census returns for 1881–1971, with the exception of 1931 forms, all of which were accidentally burnt. The 1966 Sample Census forms have been destroyed as this was not a decennial census. Census records up to 1871 at the PRO are generally available to the public and are used extensively for genealogical and historical research.[21]

The only groups to have stated a view on the 100-years rule are genealogists and historical researchers – who agreed that the period was unnecessarily long and damaging to their professional interests. In practice, information from the early census records had been supplied to bona fide historical researchers from censuses down to 1901 before the 1966 Instrument, and this continued up to 1971. On the rare occasions when information was supplied for research purposes, names and addresses were deleted to render the data anonymous, and a number of other safeguards were adopted. In 1966, the Advisory Council on Public Records emphasised the needs of researchers to the Registrar-General, and it was agreed to waive the 100-years rule for bona fide researchers on the grounds that staff resources were lacking for the census office to provide tabulations manually from the early census records. With the elimination of this waiver in 1971, only tabulations can now be offered. There have been few such requests since 1971 and, in fact, no tabulations have been provided, probably because of the high cost involved in producing them manually.[22]

The public use of 1841 and 1851 records for adducing evidence of age created the precedent for similar uses of the returns from later censuses down to 1921, a practice that was stopped in 1959. Searches were sometimes carried out in the past to help trace registration records. Searches are carried out for genealogical purposes and to help someone establish entitlement to something beneficial, such as a pension or an inheritance.[23] A similar practice is found in the United States.[24]

Access to census returns within the closed period is allowed to those working in the census office for officially-approved statistical or research purposes, most commonly research concerned with census methodology such as census form design or question-wording.

Census data files

With the introduction of computers into census processing in 1961, confidentiality procedures were extended to include rules governing the security of and access to census data files held on magnetic tapes.

Since names and addresses are not required for the production of statistics, they have never been entered on to the computer. This fact is not widely known, and the census office has on occasion received requests from genealogists and other researchers for statistics on the most common surnames. The anonymity and complexity of census data files constitute one safeguard of their confidentiality, but security regulations governing access to the census office processing centre in Titchfield and to the data files themselves are stringent.

The White Paper on census security concluded that 'the Societies' reports give no evidence to support misgivings about the potential threat to the individual from the use of computers for the Census'.[25] In fact, many of the recommendations made by the BCS and the RSS had already been standard practice in the census offices. Both societies recommended, however, that the census be the subject of independent reviews, and the government agreed to consider this recommendation in the light of the Younger Committee Report.

Census tabulations and data dissemination

The report of the Royal Statistical Society nominees made a number of comments on the publication and dissemination of census data. It supported the 100-years rule on the closure of census records and emphasised the value of their preservation for the study of social history after this time lag. It suggested that there was a need for more information on the uses of census statistics and thus the ultimate purpose of the census collection, implying that general statements about 'statistical purposes' are no longer considered sufficient. The recommendation that the census office maintain a list for public inspection of all special (*ad hoc*) tabulations produced for government departments and other organisations has been implemented. More generally, the report recommended greater emphasis on the continuous development of public relations and the provision of information on census plans. These views parallel those emerging in other countries. In the United States, for example, the Privacy Act of 1974 requires data-collecting agencies to inform respondents of routine uses to be made of the data; thus an accurate statement of the legal uses of census data will have to be provided when the 1980 Census is carried out.[26]

A very large number of tables are published through HMSO after each census (some 3000 for the 1971 Census), but in recent years an even larger number of unpublished tabulations have been available on request and the payment of a fee from the census office. A common misconception is that unpublished census data contains information that is more 'confidential' than that supplied in published reports. However, data remains unpublished primarily because the volume of statistics is too large to warrant the cost of publication in book form, especially in the case of the small area statistics that are used by local authorities for planning purposes. Confidentiality constraints are applied to both published and unpublished tables, and no data are released on a selective basis to privileged census-users – whatever data are released are publicly available to all interested census-users.

Since 1971, procedures have been adopted to ensure that census output does not disclose information about identifiable (though unnamed) individuals. A rounding technique is applied to all cells of tables based on 100 per cent counts (with the exception of basic counts of persons and households). A process of quasi-random error injection known as 'Barnardisation' is applied to each data cell based on 100 per cent counts in the unpublished small area statistics that are supplied for areas below local-authority level. Data based on samples of census results are not randomised. These data-randomising techniques have been described by Newman.[27]

Unlike the United States Bureau of the Census and Statistics Canada, the census office has never released microdata tapes from the census; that is, tapes for public use containing anonymous information on a sample of persons, families or households. Perhaps the best-known examples of census microdata are the United States 1 per cent and 0.1 per cent Public Use Sample tapes released from the 1960 and 1970 Censuses. Census-users in Britain have suggested that such microdata would offer a useful addition to census output, particularly for research purposes, where the data requirements are less predictable than for the planning applications of census statistics.[28] The census office is currently considering the viability of this type of census output and consulting census-users for their views on the utility of such data.[29] It is considered that in Britain, unlike the United States with a much larger population, the release of microdata on a sample basis does not by itself adequately prevent the disclosure of information about identifiable individuals, unless additional censoring techniques are applied to the data. Some research has been done to test the effectiveness of a number of data-censoring techniques and to assess the validity and utility of the statistics produced from censored microdata.[30] However, it is not clear, in my view, whether the Census Act 1920, written well before the advent of computers, provides for or prevents the release of microdata. It is possible that Britain would be obliged to follow the Canadian example in carrying out special legislation to provide a firm and publicly-accepted basis for such new types of data.

Statistical and research applications

With the creation of the Office of Population Censuses and Surveys (OPCS) in 1970, the census organisation became part of a larger office with broader responsibilities for social and demographic statistics. The Registrar-General's duties to collect, co-ordinate and publish statistics on the characteristics of the population were facilitated. New types of statistical and research work became feasible and some existing census work was facilitated. With these developments, the methodological distinctions between the census and other surveys of the population have become less clear-cut. This is a necessary consequence of adopting a more co-ordinated and cost-effective approach to collecting information on 'the number and condition of the people' as required by the Census Act 1920.[31] Within OPCS, the census is used as a sampling frame for surveys; for the creation of a Longitudinal Study; and for methodological studies.

Since 1961, the census has provided the sampling frame for voluntary post-enumeration surveys. These are carried out to produce coverage checks and quality (validation) checks on each census, but do not seek any additional information to that collected in the census itself. The results of the 1961 post-enumeration surveys were reported in the *1961 Census General Report*, giving estimates of under-enumeration and an assessment of data quality. The post-enumeration survey for the 1966 Census was reported in a separate volume by Gray and Gee.[32] The results of the 1971 quality checks for E. & W. are not yet out. The creation of OPCS in 1970 facilitated census post-enumeration surveys because the organisation responsible for voluntary sample surveys and the census organisation are now part of the same office, and governed by the same confidentiality rulings.

The 1971 Census was supplemented by other voluntary follow-up surveys for which census returns provided the sampling frame: the 1971 survey of people with nursing qualifications; the 1972 income survey; and the 1973 qualified manpower survey.[33] The latter two were census-linked in the sense that information from each survey was merged with that provided on census forms, giving two examples of file-merging for statistical purposes within OPCS. Information collected from the two surveys is less complete than that collected in the 1971 Census, in part because response to the surveys was voluntary, and in part because the surveys were carried out one year after the census and some respondents in the survey samples could not be recontacted. Voluntary follow-up surveys are regarded as a useful and cost-effective adjunct to the census. They enable the number of questions on the census form to be reduced, and ensure that questions which only apply to a minority of the population (such as those with higher educational qualifications) are addressed solely to members of that minority group. The census is the only data collection that can supply a complete sampling frame for such voluntary follow-up surveys; this is particularly true of groups that are relatively small and widely dispersed in the country as a whole – as in the case of people with higher qualifications. Census follow-up surveys are considered to be part of the census, so that census confidentiality constraints apply equally to the survey information.

The unique value of the census as a sampling frame is recognised by researchers, and requests for this type of use have on occasion been received from organisations carrying out research. Where the research in question was considered to be in the public interest and the researchers accepted the procedures imposed by OPCS to safeguard census confidentiality, these requests were met. A small number of surveys fulfilled these conditions; for example, the 1966 Sample Census was used as the sampling frame for health surveys. The procedure adopted in each case was for OPCS to have sole responsibility for the selection of the survey sample from census returns and for conducting the postal survey. Respondents were informed that the survey was voluntary and responses were returned to OPCS for names, addresses and other identifiers to be removed before sending the anonymous sample survey results to the researcher for analysis. The researchers did not therefore obtain, or have access to, any census information relating to respondents.

The Royal Statistical Society's report on the 1971 Census noted that the use of the census as a sampling frame was not explicitly recognised in public assurances of confidentiality and recommended that more information on census plans, including any proposed follow-up surveys, should in future be made available.[34] The White Paper on the 1981 Census states that it may be used as a sampling frame and that Parliament will be informed of any follow-up surveys.[35]

The census is thus used solely as a sampling frame for some surveys that are otherwise not connected with the census (such as the nursing survey), and also for census-linked surveys, the results of which are merged with census information (such as the income survey). The Longitudinal (cohort) Study provides another example of file-merging for statistical purposes within OPCS. In this case the data files being merged are already held by OPCS and are not the results of additional surveys.

The Longitudinal Study is based on merging census information for a 1 per cent sample of the population in 1971 with other information already held by OPCS, for example birth and death registration, notification of cases of cancer, and internal and overseas migration as recorded in National Health Service records. The study does not involve the collection of any additional information from the public, nor the transfer outside OPCS of any personal information held by the Office, nor the transfer to OPCS of any personal information from other agencies. A number of confidentiality safeguards have been designed specifically for the Longitudinal Study data files and for the resulting statistical analyses, and these take account of the confidentiality constraints applying to the census information.[36] In this case, the use of the census information is clearly solely for compiling statistics, but the research methodology involved is new. Here again, the purpose of the new research is to keep down the number of questions included in the census itself. A survey showed that $4\frac{1}{2}$ per cent of a sample of adults considered that fertility questions for married women should not have been asked in the 1971 Census.[37] The longitudinal study provides an alternative source of statistics on fertility,

mortality and aspects of the flows within the labour force.[38] The
White Paper *Computers and Privacy* notes that statistics play an essential
part in research and that file-merging for statistical purposes is justified.[39] But this is the only example of such work within OPCS; more
extensive file-merging exercises for statistical purposes that involve
census data are carried out in some other countries, and techniques of
data-linkage have been developed further.[40]

The third type of census use within OPCS is for methodological
studies, such as Kemsley's study of differential response to the 1971
Family Expenditure Survey (FES).[41] Special tabulations from the
1971 Census were produced for the 1971 FES sample, permitting statistical comparisons of FES respondents and non-respondents.

In summary, it can be seen that the creation of OPCS has resulted
in a more co-ordinated effort on the collection and analysis of social
and demographic statistics, and in new departures in research methodology. As statistical analysis and research techniques develop in
complexity, there is an increased risk that they will be carelessly and
imprecisely described by non-specialists, thus creating public fears
for the confidentiality of the information in question. There have been
numerous examples of this in census-users' research reports and press
articles on the work of OPCS, giving misleading impressions of the
type of census (and other) data released by OPCS and the uses of the
census. The solution to this problem is not easy to determine. The
provision of more information by OPCS on census plans and
increased emphasis on public relations, as suggested by the Royal Statistical Society, may be helpful. The creation of an independent data-
protection authority has also been viewed as a solution, but this would
not in itself prevent misleading reports by census-users or the press.
We shall return to this issue later, but a review of current information
on public attitude to census confidentiality suggests the problem
cannot be ignored.

Public Attitude to Census Confidentiality

The public debate surrounding the 1971 Census of Population was
concerned very largely with the confidentiality of census returns and
with whether some of the questions asked constituted an invasion of
privacy. An independent survey carried out in the week before census
day showed that only 47 per cent of a sample of 1135 household heads

in 120 constituencies believed that 'the secrets of everyone's private lives are kept fully secure by the census organisers'. Altogether, 45 per cent of the household heads sampled thought that 'there is a risk that information could fall into the hands of the wrong people'. The results of this independent survey suggest that a large proportion of the population had misgivings about the extent to which census confidentiality was preserved by the census offices.

Since confidentiality concerns the permitted uses of personal information, we might expect that providing information on the applications of census data would help reassure the public. A slip-in leaflet to the 1971 Census household form described the applications of census statistics in planning services such as housing, education, hospitals and clinics, roads and public transport, and manpower planning. The leaflet also stated that information on identifiable persons would not be revealed in tabulations produced from the census. The results of another survey carried out seven weeks after census day suggest that the leaflet was read by about four-fifths of all adults and had some impact on public understanding of the census.

This second survey was commissioned by the Census Offices and based on a sample of 2285 adults in the United Kingdom. It showed that, when presented with descriptions of possible uses of census data, 80 per cent of respondents thought the census was used 'for forecasting population growth' and 65 per cent thought it served 'to help local government planning'. However, 35 per cent still believed a main purpose of the 1971 Census was 'to provide a record of people's addresses for the government'. Asked to state who, in their view, were allowed to see information from individual census forms, 65 per cent of respondents replied 'people in the census office only', but a further 27 per cent said 'people working for government', 3 per cent replied 'qualified people in industry', and a full 7 per cent said 'anyone'.[42] Thus about one-third of the sample (possibly including the 21 per cent who had not read the slip-in leaflet) were misinformed about the purposes of the census and the confidentiality of the census returns. Assuming the survey sample was fully representative of the adult population, about one-third of all adults do not yet fully appreciate the principle of census confidentiality.

It is likely that some users of census statistics may be among those who are misinformed about confidentiality. As our review has shown, operational policies must cover a very wide range of situations in the census-taking cycle. Even users of census data are often aware only of the constraints imposed on statistical output.[43]

The survey commissioned by the census offices provided some indication of the extent to which the census was perceived to be an invasion of privacy. Altogether, 13 per cent of all adults interviewed objected to some of the questions included on the 1971 Census form; $4\frac{1}{2}$ per cent felt strongly that questions on parents' birthplace should not have been included; $4\frac{1}{2}$ per cent mentioned the fertility questions for married women; 3 per cent of all respondents objected to the questions on occupation and hours of work; other questions were named by fewer than 3 per cent of those interviewed.[44] Other questions may, of course, prove sensitive in certain cases, even though there is no objection to them in principle. For example, the question on relationship to the head of household may prove difficult for unmarried couples living together, and the fertility questions may prove sensitive to parents of adopted children. Similarly, households may feel sensitive even about listing persons usually resident at the address, for example where a lodger is present in a household, the legal conditions of whose tenure does not formally permit this.

The 1971 Census resulted in a higher number of prosecutions for non-compliance with the legal obligation to complete fully the census form than had occurred in previous censuses. The number of prosecutions for non-compliance is always a minute proportion of the total population. Even after the 1971 Census, the number was still less than 500, a tiny proportion of the total population.[45]

Of those who refused to complete their 1971 Census form, 41 per cent did not state a reason. Of those who did give a reason, the great majority (57 per cent) were concerned with the census as an invasion of privacy either explicitly or implicitly. For example, they objected to a particular question on the census form, to parts of the form, to the fact that all questions were compulsory, or to the fact that the census had become more than a basic head-count. Of those stating a reason for non-compliance, only 11 per cent could be described as having fears about the confidentiality of the information given, and many of these were concerned that a future government might not fully respect census confidentiality. A further 32 per cent gave other reasons for non-compliance, for example political reasons or the computerisation of results. If the reasons for non-compliance are indicative of the wider debate on the 1971 Census, it would seem that the invasion of privacy issue was by far the most important among those who questioned the census; in other words, the appropriateness of including certain questions in the census was questioned, rather than the confidentiality of the information once collected. The questions which attracted the greatest amount of opposition were, as shown by the post-census opinion survey, those on country of birth, fertility and questions on the person's employer and qualifications.

It is perhaps of interest that prosecutions provide the only case where census forms are allowed to leave the census office. The Parliamentary Commissioner for Administration criticised OPCS after the 1971 Census for failing to reconcile the public assurances on confidentiality with the need to produce evidence in any prosecution under the Census Act for non-completion of the form. The White Paper on the 1981 Census now makes the position clear.[46]

In the United States, the protection of confidentiality for statistical and research data requires exemption from mandatory disclosure of identifiable data pursuant to a subpoena or other compulsory legal process or under the provisions of the Freedom of Information Act. In 1961, Congress had to amend the census law to protect copies of census documents retained in respondents' files from compulsory legal process.[47] In Britain, there are no procedures for mandatory disclosure of census (or other OPCS) data and thus no need for special exemptions from compulsory legal process.[48]

The success of any data collection, even the obligatory population census, rests in large part on the willing co-operation of the public. The census office thus tries to ensure that questions asked in the census are acceptable to the majority of people. However, attitudes change over time. The idea of taking a census was itself the subject of public debate in the late eighteenth century.[49] In the early part of this century, the census included questions on 'lunatics' and 'imbeciles' that would now be quite unacceptable. Even though the census office leaves it to each household to decide who should be listed as 'head of household', the very use of the term provoked lively press comment in 1971 and may prove less widely acceptable in future censuses. The term 'head or joint heads of household' is currently proposed for the 1981 Census. The census office is always under pressure to include additional questions on the census form. Unlike the United States, Canada and Australia, however, a question on income has never been included on the census form; in the 1971 Census it was allocated only to a voluntary census follow-up survey. Census follow-up surveys, which do not share the compulsory character of the census itself, may offer a more acceptable medium for collecting information that is of

general interest but does not have the support of a substantial proportion of the public.

Current Issues

The principles and operational policies of census confidentiality have
undergone seventeen decades of maturation. But it is likely that they
will develop further, and more quickly, in the next decades as more
powerful computer technology and the improved co-ordination of
official statistics open up new possibilities and hence raise further
questions to be considered from the confidentiality viewpoint. The
creation of a data-protection authority would be an important factor
in this process.

The Younger Committee on Privacy reported in July 1972 on the
use of computers in the private sector. A separate enquiry was conducted of the public sector, resulting in two White Papers in
December 1975.[50] *Computers and Privacy* reviews in some detail the
issues, principles and problems involved in this field, and presents recommendations on procedures to safeguard privacy in the context of
widespread use of computers to store information on identifiable persons. A Supplementary Report, *Computers: Safeguards for Privacy*,
reports on the review of categories of information held in the computer
systems of government departments and other parts of the public
sector, discusses the safeguards which operate to protect the privacy
of people on whom personal information is held in public-sector computers, presents information on computer use in the United Kingdom, and discusses practice in other countries. These two recent
White Papers are of particular interest in that they set out current
government thinking on data confidentiality.

The first paper outlines the government's view of privacy in greater
detail than hitherto. Privacy of the individual is seen to be at issue in
respect of the accuracy, completeness and relevance of the data in
question; security measures and access to the data; and its confidentiality. Under the heading of confidentiality, the paper considers
the questions of improper use, data transfers and file-merging. It
does not rule out file-merging as a breach of confidentiality, stating
that 'some limited linkage of data from different systems for administrative or statistical purposes (or both) may be justified subject to
proper safeguards' (para. 17). It goes on to say that certain types of

research may necessitate combining data about the same people which are held in different systems, in order to find or confirm correlations, and that 'statistical work carries few risks for privacy because it gives information about groups of people, even though the original data related to identifiable individuals. . . . What is important, however, is that the output of statistics should guard against revealing information about identified or identifiable individuals' (para. 20).

Regarding the population census specifically, the Supplementary Report notes that '. . . certain records, such as income-tax returns, medical records, census returns and criminal records, merit a high degree of interdepartmental confidentiality – and this they receive' (para. 18), and that 'information about identifiable individuals collected in the Census of Population, under the provisions of the Census Act 1920, is not divulged by the census offices to third parties' (para. 23). Perhaps most important, the population census is not listed in Table 2, which sets out government work involving the transfer of information about identifiable persons.

More generally, the White Paper notes that the Supplementary Report 'discloses no evidence to suggest that fears about the improper use of computers in the public sector are justified by present practice' (para. 2), and that it was the potential rather than the actual threat to privacy which led the Younger Committee to recommend the creation of an independent review body. In line with this view, it recommended the establishment of a permanent statutory body (termed data-protection authority for convenience) to oversee the use of computers, in both the public and private sectors, 'to ensure that they are operated with proper regard for privacy and with the necessary safeguards for the personal information which they contain' (para. 30). The precise nature of such an agency was to be determined by an interim body, termed Data Protection Committee, but one option is a registration and licensing agency (along the lines of the Swedish Data Inspection Board, for example). The Data Protection Committee has collected views from data producers, data users, others involved in data processing, and the general public, and a report has been published with its recommendations as to the type of data-protection authority required (see Chapter 17).

The full implications of the legislation recommended by the White Paper have yet to be seen, but one consequence may be that with a licensing body or similar agency, data-holding bodies such as OPCS would have greater freedom to hold, transfer and merge data files for statistical and research purposes, with an agency to oversee these practices and to reassure the public that confidentiality and privacy safeguards are actually in force. Such an agency would have the necessary expertise to assess the relevance and stringency of the safeguards used in respect of each type of data. This would overcome some of the problems noted earlier in keeping the general public fully informed of the operational policies applied to each stage of the census cycle to ensure the confidentiality of information collected.

Whether the creation of a data-protection authority would facilitate the release of new types of census output, such as microdata, remains an open question. Aside from the question of OPCS's authority to produce such data, there are other considerations. The release of microdata would have to gain public and political acceptability, and the recommendations of a data-protection authority on this matter might be of assistance here. But there are serious problems in the design of suitably-censored microdata that would still retain sufficient validity and reliability not to prejudice the results of statistical analysis. Furthermore, census-data users tend to have divergent views on the type of information that should be contained in microdata files for research purposes. Historians, for example, are interested in detailed information on household composition and relationships, while others are interested in detailed information on the employment situation of individuals. It is debatable whether the census office could produce straightforward samples of hierarchical census microdata as in the United States. Yet the Canadian solution of producing three separate files of microdata, one for persons, one for households and one for census-defined families, has not proven entirely successful. Researchers have found that the separation of the information into three files imposes severe limitations on the type of research and analysis for which the data can be used. It is likely that further research on data-censoring techniques, and on the research interests of potential users, will be needed before microdata could be released from the census.[51] Should these problems be resolved, there seems to be no reason why similar types of microdata could not be released from earlier censuses that are held on computer tapes. In the United States, demands for such data have already been made to the Census Bureau.[52]

So far the computer tapes from the 1961 and subsequent censuses have been retained by the census office and are used to produce special tabulations.[53] The question arises as to whether the anonymous computer master files of the census results should, like the census forms, eventually be deposited with the Public Record Office. Responsibility for maintaining the tapes in machine-readable condition would thus fall to the PRO. Permanent preservation of the tapes would, of course, facilitate future historical research, as the laborious process of manual analysis would thus be eliminated. Although the census tapes could not be released for a number of decades after each census, decisions regarding their preservation or destruction will have to be taken in the near future.

While the current focus of interest is on computers and their implications for data confidentiality and privacy, another line of thought is developing on the confidentiality of class data. This may prove to be an equally salient issue in future years. It is not always assumed that confidentiality, and privacy more generally, are matters affecting the individual alone. People do not necessarily make a distinction between information used for action on 'me personally' versus data used for action on people like 'me generally'. The research and planning uses of statistical data on the population or sub-groups within it may not in some cases be very different in their effects from the use of information on individuals for administrative purposes. For example, the release of class data on groups such as the coloured population, working women or the self-employed, renders them subject to public action (whether welcome or unwelcome) which could affect them, in the same way that the release of information on individuals might render them subject to actions affecting them personally, for example by local authorities or market researchers.[54] Kelman notes that the confidentiality of research results on specific organisations, geographically delimited communities or population sub-groups (such as ethnic minorities) present special difficulties.[55]

One strand of this argument focuses on the problem of an information monopoly: the situation where large organisations (both in the public and private sectors) have the resources to obtain class data, store it on computers, acquire the specialist expertise to analyse it, and eventually formulate policies based on the results obtained. Furthermore, large organisations are often in a better position to influence or determine the nature of the data collected (either on the population as a whole or sub-groups within it) according to their interests, and hence promote a bias in the type of data available.

This line of thought is not concerned with confidentiality as currently conceptualised, but rather with the politics of information, a very much broader issue which lies beyond the scope of this review. Extending the principle of privacy to class data would totally preclude most social-science research and probably many of the uses currently made of census and other official statistics. It is, in my view, concern over the politics of information, rather than the use of computers and data banks more specifically, that lies behind some of the reactions to census and other data collections. The population census probably attracts more than its fair share of this concern, not only in Britain, but in other countries as well, because it is a highly visible and compulsory collection taking place at a given time, known well in advance.[56]

One answer to this problem may lie in the direction of encouraging and facilitating greater use of official statistics, and the creation, or promotion, of centres providing advice on the use of statistical data, or data-analysis services, free of charge to community groups. A number of such groups are already in existence, although little information is available on their impact, if any, on the information monopoly which they perceive. In France, the question of information monopoly has been squarely confronted already, with the creation of official data-dissemination centres in all regions, operating under the principle of 'l'égalité de l'information'.[57]

Summary and Conclusions

The policy of census confidentiality was first stated in 1841, but not enshrined in legislation until 1900, after a century of census-taking. The procedures adopted to preserve the confidentiality of census information, and the permitted uses of the data, have been modified and adapted to changing circumstances over the decades: the lack of effective birth registration; the availability of resources for census searches; the demands of researchers for census data; the introduction of computers to census processing; the creation of a statistical office (OPCS) with responsibility not only for the census and vital statistics but also for voluntary *ad hoc* social surveys; and changes in public attitude to privacy. Developments in Britain closely parallel the history of census confidentiality in other countries, with administrative and legal safeguards gradually being instituted over the decades.[58]

However, there is evidence that the public is not fully aware of the policy and practice of census confidentiality. The publication of a White Paper on census plans some three years before the 1981 Census should go some way towards creating a more informed climate of opinion on the census and its function of providing statistical data on the demographic and socio-economic characteristics of the population.

Public attitude is likely to be a crucial factor in future developments. Sir Claus Moser, when head of the Government Statistical Service, suggested that well-publicised safeguards of confidentiality, and some constraints on the total burden of statistical enquiries, could result in more relaxed attitudes to privacy over the next ten years. But he also considered attitudes to government to be an important factor and one that could produce a hardening of attitudes, with people increasingly challenging the right of government to ask personal questions.[59]

While it is difficult to predict future trends in public attitude, it seems certain that there will be more codes of conduct, formal constraints and statistical laws applied to the activities of agencies holding information on individuals. Statistical offices will, in my view, have to engage in a more open and public debate on the issues of privacy and confidentiality, to maintain public confidence and to retain the support of the public for their work. The recent White Paper on the 1981 Census outlines the principles of confidentiality to be applied to the next census and provides an example of the type of statement that may be required for other data collections in future years.

11 Parliament and the British Census since 1920 *

Martin Bulmer

Censuses of population are the most extensive social research inquiries undertaken in modern industrial societies. They are also the most public, because of their scale and importance, and they draw attention to the research and statistical function in a way that no other inquiry does. The bodies of data which they provide are also the largest likely to be found in data archives used by social scientists. It is therefore of some interest to examine census-taking in Great Britain in the last half century from the point of view of privacy as a social issue.

Procedures for carrying out censuses differ from country to country, though there are certain general similarities. This chapter discusses censuses in Great Britain (England, Wales and Scotland) since 1920.[1] Briefly, the conduct of the census of population, which is governed by the Census Act 1920,[2] is the responsibility of the Registrar-General for England and Wales and the Registrar-General for Scotland. Each is a government official, but with a semi-independent status, heading the government department responsible for the conduct of the census (among other duties). Censuses have been held at ten-year intervals since 1801; in the period under con-

* Original material© 1979 Martin Bulmer.

sideration in 1921, 1931, 1951, 1961 and 1971. (No census was held in 1941 because of the Second World War.) In 1966, additionally, a five-year sample census of 10 per cent of the population was held. A five-year census was proposed in 1976, covering the whole population but using an interlocking sample design to reduce the number of questions.[3] This was approved by Parliament, but shortly afterwards cancelled as part of a package to reduce government expenditure. The next British census will be held in 1981.

Detailed planning of censuses is in the hands of the Registrars-General; their proposals then require ministerial approval. Government proposals for the taking of the census are then put to both Houses of Parliament for approval by affirmative resolution (though there has been some lack of clarity in the past about the precise procedure to be followed). It is thus possible to trace in the official record of Parliament, *Hansard*, concern about census matters expressed by politicians.

The evidence for this chapter has been gathered from *Hansard* volumes for the House of Commons, where the most important debates have taken place. It is of two kinds. Firstly, there are the debates in 1920 on the legislation which became the Census Act and then, subsequently, at each census the debate on the affirmative resolution to allow the census to be held. This usually has taken place twelve to eighteen months before the date of the census itself, always held in April, except in 1921. Secondly, Parliamentary questions provide another indicator of public concern. In the British parliamentary system, matters are brought to the attention of ministers, and/or raised to gain publicity, by Members of Parliament asking questions for (oral or written) reply by the government in the House of Commons. In the analysis that follows, Parliamentary questions are examined for the three years around each census (the year before, the year of the census and the year after).

The first point to make is that the taking of the census, as an event and as a matter of statistical policy, has not greatly exercised politicians in the British House of Commons. It has been a minor issue without much political attraction until recently: the amount of time devoted to it has been comparatively slight. Interest in the subject has been low, as is shown by the data in Table 11.1.

The table makes very clear the very small amount of time devoted to census matters every ten years (or latterly five years); the small number of speakers; and the absence of controversy – until 1975 there was no vote taken. Even in 1970 the amount of Parliamentary time allotted was not used up and the debate ended over an hour before it needed

TABLE 11.1   *Debates in the British House of Commons on the census, 1920–75*

Year of debate	Year of census	Number of columns in Hansard	Duration	Number of MPs who spoke
1920 (Census Act)	1921	37		
1930	1931	6		3
1950	1951	31	1 hr 39 min	11
1960	1961	17½	54 min	5
1965	1966	27	1 hr 15 min	5
1970	1971	28	1 hr 14 min	5
1975	1976 (later cancelled)	36	1 hr 50 min (Division, 66 Yes, 13 No)	8

Source: *Hansard*, House of Commons.

to. This is particularly surprising in view of the ensuing controversy when the census actually took place. This perhaps explains why in 1975 there were more MPs wanting to speak than there was time to hear. Until the 1975 debate, there was little real edge to the argument and few really critical points being made. For example, in 1960 both the government (Conservative) and the opposition (Labour) were very acquiescent, each side congratulating the other on the need for a census and not scrutinising the details very closely.

Nevertheless, certain trends are discernible on privacy and confidentiality. The evidence shows that, in recent censuses, privacy and confidentiality have become very much more salient issues. Though present to some extent in 1920 and 1950, it is only in 1970 and 1975 that they emerged strongly.

One indicator of this is the scope of questions which may be asked in the census. This scope is defined in the schedule at the end of the Census Act 1920, 'Matters in respect of which particulars are required'. They are:

(1) Names, sex, age.
(2) Occupation, profession, trade or employment.
(3) Nationality, birthplace, race, language.
(4) Place of abode and character of dwelling.

(5) Conditions as to marriage, relation to head of family, issue born in marriage.

(6) Any other matters in respect to which it is desirable to obtain statistical information with a view to ascertaining the social or civil condition of the population.[4]

The original bill presented to the House of Commons included additionally two other items, education and infirmity and disability. These were withdrawn following objections from several MPs. The objections of Mr Inskip remind us of how different are contemporary censuses from those of sixty years ago.

Imagine Hon Members [he said in criticism] having to cross-examine maids or any other persons in the house as to whether they were suffering from infirmity or disability, because some medical expert with the best will in the world said it was desirable that a census should be taken of persons who were so suffering.[5]

Mr Rawlinson represented those who at all periods have tended to sensationalise and distort the purposes of census-taking in order to attack it. He alleged that there was nothing to prevent the population being asked whether they suffered from venereal disease if the item on infirmity and disability were included.

Controversy also occurred over the wording of Clause 5. In its original form, it included the word 'parentage' and did not include 'born in marriage'. Members objected to heads of households having to ask people who their father was (thereby discovering whether they were legitimate or not). Mr Rawlinson asked whether heads of households were expected to inquire of a servant who her father was, and face the mutual embarrassment of discovery that she was illegitimate. An amendment to delete the word 'parentage' was agreed. In addition, the words 'born in marriage' were added to 'issue', thereby avoiding embarrassment over illegitimacy of children.

The final clause was also criticised for its open-ended nature, giving *carte blanche* to the census authorities to ask whatever they liked. Lieutenant-Commander Kenworthy asked: 'are they going to take my fingerprints? In view of the way we are now docketed and indexed and so on, and the whole system of internal espionage, spying on the private life of the people, which is a custom that has sprung up in the [First] World War, are they going to use the cloak of the census still further to pry into the private lives of people?'[6]

In practice, such fears have had no basis in reality. Health questions have not been asked since the 1920 Act. The last time was in 1911, when heads of households were asked whether any person was blind, deaf, dumb or lunatic. Educational questions have been included since 1951, arousing mild criticism from time to time. However, at each census debate, ministers presented to Parliament an outline of the questions to be asked, including an indication of those which were an addition to the previous schedule. Thus in 1970, the minister discussed in detail twelve new questions to be included and drew attention to three from the previous census which had been left out.[7] Until recent years, the most sensitive question has been one (included for the analysis of fertility) asking married women, if married more than once, the month and year of their first marriage. Some MPs argued that this was an embarrassing intrusion on privacy.

Up to 1971, attempts to add extra questions have been as noticeable as criticisms of new ones. A hardy perennial is the suggestion that a question on Welsh-speaking be included in the census forms distributed in England, to identify Welsh-speakers living outside Wales. In 1960, Mr John Parker made a sustained argument for the inclusion of a question on religion, principally to facilitate the better planning of denominational education. He argued that such a question was asked in many countries and that there was no difficulty in collecting the information. It was less sensitive than asking married women about their marital history. The ministerial reply is interesting in throwing light on the sorts of criteria used to judge potential census questions. Decisions are taken on what questions to include (he said) on the basis of what questions

> are likely to be answered truthfully and what use will be made of the results when obtained . . . There is considerable resistance to giving this kind of information, and we are advised that the question would probably be widely resented and in consequence we would not be likely to get the sort of truthful answers which we seek to obtain in the census.[8]

In the recent past, strong criticism has been levelled at certain questions by the Parliamentary Liberal Party, numerically small but vociferous on census matters. In 1970, Mr Eric Lubbock criticised questions on parents' country of birth and on year of entry to the United Kingdom which, he said, were not warranted by the powers given to the government under the Census Act. In 1976, Mr Alan Beith particularly criticised the proposed question on parents' country of birth and on residence five years ago. Parental birthplace, he argued, does not tell one much about problems of immigration or problems of language, and contributes to the notion that anybody with a parent born abroad is a problem. Moreover, the question 'is strongly opposed by the organisations concerned particularly with the welfare of immigrants, who fear that these figures may be used in the wrong way'.[9] (The minister interrupted to say that the question had been specifically asked for by the Race Relations Board and the Community Relations Commission.) In the House of Lords debate of 1975, Lord Avebury (formerly Mr Eric Lubbock) argued in effect that the question should not be asked.

A number of other themes recur in the census debates in Parliament over the years. Some are perennial issues, like cost or procedure. Others are specific to statistical data gathering such as why, if government already has so much data about the population, it has to institute another specific and intrusive inquiry like the census. Ministerial statements, which in some years have taken up as much as half the time of the debate, have gone to great lengths to explain the need for census data, why existing sources are inadequate, and the confidentiality safeguards for collecting, storage and publication.

A full statement of the case in 1970 is representative of recent debates. The minister said that

> we realise very well that the taking of a census involves some invasion of people's privacy. But government, central and local, is under continual pressure to develop the social and other services, to improve the planning of the economy and to make sure of the right priorities in capital investment. How can all this be done without having available the hard facts on which to work? The necessary information in many cases can only come from the private citizen. But this reliance on individuals to give their personal information in turn imposes a responsibility on us to create complete safeguards against any breaches of confidence when the information is collected and handled.[10]

This was a Labour minister, but the policy has been bi-partisan. A Conservative minister in 1960 said:

It cannot be emphasised too often that, as in the past, the census schedules that the householders complete are strictly confidential, that the information in them is used solely for compiling statistics, and that no details of individuals are disclosed to any persons or departments outside the census staff.[11]

This bi-partisan policy was well summed up by Patrick Gordon Walker in the 1961 debate.

British people will put up with anything so long as it is reasonable and sensible, but otherwise they will not, and therefore it is extremely important to explain these matters and particularly the difficult questions . . . It is important to explain that the government need the information and also to explain its confidentiality – that it is as secret as the Ballot itself. This must be continuously put across.[12]

By 1970, however, cracks were beginning to appear in the unified façade, which by 1975 had widened. In the latter year, Dr Gerard Vaughan for the Conservatives asked about alternatives to the census. He referred to population registers in Sweden, the Netherlands and West Germany (which Britain does not have) and to continuous surveys in Canada and Britain. Was the census, he asked, really necessary on its present scale?

The privacy question, raised by Mr Lubbock in 1971, was pressed by the Liberal spokesman, Mr Beith, much more strongly in 1975. He questioned the need for compulsion in answering the census, suggesting that after the basic questions on population, completion of the remainder of the census schedule should be voluntary.

The government have begun to accept the principle of voluntary censuses in the follow-up and sample surveys. Why not go the whole way? In any case, much of the census is being done on a 10 per cent basis, so that we are not dealing with total figures for many of the questions.[13]

Criticism of the census is not new. As D. V. Glass has documented, questioning the need for a census and criticising the census-taking authorities goes back well beyond 1801.[14] It does appear, however, from recent Parliamentary debates that census-taking has become a more controversial activity. The degree of criticism is much greater, particularly before the 1976 Census (subsequently cancelled for reasons of economy). Strident attacks have been made on the inclusion of particular questions, often themselves innocuous. The compulsory nature of the census has been questioned for the first time in recent years. It is only fair to add that both kinds of criticism have been firmly rejected by the government of the day. If anything, however, these debates underestimate political concern, for they take place twelve to eighteen months before the census is held.

This concludes the discussion of formal Parliamentary debates on the British census. It is now useful to turn to the data on Parliamentary *questions*, which cover the period of the census itself. In particular, this may throw some light on the considerable public controversy surrounding the 1971 Census, which led to several studies of privacy and social data, with recommendations, notably a government White Paper on census confidentiality[15] and the SCPR working party report (Chapter 5 above). These too are an indication of the changing climate in which censuses are nowadays conducted, for in the Netherlands and the United States, as well as in Britain, the most recent census was attended by some public controversy.

An analysis of Parliamentary questions about the census by frequency, month and year is contained in Table 11.2 and Figure 11.1. This brings out clearly both the increasing number of questions asked about the census, especially marked in 1971, and their clustering around the time of the census, which may be taken as an indication of greater current controversy. Only in 1921 and 1951 was there a similar clustering, and then the number of questions asked were fewer.

Even more striking than a count of the questions, however, is the result of a content analysis of the questions asked, the results of which

TABLE 11.2 *Numbers of Parliamentary Questions asked about the Census of Population, 1921–71*

Census of	Year before	Year of census	Year after	Total
1921	2	29	6	37
1931	9	27	2	38
1951	3	25	—	28
1961	—	5	5	10
1966	1	12	3	16
1971	5	58	8	71

Source: Hansard, House of Commons.

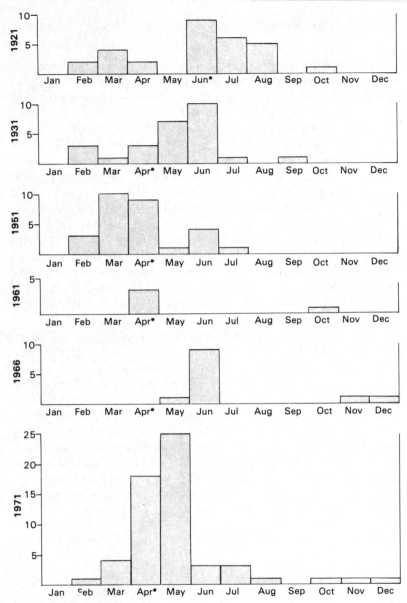

* indicates the month of the census.
Source: Hansard, House of Commons.

FIGURE 11.1 *Number of Parliamentary Questions asked about the Census of Population in each of six census years, 1921–71, by month*

are shown in Table 11.3. Though the sheer number of questions is one indication of concern, their content is more important. There is a significant difference between questions about the employment of enumerators or the timetable for the publication of results, on the one hand, and questions about the justification for including a particular topic or about the confidentiality of data. In Table 11.3, questions are broken down into nine types. These are:

(1) Question content and wording: why particular questions are asked, or not asked; the wording of particular questions etc.

(2) Compulsory nature of the census: why the census is compulsory; what are the penalties for failing to complete the schedule; how many people have refused to co-operate and how many have been prosecuted etc.

(3) Confidentiality: safeguards for the security of the data; undertakings to respect it given by census staff; leakages of confidential information etc.

(4) Languages: questions in Welsh (Wales) and Gaelic (Scotland); translation and information for foreign-language speakers, especially from Indian sub-continent.

(5) Recruitment: pay and conditions of employment of enumerators.

(6) Administrative arrangements involving timing, cost, printing etc.

(7) Timetable for publication of data, inquiries about the availability of specified tabulations etc.

(8) General questions about the authority for taking the census, the need for a census, the responsibility for it.

(9) Other: a wide variety of miscellaneous questions on census matters.

Table 11.3 brings out clearly how these have varied from one census to another. In 1921, for example, one quarter of all questions concerned suspected corruption involved in issuing an announcement of the postponement of the census together with an advertisement. In 1931, one-third of all questions concerned the recruitment and pay of enumerators, particularly with reference to the unemployed. In 1951, no one topic predominated. In 1961 and 1966, the timing and speed of availability of publication were the most frequently raised topics. In 1971, there was a striking concentration on questions concerning the content of the census, confidentiality, the use of compulsion and language issues. This is clearly shown in Table 11.4. The rising trend of interest in questions concerned with the content of the census, its confidentiality, the use of compulsion, and the recognition of language problems, is clear, apart from the quiet year of 1961 when few questions as a whole were asked. It shows the way in which the line of Parliamentary questioning has changed. This can be illustrated from the content of particular questions. In 1931, for example, an MP was asking (apparently seriously) why the census could not be used to record the number of dogs, cats and horses. In 1971, several questioners doubted the desirability of questions asking the name and address of employer, country of birth or parents' country of birth. In 1921, a questioner asked why women were to be employed as enumerators when there were unemployed ex-servicemen looking for work; by 1971, an MP was asking what

TABLE 11.3 *Analysis of content of Parliamentary Questions about the census in year preceding census, year of census and year following census, for censuses between 1921 and 1971*

	1971	1966	1961	1951	1931	1921
Question content and wording	9	3	—	2	3	1
Compulsory nature of census, penalties	8	—	—	—	1	—
Confidentiality provisions, safeguards and breaches	13	2	2	5	1	—
Language: questions, translations	4	2	—	1	1	—
Recruitment, pay and conditions of employment of enumerators	10	—	—	6	15	10
Timing, cost, administration of census, printing etc.	9	3	—	5	6	16
Timetable for publication, or availability of tabulations	7	4	6	3	8	7
General questions about need for or responsibility for the census	2	—	1	3	—	2
Other – miscellaneous	9	2	1	3	3	1
Total	71	16	10	28	38	37

Source: Hansard, House of Commons.

powers there were to prevent an enumerator revealing confidential information. In 1951, an MP suggested breaching the secrecy of the census to track down those evading military service. In 1971, ministers were being pressed with questions about leakages of information, apparent breaches of confidentiality and the taking of legal action against enumerators.

This change in the type of question, and the markedly more critical

TABLE 11.4 *Analysis of Parliamentary Questions showing questions concerning census content, compulsion, confidentiality and language, 1921–71, for three years around census*

	1971	1966	1961	1951	1931	1921
Number of questions concerning these topics	34	7	2	8	6	1
As percentage of all questions about the census	48%	44%	20%	29%	16%	3%

Source: Hansard, House of Commons.

tone, is illustrated by three questions. In 1931, an MP wanted to know why census confidentiality could not be breached to allow elderly persons to verify, from earlier censuses, their age to establish their entitlement to an old-age pension. In 1961, a questioner pressed for the destruction of all individual census returns after processing. In 1971, a questioner raised a number of fairly technical points about the under-enumeration of immigrants and the coverage of this group in the population. Census-taking over fifty years, judged by the sorts of criticisms which British MPs have levied at it, is a somewhat changed activity.

12 Invasion of Privacy: the Case of the United States Census*

Conrad Taeuber

In this chapter, invasion of privacy is discussed in relation to the confidentiality of census records and to the propriety of asking the public to answer the questions. It is also desirable to differentiate among three types of data collection and compilation of the United States Bureau of the Census:

(1) National Censuses provided for by Title 13 of the United States Code in which replies are mandatory.
(2) Other Bureau surveys taken at more frequent intervals under the provisions of Title 13 in which the replies are voluntary; and
(3) Surveys conducted by the Bureau for other agencies of the Federal Government under provisions of their laws, in which the Bureau is involved primarily as a collecting and compiling service.

The requirement to maintain confidentiality can be defined more clearly than many other aspects of the Bureau's obligations. The law which requires confidential protection of information given by any

* Reprinted with the permission of the author and the publishers from *Eugenics Quarterly*, **14**, no. 3, 1967, pp. 243–6.

respondent to the Bureau of the Census is quite specific. Section 9 of Title 13 states, in part, that neither the Secretary of Commerce nor any other officer or employee of the Department (including, of course, the Director of the Census) may:

> (1) use the information furnished under the provisions of this title for any purpose other than the statistical purposes for which it is supplied; or (2) make any publication whereby the data furnished by any particular establishment or individual under this title can be identified; or (3) permit anyone other than the sworn officers and employees of the Department or bureau or agency thereof to examine the individual reports.

These provisions do not apply, of course, to information which is secured by the Bureau from public records.

For the enforcement of the above limitations on the possible uses of data in such a way as to violate confidentiality, Section 214 of Title 13 provides:

> Whoever, being an employee . . . , publishes or communicates, without the written authority of the Secretary or other authorised officer or employee of the Department of Commerce or bureau or agency thereof, any information coming into his possession by reason of his employment under the provisions of this title, shall be fined not more than $1000 or imprisoned not more than two years or both.

A Presidential Proclamation at the time of the 1960 Census assured the public that: 'There need be no fear that disclosure will be made regarding any individual person or his affairs.' It stated also that:

> Individual information collected in the Eighteenth Decennial Census will not be used for purposes of taxation, investigation or regulations, or in connection with military or jury service, the enforcement of school attendance, the regulation of immigration, or the enforcement of any individual, state or local law or ordinance.

In accordance with these provisions, steps are taken to avoid any direct or indirect disclosure of information about any individual. Details will not be published for any area or group unless the number of cases in the group is such that no one could be identified from the information about the group. Normally at least three cases must be present before any details can be published for the group. The minimum number may be larger in some instances. Even if the minimum number is met, publication may still be withheld if one unit (for example, a business establishment) is so dominant in the group that publication of the total would effectively reveal the figures for the dominant unit. Disclosure analysis also requires that there be no inadvertent disclosure, as when figures for a total and one part of the total might each meet the requirements for publication, but the publication of these two would enable a person to secure information for another part of the total which is being suppressed to avoid disclosure.

The release of information in the form of the 1/1000 (0.1 per cent) sample from the 1960 Census was carefully screened to comply with all the requirements of confidentiality. The records in that tape give no information which would identify the area in which the person lives except by broad region and size of place. Moreover, information such as that relating to occupation and industry is given in such broad categories that it would not be possible for anyone to identify a person with a highly unusual occupation who might have been included in this small sample.

The provisions regarding confidentiality of census information apply whether the information was collected under the mandatory powers or in connection with a voluntary survey. Again and again the courts have upheld the Bureau in its refusal to supply information about an individual to regulatory, administrative or judicial agencies. Some years ago one of the regulatory agencies endeavoured to secure individual information about a business establishment from the census. When this was refused, the agency endeavoured to secure the copies of the reports to the Census Bureau which the firm had kept in its files. After the matter had been reviewed in the courts, the Congress adopted an amendment making it clear that it was the intent of the Congress to protect these file copies in the firm's possession in the same manner as the originals which had been filed with the Bureau of the Census.

These stringent provisions for the protection of information about an individual affect any discussion of the invasion of privacy.

The Presidential Proclamation issued in March 1960 said:

Life and liberty in a free country entail a variety of co-operative actions for the common good. The prompt, complete, and accurate answering of all official inquiries made by census officials should be regarded as one of the requirements of good citizenship.

There are no similarly clear-cut rules for determining when it is proper to ask a person to yield his privacy in order to provide information considered essential by the government. The balance between the individual's right to privacy and the government's need for information is often a delicate one. We attempt to give full weight to these considerations by limiting the questioning to those items for which there is a demonstrated need and which the public generally is willing to accept as appropriate to the census. One reason for our preference for a mail approach to census-taking is that this approach reduces the extent to which a neighbour comes to ask questions for the census. When an enumerator comes to collect the information, she is asked to assure that it is given in private; that is, that the information is not collected in the presence of a third party who has no right to it.

Making the proper choices requires a good deal of judgement. We solicit the help of advisory committees, hold public meetings with interested persons, and conduct the planning for a census in such a way that there is widespread opportunity for comment and discussion. There are differences of opinion. A few persons believe that the census should be confined to a head-count for apportionment purposes, citing this as the constitutional basis for the decennial census. Others point to the need for a broad range of information about social and economic conditions and the changes which are occurring.

Views concerning the limits of permissive invasion of privacy change from time to time. It is unlikely that a proposed question on income in 1970 would arouse the reaction that appeared when such a question was suggested for 1940. The value of this information has been so clearly demonstrated that this is now considered to be a field in which the inquiry is entirely appropriate. The decision not to include a question on religion in the 1970 Census was taken in the light of the demonstration that at this time a significant proportion of the population would regard such a question as an improper invasion of their privacy on the part of the government.

In contrast to a census in which replies are mandatory, the Bureau's current surveys generally are not taken under powers to compel a reply. Nevertheless, the same provisions of confidentiality apply. Every proposed new inquiry is subjected to careful consideration from the point of view of essentiality, as well as the possibility that the query would be considered an improper invasion of individual privacy by a significant number of people. Collecting information on possible public reaction is an important part of any pretest. In sample surveys the interviewers usually have more opportunity to explain the relevance of an inquiry that is challenged by a respondent than is the case in the census and thus may be in a better position to justify a line of questioning which initially arouses opposition.

The Bureau's services as a collecting agent for another governmental organisation are becoming an increasingly important phase of its work. Such work for another agency may be undertaken under the provisions of census law or under the legal authority of the other agency. An effort is made to inform respondents as fully as possible as to the agency concerned and the uses which will be made of these data. Here, too, the rules of confidentiality apply to all information submitted to the Bureau, except where the respondent is specifically informed in advance that his individual return may be given to the agency for which the survey is being taken.

In such surveys for other governmental agencies, the nature of an inquiry and the context within which questions are asked may lead to the inclusion of items which would not be considered suitable in a census or a survey done by the Bureau as part of its own programme. Even here, however, it is essential that there be a broad general agreement that the questions are relevant and do not constitute any improper invasion of the individual's privacy. In many instances the subjects of such an inquiry, however, have certain characteristics or conditions which make them especially receptive to the questions involved – as a sample, the aged who might be asked about income and medical care. Questions addressed to a particular group may be more acceptable to that group than to the general public.

Careful adherence to the provisions listed above frequently leads the Bureau into conflicts with persons and organisations which have an interest in utilising the data collected by the Bureau. The provisions against disclosure of individual information make no distinction between good and bad uses, nor do they give the Director of the Bureau the option of deciding that a piece of information might be used to the advantage of the individual and, therefore, may be released to a third party without the prior written authorisation of the individual concerned. The Bureau is occasionally requested to supply information concerning a person with the justification that some benefit would accrue to the person if this information is given to the requestor, for example, an inheritance. Such requests must be refused along with those which on the face of it might appear to be injurious to the person involved.

The advent of the electronic computer has led to the suggestion that information collected by different agencies about a person or a firm might be merged, thus reducing the burden of duplicate reporting and increasing the amount of information which becomes available for analysis. Fears have been aroused that such a merging of records might lead to improper uses of information given for specific purposes and that individuals might thereby have their privacy invaded under circumstances which make it impossible for them to exercise any control over the use of information about themselves. Two points may be made in this connection. First, the Congress has taken a considerable interest in this matter and will doubtless review proposals with care to insure the maintenance of rigorous guarantees of confidentiality of information pertaining to individuals. Second, the state of the art is such that much time must elapse before significant advances can be made in merging information from large data files.

Unless we can develop and maintain the confidence of the public in our willingness and ability to provide confidential treatment of information given to us in confidence, we cannot continue to ask individuals to give us information which they would not willingly give to any other individual.

When the government asks individuals to waive their privacy, it must be able to give assurance that the information will be used only for statistical purposes. The inquiries must be relevant to the government's needs and it must be possible to give the respondent an adequate reason for asking him to give up some part of his privacy for the public good.

13   The Protection of
Privacy and the
United States Census*

William Petersen

Privacy is a contemporary issue and one which has implications for social research in general and censuses in particular. This chapter considers the impact of privacy concerns upon the content of the United States Census. The many books published in recent years on the issue of privacy range from serious commentaries to a best-selling vulgarisation.[1] Their common theme has excited organisations from the John Birch Society to the American Civil Liberties Union. Government agencies at various levels have investigated the matter and made recommendations.[2] The frequently paranoiac tone of many discussions can be illustrated with an editorial from the *New York Times* (6 August 1966):

> Can personal privacy survive the ceaseless advances of the technological juggernaut? . . . The Orwellian nightmare would be brought very close indeed if Congress permits the proposed computer National Data Center to come into being. . . . Perhaps in the long run the fight to preserve privacy is a vain one. But, like the

* Extract from W. Petersen, 'Forbidden Knowledge', in S. Z. Nagi and R. G. Corwin (eds), *The Social Contents of Research*, New York, John Wiley, 1972, pp. 297–304. Copyright © 1972 John Wiley & Sons, Inc. Reprinted by permission of John Wiley & Sons, Inc.

struggle to preserve life, it must be continued while any shred of privacy remains.

Perhaps the most authoritative official statement on the issue is the one by a special committee assembled under the President's authority. According to this pamphlet, an inherent conflict exists between, on the one hand, 'the right of the individual to decide for himself how much he will share with others his thoughts, his feelings, and the facts of his personal life' and, on the other hand, the right of society 'to know anything that may be known or discovered about any part of the universe'. The committee's statement is heavily weighted to favour the second of the rights, beginning with the disclaimer that 'most current practices in [behavioural research] pose no significant threat to the privacy of research subjects'. To reduce this threat as much as possible, the participation of subjects must be based on their informed consent 'to the extent that it is consistent with the objectives of the research'; but 'in the absence of full information, consent [may legitimately] be based on trust in the qualified investigator and the integrity of his institution'. The scientist must design research so as to protect his subjects' privacy 'to the fullest extent possible', considering whether 'the benefits outweigh the costs' – that is, the benefits to society through the researcher as opposed to the costs borne by the subject.[3]

The analysis and proposed norms are reminiscent of those with respect to the physical protection of patients subject to therapeutic experimentation. Two important differences, however, should be noted. First, the authority of the medical profession, contrary to that in the social disciplines, is great enough to impose ethical standards on most of the individuals doing research. Second, the research done in medicine and allied sciences generally helps realise such universal goals as the extension of life or the reduction of pain; but there is seldom so clear a public benefit from, for example, sociologists' research on race relations, or political scientists' on 'voting behavior', or even economists on the causes and cure of inflation. If we grant that other values must sometimes be sacrificed to the furtherance of knowledge, we must also be careful to distinguish this from mere ideology.

The contrast between widespread popular distrust of datagathering agencies and the sometimes bland, self-serving defence by their representatives obviously affects research in many ways. In this discussion the issue is *not* the allegedly widespread use of wiretaps, ·

concealed microphones and hidden cameras. Such supposed facts are here seen only as buttresses to the general lack of confidence that can, and often does, envelop any empirical work, especially one associated with a government institution. If any information that any research organisation or official agency collects can (will?) be misused, one solution is to prevent its collection altogether. And that mood of suspicion thus seemingly warrants, however irrationally, an attack on the collection of data that are obviously useful and that, moreover, hardly threaten the privacy of anyone.

Two such instances are presented: the objections to classifications by race and the recent attacks on the census. Until the mid-1960s one important goal of civil rights organisations was to remove racial designations from public forms and the data compiled from them. They achieved a few notable – if sometimes temporary – successes.[4] The reasons for this opposition to identifying a person's race on public documents can be usefully reduced to three main arguments:[5]

(1) *It is morally wrong for a government to require a man to identify himself by race. It is an invasion of privacy.* It was mainly on this basis, for example, that the American Civil Liberties Union sought to have the question on race deleted from the 1960 Census schedule. It would be difficult to maintain, however, that the colour of one's skin is any less an element of one's persona than the colours of one's hair and eyes, which appear routinely on such documents as a driver's licence or a passport – and excite no one's opposition. And in a period when consciousness of group identity is rising, when political programmes to alleviate social problems are often linked to certain races (even if sometimes half-disguised as 'the underprivileged', 'the inner city', or the like), it is even harder to dissociate personal differentiation from the parallel subgroups of the population. Both at the individual and the social level, race significantly distinguishes one from another, and government programmes of all kinds (for instance, both segregated schools and desegregation) operate in accordance with this differentiation. Is it reasonable or useful to draw an ethical line at a mere census enumeration, in order to preserve our ignorance of this important classification? I think not.

(2) *Race identification on forms is often used to discriminate against the individual identified on the form.* Persons who defend this proposition typically do so on pure faith. Apart from a small number of lower-level

positions in the federal bureaucracy, few jobs of any kind are filled without a personal interview. In the typical circumstances the lack of a racial designation on an initial form could hardly be much of an impediment to discrimination in either employment or the distribution of welfare, education or any other social services. (And if the bare possibility of discrimination is taken to be a sufficient warrant to eliminate the designation of race, this need be done only on personal documents. For example, birth certificates issued in New York State carry no race identification, but confidential records that include this information are maintained so that group data can be compiled.)

(3) *Statistical summaries by race are often used to reinforce stereotypes and prejudices — for example, racial breakdowns of crime, venereal disease and dependency statistics.* Thus, for example, according to a member of its national staff, 'the NAACP opposes the compilation and publication of racially classified data on crime and illegitimate births because such information sheds no significant light on the causes, because it serves no useful purpose in curbing these offences, because it is subject to distortion and misrepresentation, and because it is utilised to thwart the drive toward an egalitarian, pluralistic society'.[6]

In the past the principled opposition to certain types of knowledge, the stance known during the last century as know-nothingism, was generally associated with reactionary politics. Liberals typically held that knowledge *per se* is valuable and, in particular since prejudice is fostered by ignorance, that more and better data about the various ethnic groups generally helps to improve the relations among them. Indeed, according to the American credo the administration of justice should be colour blind, as well as access to employment, public institutions, and all other services not reasonably designated as private. However, it was an aberration from this democratic norm to apply it to the gathering of knowledge, and some of the liberal organisations that in the 1950s expressed their own type of know-nothingism half-reversed this position during the 1960s. To develop social policies that would better the lot of racial minorities, in any case no easy task, was made more difficult by the resultant confusion.

The earlier policy of inhibiting the dissemination of certain types of knowledge was so general that it affected even newspapers. Following the example of such prestigious organs as the *New York Times*, many papers in the United States began to omit all racial identifications from persons in the news. Even so, the subsequent spectacular rise in the crime rate, especially among Negro youth in northern cities, did not escape public attention; and the conscientious deletion of the offenders' race from news stories probably did more to reinforce the stereotype of the Negro criminal than the contrary. During the same period, moreover, many more Negroes were appointed or elected to places of honour, and as long as the policy was in effect, their race was often specified through a photograph. After several years the practice broke down – partly by such evasions, partly through newspapers' sympathetic reports about black militants, who shrilly demanded that they be identified by race.

More generally, statistics by race are crucial to these efforts to achieve the 'egalitarian, pluralistic society' that the NAACP is working for. If the designation by race were to be deleted from the census schedule, as the ACLU advocated, one could still write philosophical essays on the virtues of equality, but it would no longer be feasible to show that Negroes get less schooling and worse jobs, that their health is poorer and their lives are shorter, that in general the discrimination they suffer has measurable effects. Even more important, without such statistics it has been impossible either to compare the effects of the varied, often experimental, ameliorative programmes, or to check on compliance with legislation designed to end discrimination. Since the passage of the Civil Rights Act of 1964, which stipulated that 'no person shall, on the grounds of race, colour, or national origin, be excluded from . . . any programme or activity receiving federal financial assistance', the lack of group data on race has been of great assistance to bigots. For it is generally difficult, if not impossible, to prove that one particular person was denied benefits of any kind because of his race rather than a legitimate criterion of discrimination. However, if the distinctions so made reveal a pattern, then the burden of proof falls on the responsible administrator; he must try to show, contrary to the evidence, that racial discrimination was not practised.

Colleges and universities that receive federal grants and contracts (hardly any do not) are now required not merely to enroll or employ qualified Negroes who apply to them but to take what is termed 'affirmative action' – that is, to seek out Negroes and invite them to apply. But the university administrators charged with carrying out this directive are plagued by the fact that, in accordance with the immediately prior norm, Negroes are often not identified as such in lists of high school graduates, college students, university faculty and the like.

An even more striking contradiction exists in two parts of the Civil Rights Act of 1964. According to Title VIII, 'no person shall be compelled to disclose his race, colour, national origin, . . . nor shall any penalty be imposed for his failure or refusal to make such disclosure. Every person interrogated orally, by written survey or questionnaire, or by any other means with respect to such information shall be fully advised with respect to his right to fail or refuse to furnish such information.' If this were applied to the census – and the wording of the act suggests no reason why it should not be[7] – answering the question on race would be stipulated to every respondent as voluntary, although under other laws replies to all items in the census schedule are mandatory. The very ambiguity, if it were to be exploited in litigation challenging either proviso, would damage the tabulations by race.

The sometimes hysterical opposition to the collection of data by race became more intense when it was proposed to include a question on religious affiliation in the 1960 Census. Indeed, the proposal was met with indifference by the vast majority of the population, and it was actively supported by social scientists and many Catholic groups. However, the opposition of Jewish organisations, supported by one or two liberal associations, was sometimes offered by recalling, however irrelevantly, the genocide in Nazi Germany; and this emotionality has characterised much of the subsequent discussion.[8] In response to this largely irrational opposition from a minuscule portion of the population, the Census Bureau withdrew its proposal. It also rejected a renewed suggestion to include a question on religious affiliation in the 1970 schedule, partly because of the harm it would do to the Bureau's public relations, partly because its officials 'were not sufficiently impressed with the stated need for the data to face the antagonism of those that are opposed to its collection'.[9] Yet the issue is essentially parallel to that concerning race, even down to establishing accountability. A vast amount of public money is allocated by both criteria (in the case of religion, mainly by the facts that churches pay no taxes and that private donations to them may be deducted from taxable income), and with the religious statistics presently available there is no way of even estimating whether, by any criterion one chooses, the presumed public interest is served.

Undoubtedly, the main reason the Census Bureau did not choose to take on another dispute is that it was already under general attack.

Although this was part of the general furore over the right to privacy, the issue of confidentiality is in fact irrelevant – except in the mouths of demagogues. However improbably, the Census Bureau has established a perfect record, never once accidentally or illegitimately revealing a single datum tied to an individual; but this has not inhibited those who say they are protecting the people's privacy.[10]

The first move in Congress against the census was in a bill offered by Congressman Jackson Betts (Rep., Ohio), which would have limited the mandatory questions to seven: name and address, relation to head of household, sex, date of birth, race or colour, marital status, and visitors in the home at the time of the census. Many of the questions in the schedule, Mr Betts argued, have no relation to the constitutional provision for a census, serve no public purpose, and violate the privacy of citizens; and such 'probing of people's affairs is certainly unwanted and unnecessary'. His stand catapulted him into national prominence, and the lesson was not lost on others in Congress. By mid-1968, sixty-five bills to limit the 1970 Census, originating with Representatives of forty-three states, had been introduced in the House, and nearly a third of the Representatives were on record as sponsors of one or another of these bills.[11]

This massive opposition, it must be emphasised, had nothing to do with any special features of the 1970 Census. On the contrary, as compared with previous counts, it was planned to use sampling to relieve respondents of the duty of answering a larger portion of the schedule, so that in the 1970 Census four-fifths of the household heads were asked only twenty-four out of the total of eighty-nine questions. Nor did the questions differ in being unusually intrusive, in spite of nation-wide propaganda to the contrary.[12]

A pretest of the 1970 Census in Dane County, Wisconsin, was undercut by a mail campaign and advertisements in local newspapers, both organised by 'The National Right to Privacy Committee', of which Vance Packard and William F. Rickenbacker were co-chairmen. A pretest in Chesterfield and Sumpter Counties, South Carolina, was publicly attacked by Senator Strom Thurmond. At one time it seemed that there might be no enumeration in 1970. When the attacks reached a climax in 1969, the schedules were already printed; and if a new law had called for substantial changes, it would not have been possible to prepare and distribute new questionnaires before 1971. That may have been the main reason that the various anti-census bills failed to pass. This does not mean, however, that the attack is over. On the opening day of the 91st Congress, Congressman Betts introduced HR 20, almost identical to the bill he had sponsored in the previous Congress except that the mandatory questions were reduced to six, with 'race or colour' eliminated from his earlier list.

Even if the attacks were to cease immediately, some damage has been done. A census in a democratic country is more accurate than its counterpart in a totalitarian country simply because the count is based on the willing co-operation of the people, who are certain that the information they reveal for statistical purposes will not be used against them. Once irresponsible and false charges against the Census Bureau eroded this certainty, the accuracy and completeness of the returns were bound to suffer. Census Bureau officials, one should note, acclaimed the enumeration as the most accurate ever completed in this country – an assertion intended, one can assume, to undercut the hostility. However, officials of several areas that had been centres of opposition to the Bureau's activities were indignant because they would lose federal funds through what they termed, possibly correctly, a serious underenumeration.

To defend the mammoth, technically expert, politically neutral compendium of essential data that we know as the census would be unnecessary if a judgement were based only on accurate information and rational criteria.[13] No American institution – whether federal, state, or local government, business firm or trade union, church or school – could be competently administered without the guide to management furnished by census figures. The fact that everyone benefits from the enumeration means, however, that the census has no special constituency. Its main defenders against the attacks were various professional societies in the social sciences, almost all of which issued statements or even tried – not very successfully – to organise a counter-movement. As one employee of the Census Bureau remarked following some positive testimony before a congressional committee, after a decade of issuing hundreds of manifestoes on almost every political issue, expressing ill-informed opinions in highly emotional language with the full authority of their academic standing, professors have opened up a vast credibility gap between themselves and Congress. In reply to Congressman Betts, when academia had something important and valid to offer, its genuine expertise was largely ignored.

14 Census-taking and the Debate on Privacy: a Sociological View*

David R. Cope

The 17th Decennial Census of Population and Housing was held in Great Britain on 25 April 1971. It was the largest census exercise ever attempted in Britain. A wide range of questions was asked, covering housing and household facilities, employment, education, birthplace and nationality, and several other topics, as well as more conventional questions on age, sex and marital status. Some of the questions asked were the same as those which have been asked for 100 years or more. Others covered topics which have become the focus of national or local government planning activities, such as educational achievement and journey to work. Some others, in particular a question on parental birthplace, were designed to provide information on issues of contemporary political concern.

The results of the census were held to 'form the sound basis for all sorts of research and planning',[1] but the period surrounding its taking was marked by a degree of public debate and hostility which undoubtedly caught the census authorities and the government by surprise. Comment on the 1971 Census was paralleled, in the history of census-taking in Britain, only by the acrimonious reception given in

* Original material   1979 David R. Cope.

some quarters to the proposals to hold a national census which preceded the first inquiry in 1801.[2] Opposition to the census took a variety of forms from questions in Parliament to the ritual burning of census schedules in Trafalgar Square. A very few individuals resolutely refused to fill in their schedules and the statutory procedures for non-compliance in the 1920 Census Act were used against them.

In the years after 1971 there have been a number of actions taken by both the government and the Office of Population Censuses and Surveys as a direct response to the reception which the 1971 Census received. The British Computer Society and the Royal Statistical Society were invited to comment on the procedures involved in census-taking and the processing and presentation of results. Their report, published as a White Paper in 1973, received a response from government which can only be described as cool.[3] During the 1970s, the Office of Population Censuses and Surveys began to pay much more attention to public relations and the image of census-taking. An Information Branch and Press Office were created, and more information was collected on the end uses of census data by researchers in other government departments and in local authorities, university and other research institutes. Some in-house studies of the issues involved in public response to surveys were also carried out.[4] The increased seriousness with which the census office views the possibility of public disquiet over census questions is best reflected in the rigorous treatment being given to the potential inclusion of a question on 'racial origin' in the forthcoming 1981 Census.[5] In discussing this question, the White Paper on the 1981 Census, for the first time, called for public discussion on the desirability of inclusion of a particular question in the population census.[6]

It would clearly be wrong to imply that public and governmental concern over data privacy stemmed only from the population census. At the time of the 1971 Census, the Younger Committee on Privacy was in the middle of its investigation.[7] The survey into public attitudes to the subject which the committee commissioned was carried out in close proximity to the date of the 1971 Census and the results were to a degree influenced by the reception that the census had received.[8] The committee's report, published in 1972, was followed three years later by two White Papers on *Computers and Privacy*[9] and in 1976 by the setting-up of the Data Protection Committee which recently presented its report [see Chapter 17].

The protracted debate on privacy and access to information which had developed in the United States in the late 1960s, influenced by publications such as that by Westin,[10] also began to have its effect on this side of the Atlantic. A succession of abuses, mainly connected with the creation of credit and debt registers, led to a disquiet which was fuelled by the teething troubles accompanying the widespread introduction of computerised accounting and billing procedures. As a result, a number of organisations, notably the National Council for Civil Liberties, became increasingly involved in pressure-group activities over privacy issues.

Caught unawares by the sudden attention devoted to their activities, data-collection agencies, whether in central or local government, market research, or academic and general research, responded initially by a series of reports and conferences on the question of privacy and confidentiality. The response of central and local government agencies is particularly important because they are far and away the largest collectors of data, especially of data which may later be made available to other researchers for secondary analysis, as is frequently the case with the census.

Two themes emerged from the round of investigations and discussions. The first was the need for a greater public awareness of the actual use made of census and other data; of the distinction between administrative and statistical uses and of the safeguarding procedures used to protect the integrity of data once it has been collected. The second theme was an exploration of technical means to guarantee such integrity and the non-disclosure of data on individuals in statistical tabulations.

Having attended a number of discussions on these topics and learned the mysteries of 'Barnardisation' and 'Dutch Rounding'[11], it became increasingly clear to the author that these technical proposals were being put forward in a vacuum of knowledge about the phenomenon to which they were a response – public conceptions of 'the private'. To counter each fresh assault on their activities, data gatherers put forward yet more complex procedures for guaranteeing the confidentiality of collected data and were confused when these failed to stem public expressions of disquiet. The technical proposals inevitably involved restrictions on the uses to which collected data could be put and there was a danger that the usefulness of the data would be limited while public concern was in no way alleviated. There had already been some cynical response to the claim that the 1971 Census data would help to improve the quality of planning decisions.[12] Restrictions on the use of data might give these doubts a firm validity, leading to a downward spiral of public confidence. Similarly, any attempts at public education could be expected to succeed only if the nature of public concern were clearly understood beforehand.

With one or two exceptions, mainly American, the subject of privacy has not received much attention from sociologists and social psychologists. Until very recently, there has been a surprising disparity between the amount of public concern and debate and the level of academic analysis. The overall neglect of the topic is true *a fortiori* in Britain. There have been only three empirical investigations of aspects of the topic in recent years – the Younger Committee Survey, a study on response rates to surveys by the Market Research Society and the report of a working party organised by Social and Community Planning Research.[13] A number of reasons for this neglect can be put forward. Privacy issues may be seen as unimportant compared with other topics.[14] To a certain extent, again, privacy considerations may seem too transient and ephemeral to merit and facilitate close study. Privacy's peaks of prominence in the 'public agenda'[15] in the past decade have frequently been followed by as marked a decline to comparative obscurity. Another viewpoint sees privacy as not being a matter which can be isolated for study in its own right but as a topic which is simply a specific case of a wider object, such as rights over property. Privacy is seen as concerned with the ownership of information, as opposed to material possessions. An alternative interpretation sees privacy rights as part of the set of rights which inhere to the individual *qua* individual – an autonomous, free human being, by definition, has these rights.[16]

Approaches to the study of privacy have ranged from social-psychological analysis of individual perceptions of the private to macro-scale interpretations of socio-historical trends in factors such as the relationship of the individual to the state.[17] Until recently, the majority of work has tended to be carried out at the micro-scale end of this range, leading to prevalence of a view that privacy is a somewhat idiosyncratic phenomenon, a product of individual vagaries and therefore not amenable to useful analysis at the aggregate, sociological level. Two reinforcing trends seem to be reducing the validity of this view – studies of large-scale, historical trends, such as the work of Sennett,[18] and an emerging recognition of the significance of studying individual contextual circumstances for understanding important facets of social behaviour.[19]

Undoubtedly a major factor detracting from analysis of the concept of privacy has been the imprecision which surrounds definition of the subject. Virtually all commentators on the subject point out the range of interpretations which different writers have adopted and a number provide succinct summaries of the nature of the definitional differences.[20] It seems best to give up the barren search for an all-embracing definition and agree with the 'Justice' Committee on Privacy[21] that the public have a clear idea as to what is meant by the term even if it resists definitional rigour. In this respect it is somewhat like the concept of 'community', which is similarly surrounded by definitional haziness.[22] It is, however, important to distinguish the concept of privacy from the closely-linked but more technical consideration of confidentiality, which is concerned with the safeguards and security which attach to information once it has been imparted or collected.[23] There are links between the two – a willingness to allow an intrusion of privacy may frequently be conditional on the receipt of assurances about the confidentiality of the information released. This willingness cannot be taken as automatic – an oversight to which those who advocate 'technical' solutions to concern about privacy are particularly prone.

From the definitional tangle over privacy emerge two 'themes' which have a particular relevance to the present discussion. These are the understanding of privacy as the right to be alone and to be left alone – not to be troubled by outsiders – and the understanding which emphasises the right to control dissemination of information about oneself or a group which includes oneself. These themes, which have been separated here for the sake of analysis, are again linked in reality, particularly in the case of questionnaire surveys which involve both 'disturbing' people and then seeking to elicit information from them.

In the discussion of privacy aspects of the population census which follows, some use has been made of the recent exposition of Irwin Altman on the conceptual analysis of privacy.[24] Although subjected to some more recent criticism[25] and originally developed in the context of environmental privacy, it offers, with modification and addition, a useful theoretical structure. In themselves, each of the components which Altman advances in interpreting privacy-related behaviour are not startlingly profound, but taken together they would seem to have a direct relevance to understanding how privacy issues may be raised by an inquiry such as the population census.

Altman emphasises privacy as involving bidirectional processes. Actions may flow from the outside towards the self. This is the intrusion aspect, the 'right to be let alone', mentioned above. Conversely, Altman maintains, each individual interprets and maybe modifies, in terms of privacy considerations, the socialising interactions which flow from the individual outwards, including the selective imparting of information. Some intrusion flows may be specifically designed to elicit an outward flow in response and the census and most other surveys are cases in point.

For Altman, it is important to recognise the significance of different 'levels' in any discussion of privacy. Interactions between individuals may differ from those between individual and group and from those involving only groups. In the case of questionnaire surveys, it can be seen that the nature of the level may be important in the determination of whether a survey should be conducted by interviews or by impersonal means such as a postal questionnaire. To date, the great majority of the work on privacy has concerned itself with individual relationships. There are, however, indications that considerations of group integrity are becoming of increasing significance and this is a topic touched on by Hakim on page 155.

Altman interprets the importance of privacy from a strongly functionalist viewpoint and maintains that it has two functional attributes in particular. The first of these he defines in terms of personal identity and integrity. This involves the defining of some necessary minimum boundaries of what is private in order to establish a sense of individuality and completeness. The derivation of Altman's theses from a concern with physical environmental factors perhaps shows clearest here. The second function identified is the means which possession of a defined area of personal information (or space) offers for socialisation by selective imparting of that information (or admission to the space). The information which an individual will voluntarily impart about himself (or a group of which he is a member) will usually vary, depending on the relationship which the individual has with the recipient of the information. Altman regards this selective information flow as a very important relation/action defining mechanism in society.

This interpretation can be extended by introducing the dimension of control of information for conflict situations. Knowledge of personal facts is widely seen as giving the possessor of that knowledge certain power over the person to whom the facts appertain. Conversely, one of the most widespread and conventional ways of defining a conflict situation, at all levels from the individual to the nation state, is to withhold information which might otherwise be freely given, or to erect barriers and block channels to prevent facts from being manifest. In the context of an inquiry such as the population census, information may be withheld, not through any intrinsic sense of its privacy, but because the individual concerned sees himself in conflict with 'bureaucracy' or 'government'.

Generally, a maximum of privacy leads to a maximum of freedom of choice and freedom of action in social relationships. The less that is previously known about a person or group, the less the pre-emptive response that can be taken to potential action by that person or group. The distinct advantage that total control over privacy would confer on its possessor in social action is recognised in Altman's final attributed characteristic of privacy. This is that it is 'non-monotonic'. Both too much and too little of it is perceived as dysfunctional. Westin also comments on this quality of privacy and gives some examples of how societies prevent individuals from enjoying total privacy. He argues that this can be socially and individually harmful.[26] An interesting consideration here, which neither author addresses, is whether an individual or group in a situation of having 'too much' privacy, perceives it as such or whether such a situation is defined by the actor(s) in other terms, such as 'loneliness' or 'ostracism'.

Altman appends to his exposition the caveat that any particular example of concern for privacy will have to be interpreted with full awareness that the matter is subject to considerable variation in all its dimensions depending on the personal experiences of the actors in the particular situation. Without a knowledge of the contextual background which each actor brings to the situation, an observer may be at a loss to offer any coherent explanation of observed behaviour. The unfortunate conclusion from this is that, whatever the precautions taken to minimise the privacy-intrusive nature of census-type enquiries, there are always likely to be some surprise responses in store, a fact to which almost anyone who has conducted such an investigation will attest.

One of the more intriguing questions raised by an examination of privacy and which, with closer investigation, might have relevance to some of the specific problems raised by census-taking, is the extent to which a 'need' for privacy is a universal feature of all societies.[27] Not surprisingly, this quickly leads to a discussion of whether concern for privacy derives from innate biological mechanisms or is culturally prescribed.[28] It is undeniable that there are widespread variations in what is regarded as private in different societies and between different groups in the same society. This fact does suggest a cultural origin, or at least a powerful cultural conditioning of any non-sociological source of the desire for privacy. Westin addresses himself to this question in some detail and concludes that the only area of human activity that seems universally to be associated with privacy norms is sexual behaviour and that even here there are wide variations in norms.[29]

In some of its manifestations, privacy norms vary quite markedly between societies which are very similar in other respects. For example, Britain and Holland have much in common on many scores, but conventional attitudes to some aspects of environmental privacy depart strikingly. This will be forcefully apparent to anyone used to the net-curtained concern about being overlooked which characterises most British households, when they are confronted with the deliberate exposure of interiors by bright lights and carefully drawn-back curtains which occurs in Holland. There have, however, been problems over information-privacy matters in Holland which affected the taking of the last census.

In the area of data access and information privacy, British researchers frequently look enviously at Sweden, where so much more seems to be freely available and where continuous population registers are regarded as more or less unexceptional. There are some misconceptions widespread about the exact extent of free access to information in Sweden. While it is true that a register giving details of every individual's income and sources of income is open to inspection, there have been some problems with response rates in surveys which have asked an income question, and recently the 'personnummer' system on which the registration procedures are based has been questioned by the current Prime Minister, Thorbjörn Fälldin.[30] Despite this, it remains true that attitudes to data collection and dissemination are apparently more relaxed than in Britain.

A recent discussion which the author had with researchers at the University of Rome revealed that the journey-to-work statistics in Italian surveys grossly over-estimated the numbers who used a car and that there was a marked shortfall in numbers of those walking to work. The researchers attributed this to it being highly insulting to suggest that an Italian actually walked to work! The comparison of national attitudes within Europe and North America on what constitutes private information and on the nature of responses to different subjects in questionnaire surveys could prove most valuable in forming an understanding of how privacy concerns arise and become the subject of public debate.[31]

The interpretations outlined in the previous section will now be taken and applied in greater detail to the census of population – its nature, purpose, the circumstances surrounding its taking, its coverage and the responses which the 1971 Census elicited on the subject of privacy

In terms of method, the British population census is something of a hybrid. It usually involves personal contact with at least one member of every household in the country by an enumerator but, at the same time, relies on self-completion of the majority of the questions by the 'head-of-household'. In the great majority of cases, the completed form is then checked through by the enumerator, who may point out omissions and is required to give advice when respondents are uncertain as to what is required of them. The possibility that information revealed by a respondent might be used by an enumerator who was personally acquainted with the respondent was one of the major issues in the entire debate on privacy which surrounded the 1971 Census. Procedures did exist for returning the schedule direct to the census office, bypassing the enumerator, but awareness of this was not widespread and it is fair to say that the census office did not go out of its way to publicise this option as it inevitably involves more work in relating a form back to its area or household of origin. A similar concern arose in the Swedish census of 1960 where the landlord of blocks of flats had the statutory responsibility for collecting the forms of all the tenants. Subsequently, tenants were able to return their forms direct.[32] In Britain, the concern expressed in 1971 has led the census office to adopt complex and expensive 'busing' procedures for the 1981 Census, not only to ensure that the enumerators are unknown in the areas they are enumerating but also to move completed census forms for processing to regional centres outside the area from which they come. A special case of this concern about enumerators arose from the use of workers such as income-tax or rates collectors as enumerators in some areas.[33]

These are examples of situations where, using Altman's analysis, the 'level' of the information interaction was important. At least ostensibly, there would have been no complaints about intrusion of privacy had the enumerators been completely unknown to those they were enumerating or had no instrumental relationship with them. Familiarity was here associated with a desire to curtail the interaction of information flow. It remains to be seen whether the complex procedures referred to will eliminate this particular concern in the 1981 Census. It may have been that the specific issue raised was merely a convenient means of articulating a more general, unspecific, concern about privacy rights. It will also inevitably not be long before someone points out that given existing levels of geographical mobility in Britain, even with the arrangements described, someone, somewhere, will be known to his or her enumerator or form processor!

The fact that the census relies on self-enumeration means that the schedule remains with the household for anything up to a week, giving ample time, at least in theory, for perusal, awareness of its contents and the possibility of raising privacy issues after contemplating it at length.[34] In this respect, responses may well differ from those which might greet similar questions asked in personal interviews, where immediate replies are solicited.

The wide-ranging nature of the census questions, together with the fact that they inevitably, in several cases, touch on areas of potential disquiet and concern, is of immense importance in understanding the response of individuals on the privacy issue and will be referred to again later on.

The census, along with some other general inquiries such as the Electoral Register, but unlike social surveys, is compulsory. This mandatory nature must affect sensitivity on the privacy issue and it has been one of the major aims of those voicing their opposition to censuses, both in this country and abroad, to make the census a voluntary exercise, or at least partially voluntary. A voluntary census would not in itself allay the concern of those affected by privacy as the 'right to be let alone', as opposed to the right to control information dissemination. The enumerator would still call to deliver and attempt to collect the form and there would still be the possible discomfort raised by reading it, even if the opportunity existed to refuse to complete or return it. It is not surprising that various social surveys conducted by local authorities in recent years, very similar in topic coverage to the census but without enjoying its legal compulsion, have had much higher refusal rates than the very small number of cases which occurred with the national census.[35] To some extent, the refusal rates of such surveys might be taken as an indicator of the proportion of the population who are 'put upon' by the national census and intimidated into compliance by its mandatory nature. The indication would be that up to one household in ten is so affected.

What is quite clear is that although the ultimate legal compulsion and preceding cajolery on the part of the census office may encourage all but a handful of respondents to overcome their scruples about privacy by returning the form as a whole, this legal panoply is not sufficient to prevent noticeable omissions, and less noticeable falsification, of replies to certain questions. This much can be gleaned from published census volumes which sometimes show 'not stated' categories in their tables. Not all of these will be the result of unwillingness to answer the question on the grounds of privacy, of course. The reply to the 1971 Census question on parents' country of birth is a good example. Nearly $1\frac{3}{4}$ million cases occurred where either one or both parents' country of birth was not stated. Although this represents about 3.2 per cent of all respondents, the effect is more serious if it can be claimed that the 'not stated' category disproportionately contains one group in the population, such as recent immigrants. Data on deliberate falsification of returns is not to hand. There was some encouragement of this at the time of the 1971 Census, and similar murmurings have already occurred in response to the preparations for the 1981 Census.[36] Unfortunately, the results of the fertility questions in the 1971 Census have not yet been published, except for Scotland, so it is difficult to gauge non-response on this other sensitive topic included in the 1971 Census.

The fact that the census is conducted by an agency of government must, despite the assurances attached to the schedule that personal information in it will not be passed on to any other agency of government, influence privacy considerations. The 'government', conceived of widely, may frequently be an object of hostility and the way in which expression of hostility may influence conceptions of privacy has already been discussed. Hakim, in Chapter 10, quotes the results of the post-1971 Census-use survey.

No matter what steps may be taken to guarantee anonymity and confidentiality in reality, if the census operation is widely believed to be suspect, there will be reaction against it. It has already been mentioned that public knowledge about the nature and aims of the census is somewhat limited and frequently misguided. This is perhaps only to be expected of an event which takes place at most once every five or ten years.[37]

An inspection of press reports about the 1971 Census shows how the debate surrounding it was a classic case of the development of rumour and counter-rumour. The sociology of rumour, though a fascinating topic, has received little attention in recent years.[38] One thesis which has emerged from empirical studies is that the level of rumour in a society about a particular event or situation is directly related to the perceived importance of that event or situation and inversely related to the amount of information available about it. The census itself might not be classed as very important, but there is no denying that many of the topics that are covered by questions are generally seen as very important. Because of its infrequency, the general level of information about the census is low, so the degree of rumour may be expected to be high, as is the potential for adverse confusion with other, superficially similar, activities involving data collection.[39]

The spread of rumour and misinformation undoubtedly contributed to the hostility which greeted the 1971 Census, and the theory of levels of rumour just described suggests two ways of reducing that associated with the census. It would be hard to reduce the perceived level of importance of some of the topics covered by the census but, as mentioned, the 'benchmark' type questions are generally accorded a higher level of legitimacy than policy-related questions. A census restricted to 'benchmark' questions might therefore be received as unexceptional and might not give rise to rumours as to the proposed or potential use of the data it collected. It may, of course, be unacceptable to reduce the policy content of the census simply to achieve a lower level of rumour and therefore higher level of immediate acceptability, but there is beginning to emerge a school of thought which argues that policy-related matters are better handled by smaller, voluntary inquiries, linked to a national 100 per cent census inquiry restricted to basic items.

The second way of reducing rumour is to increase familiarity with the census and census-taking procedures. The pre-census publicity in 1971 was greater than ever before, but the high levels of ignorance as to its nature have already been mentioned. Professor Benjamin has commented that the census office has always seemed to be on the defensive, responding to criticisms once they have been made, rather than taking pre-emptive action.[40] There may well be a reluctance on the part of the census office to open what they see as the Pandora's box of privacy by too much publicity, or premature publicity, and publicity that means incurring extra costs. The recent establishment of a

Press Department in the census office might well lead to increased and improved publicity on all aspects of its activities.

It might be argued that one way to increase familiarity with the census would be to hold more of them. However, there is considerable evidence that one reason for increasing levels of non-co-operation in surveys of all kinds is a feeling in respondents' minds that they have been asked the particular question, or surveyed in general, too often.[41] A minimum of a five-year inter-censal period should be sufficient to avoid feelings of over-exposure of this sort, but the holding of the national census does not take place in a vacuum but alongside many other surveys and inquiries of every degree of officiality and competence from the Electoral Register to life-assurance salesmen masquerading as survey or market researchers. Familiarity does definitely breed contempt in this case and some form of moratorium or control system on survey research, at least in some areas, may come to be necessary. This raises issues which are beyond the specific concern of this chapter and are discussed in some detail in Chapters 3 and 16.

It might be hypothesised that there is a bipolar structure of dysfunction in terms of the frequency of surveys and their public acceptance as unremarkable. A very low frequency might lead to the public investing those surveys which were conducted with an unexplained significance; rumour would spread and so too would objections on privacy grounds. At a middle level of frequency there would be familiarity without annoyance from over-exposure; privacy objections would be at their lowest. High frequencies would lead to annoyance, high refusal rates and general objections on the grounds of privacy as to the right to be let alone, as much as to the right to control the dissemination of personal information. Obviously, the mid-point of this continuum may change over time and it may well be that at present there is a trend towards a lower tolerance level of survey exposure.[42]

A final factor which may affect the spread of rumour is the use of sampling at the field stage by distributing schedules with varying question content to different households on a random basis. As well as having advantages in reducing the bulk of processing, this may be done to cut down the average content of schedules to lessen the burden on the public and consequently to minimise objections to the census. However, the principles of random sampling are not readily appreciated by the general public and people may conclude that there is some design behind the fact that, for example, they have received a schedule with questions on fertility, while a neighbour or workmate is being queried on journey-to-work.[43]

Clearly, the nature of attitude formation is of great significance in understanding public response to an exercise such as the census. The role of the media and of politicians must influence the public image which the census achieves. Depending on one's viewpoint, the activities of press and politicians tend to be interpreted either as a response to a genuinely articulated concern or as the awakening of a latent concern which would otherwise have remained undisturbed.

The political reception given the census deserves closer study. The assertion that politicians and parties may contrive a concern about privacy to advance their own interests does receive some support from the curious episode in which the Liberal Party attacked the 1971 Census. At this time, the party's impact in British political life was waning and the issue probably seemed to offer the opportunity to make political mileage from a situation where the government party was unable to exploit their own pro-privacy orientations because of their responsibility for administering the census, while the ideological commitment of the main opposition party was much less strongly against the objectives of the census.

In its public presentation, the response of only a few MPs may be critical in assuring that the census receives unfavourable publicity. There may well be value in a special programme of documentation and seminars for MPs, emphasising the beneficial uses of census data and the actual procedures used in handling the collected information. This publicity exercise should not cease after the taking of the census. As results become available, special, easily-digested abstracts, perhaps based on the constituency tabulations, should be sent to MPs, detailing the origin of the information from specific census questions.

Much of the discussion of privacy, confidentiality and the ethics of data collection which has occurred in recent years has been in response to a conviction that demands for privacy protection are likely to become increasingly strident, access to official data increasingly surrounded by obstacles ostensibly erected to preserve confidentiality and that, as a consequence, the basis of empirical social research might well be adversely affected.[44]

It is possible to detect conflicting trends in the access to, and desire for, privacy. On the one hand, in terms of environmental privacy, improvements in housing standards and the switch from public to private transport have, generally speaking, made access to high levels of privacy both more widely available and more desired. On the other hand, there has been acceptance of the legitimate involvement of government and other public authorities in wider and wider areas of activity, accompanied by, at least to an extent, an acceptance of the need for data collection to make such involvement efficient and equitable. Such acceptance would always seem to lag behind the acceptance of the role of government in the particular activity, so that there is always a measure of tension between the expectations that the public may have and the means open for its achievement. There are few indications that the process of greater personal access to privacy has come anywhere near the point of inflexion postulated in Altman's non-monotonic interpretation of the desire for privacy, when there might be a diminution in the demands made for greater privacy.[45]

Part Four

Protecting Privacy and Safeguarding Social Research

15 Maintaining Public Confidence in Quantitative Social Research

Martin Bulmer

A good deal of the popular criticism of social research by public 'defenders' of privacy is in varying degrees inflammatory, ill-considered, ignorant of the realities of research and statistical work, and even irresponsible. Nevertheless, the community of social researchers owes it to the public to take privacy as a serious issue because there are real and important problems and even conflicts of principle, and because the very moderate infringement of privacy which social research represents has to be justified and its potential abuse regulated. The remaining chapters of the book consider how privacy may be safeguarded in social research and how public confidence may be maintained.

The first point to make is how very rarely abuse of privacy has ever occurred in social research. There are exceedingly few documented cases of misuse of data or breach of privacy or confidence by professional social researchers. Hakim in Chapter 10 demonstrates the very creditable record of the British census office in this respect, while J. W. Duncan has recently provided a most comprehensive review of privacy and confidentiality safeguards in relation to United States Federal statistics.[1] Non-governmental social research has an equally creditable record, reinforced by the ethical codes of learned societies and professional associations.[2]

Privacy, despite this, is clearly an issue, and conducting censuses and surveys in the last two decades of the twentieth century is likely as a result to become somewhat more difficult. What principles should guide research practice and the safeguards which are evolved? The US Privacy Protection Study Commission of 1977 suggested three general principles which should govern privacy protection policy: minimising intrusiveness, maximising fairness, and creating legitimate, enforceable, expectations of confidentiality.[3] The first and last are most relevant to social research.

Minimising intrusiveness, as Part 2 and Chapter 16 which follows show, is a constant concern of survey practitioners. It is also very salient in the minds of those who conduct censuses. But it may be difficult to persuade the public that a census is less of an intrusion than some other data strategies, even though this is the case. One popular criticism of the taking of a census asks why it is necessary to hold a census when other government departments already hold most of the records and statistical information collected in the census. Why not bring all these together and avoid the need for a census? There are a number of reasons. It is not true that answers to all census questions are to be found somewhere in existing holdings of administrative data. Even if such data are held, there would be likely to be acute definitional problems of compatability (for example, what is a 'household'), of discrepant time periods, and of incompatible grouping of categories on variables. If these could be overcome, collating such data would probably be far more expensive than conducting a census. To merge such data to establish a comprehensive statistical picture would in any case probably break confidentiality assurances given when the data was collected. For all these reason, censuses continue to be necessary and governments find them superior to relying solely on administrative data.

One system for rationalising administrative data, so far not implemented, would be to centralise government statistical record-keeping in a single agency. In Britain and the United States at the present time, the statistical compilation of administrative data is decentralised in separate government departments, usually responsible for a particular function such as finance, health, education, employment and so on. In the United States in the 1960s, however, it was proposed to establish such a 'national data centre', a national statistical agency holding centralised statistical records for the whole population.[4] The proponents of such a centre had clearly not anticipated the privacy implications of what they were proposing. The gains from centralisation on grounds of efficiency may be outweighed by the threat to privacy and even to democratic government which such an agency might pose. In the event, the United States national data centre was not established.

Different societies undoubtedly view centralised statistical record-keeping and record-linkage in different ways. In some countries, such as Scandinavia and the Netherlands, there exist central population registers which hold records of basic information about all members of the population which is regularly updated. Table 15.1 provides a summary of the data held in the Norwegian Central Register. Such a register may form the basis for a statistical file system that can be used for research, and Aukrust and Nordbotten have described how this system was developed and have evaluated its research uses, which are extensive.[5] Such purpose-designed centralised statistical systems are rather unusual, though if they can be established with adequate safeguards their potentialities for social research are considerable.[6]

What strikes the Anglo-Saxon observer is the equanimity with which in Scandinavia the state holds in one central place such large amounts of individual data about each citizen. The decentralised pattern in Britain and the United States reflects in part considerable public suspicion of the state. Perhaps in Scandinavia there is a different attitude to the state, as the protector of the small man and the underprivileged.[7] Certainly the fact that in Sweden each citizen has a universal identification number, which is used in a very wide variety of contexts including tax returns and season tickets without apparent public concern, would support such a view.[8] In Britain and America in peacetime, the use of such a number would be quite widely resisted, if introduced for administrative purposes or for statistical record-keeping, or both. The proposal for a United States National Data Centre foundered in part because it was discovered that such a centre could not be run without some form of individual identification of records in order to permit record-linkage.

In Britain, no single universal identifier is available. Organisations commonly use some combination of name, address and date of birth.[9] In the United States, however, the social security number (SSN) issued to United States citizens by the Social Security Administration is not only a widely-held personal identifier, but is often requested by other organisations – both governmental and non-governmental – to comply with their administrative processes. Potentially it is a means of linking records from different sources, although there are various defects in the SSN system which affect its reliability. There was at one stage a proposal that each citizen's SSN be required on the 1970 Census form, although this was not implemented. Considerable controversy has been generated about the use of the SSN as a universal

TABLE 15.1   *The basic categories of data held in the Norwegian Central Register of Individuals, and their updating frequency*

	Attribute	Continuous	Annual	Every nth year
			Frequency of registration	
(1)	Birth date, place	X		
(2)	Commune of residence	X		
(3)	Name	X		
(4)	Address	X		
(5)	Marital status	X		
(6)	Date, place of death	X		
(7)	Data on in-/out-migration	X		
(8)	Birth number of mother	X		
(9)	Birth number of father	X		
(10)	Birth number of spouse	X		
(11)	Income data		X (from 1967)	
(12)	Property data		X (from 1967)	
(13)	Tax data		X (from 1967)	
(14)	Baccalaureat		X (from 1968)	
(15)	Family data			X (Decennial census)
(16)	Education	X		X (Decennial census)
(17)	Occupation			X (Decennial census)
(18)	Data on branch of economy			X (Decennial census)
(19)	Housing data			X (Decennial census)
(20)	Electoral participation			X (election years)
(21)	Social support		X (from 1966)	
(22)	Criminal action		X (from 1966)	

Source: O. Oyen and J. Brosveet, *Norwegian Data Law and the Social Sciences*, CESSDA/IFDO Conference on Emerging Data Protection, Cologne, August 1978, p. 3; O. Aukrust and S. Nordbotten, 'Files of Individual Data and their Potentials for Social Research', *Review of Income and Wealth*, **19**, 1973, p. 199.

identifier, a practice which the Social Security Administration itself does not encourage but over which it has little control.[10]

An authoritative review of the impact of computerised record-keeping on American society advised in 1972 caution about adopting a national citizen identifier number for each citizen. Most organisations, Westin and Baker concluded, were not yet operating with rules about privacy and confidentiality of data which reflected the new social values of the previous decade. 'Protest over the way organisations actually conduct their decision-making about people is a major facet of the sociopolitical struggles of our era. Regardless of the actual usefulness of a personal identifier in increasing the effectiveness of record-keeping processes, . . . adopting the SSN officially as a national identifier or letting its use spread unchecked cannot help but contribute to public distrust of government.'[11]

The intrusiveness of social inquiry is minimised in other ways. As the previous section demonstrates, what is not included in a census may be as significant as what is included. Given the compulsory nature of the inquiry, such scrutiny is essential in a democratic society where the executive or legislature consents to the census on behalf of the people. But governments may also be rigorous in scrutinising the nature and extent of voluntary inquiries (mainly social surveys) which they undertake. In Britain, for example, Sir Claus Moser, when head of the Government Statistical Service, commented:

> As regards privacy, I believe it to be our duty, as government statisticians, to take with the utmost seriousness and understanding the concern felt by many people. It is therefore only right for us to follow very thorough scrutiny procedures to ensure that all our surveys and questions are really needed. Our Central Statistical Office Survey Control Unit is geared to this end amongst others; and I wish that surveys commissioned in other sectors of society, commercial and academic, were subject to as much scrutiny as we now impose upon ourselves. The public is perhaps being over-surveyed, but I doubt whether government is the main culprit.[12]

The next chapter discusses these problems of regulating survey research in more detail.

Like liberty, privacy in social research may be safeguarded negatively, by minimising intrusiveness. But it may also be safeguarded positively by creating legitimate, enforceable expectations of confidentiality. In this area, the main thrust towards further and better

safeguards has come from within the research and statistical community itself, as the following chapters demonstrate. Indeed the
census, with its cast-iron assurances about individual confidentiality
(within the limits of human fallibility) has withstood even extreme
attacks. For example:

> when the United States was at war with Japan in 1942, the War De-
> partment asked the Census Bureau for the names and addresses
> of all Japanese-Americans who were living on the West Coast at
> the time of the 1940 Census. Persons of Japanese descent were
> being rounded up and transported inland for fear that some of
> them might prove disloyal in the event of a Japanese attack. Be-
> cause of Title 13 of the U.S. Code, however, which prohibits dis-
> closure of census data furnished by individuals, the Census Bureau
> could, and did, refuse to give out the names and addresses.[13]

The legal immunity of other types of social research data, however,
is less secure, which poses an important challenge to the social research community to devise better and more adequate safeguards.
Boruch in Chapter 18 provides an authoritative review both of the
legal position regarding research data in the United States, and of
the various technical and statistical methods which have been developed in order to protect the privacy of the respondent and the confidentiality of data sets. Different techniques are likely to appeal to
different audiences. Some are of particular interest to professional
researchers. Of greater interest, perhaps, are those which not only
are technically ingenious but also can demonstrate to a lay person
that the adoption of the procedure is a real step toward the preservation of individual privacy. The most dramatic example of this is
the case of randomised response, where the interviewer does not
know which question the respondent is in fact answering! It is also
evidently the case with microaggregation, where data is not released about identifiable individuals but about 'average persons'
formed from the characteristics of very small sub-samples.

If good practice is to be universally established, and potential
abuses prevented, some form of regulation of the activity of social
research would seem to be necessary. The greater the degree of
regulation, the greater public confidence is likely to be. Three ways
to achieve the objective of ensuring good practice seem to be open,
and two of them are considered in some detail in the next two chapters of the book. The three strategies are:

(1) Self-regulation, by the appropriate professional academic associations such as those of sociologists and psychologists; or by organisations such as market-research or computing societies, drawing their membership from a wider field. The present scope of such self-regulation in Britain is described in Chapter 16.

(2) Some form of state licensing of social research, either directly by qualified individuals or organisations, or indirectly through the legal recognition of professional associations. The latter course, if it followed the model of the medical and legal professions, would involve giving professional associations the right to determine minimum qualifications for those qualified to conduct social research, to establish an enforceable code of practice and ethics upon its members, to make membership of one or more associations a necessary condition of practising social research, and to give the association(s) the right to discipline and expel members who infringed such a code.

(3) Establishment of a means of regulating the *activity* of research, rather than – as in (1) and (2) – controlling the individuals who conduct such research. The means of achieving this could be through a regulatory commission, which is considered in both Chapters 16 and 17. The proposal for the establishment of a Data Protection Authority in Britain would be a major innovation; Chapter 17 spells out its implications for statistics and research. (The scope of this chapter is rather wider than the rest of the book, since it discusses not only data collected in censuses and surveys, but also the statistical use, in aggregate form, of administrative data collected for administrative purposes. Privacy and confidentiality safeguards for the statistical use of administrative data have been discussed extensively in a number of studies.[14] Many of the conclusions of such work are also applicable to data from surveys and censuses *once they are collected*, since procedures for the storage and analysis of quantitative research data derived from different sources are in principle very similar.)

Conclusion

Public goodwill and co-operation in social research will be retained only if the safeguards for the collection and storage of data, freedom of research data from abuse for other purposes, and confidence in those who conduct research, can be seen to be strong.

In order to govern and serve us the institutions of our society demand ever more information about individuals. But this exchange is not between equals, and the relative powerlessness of the individual citizen as against the data collecting and storing agencies of the modern age is perhaps the most disturbing problem of all. Whether the law can provide the protection that some desire remains to be determined; the many ambiguities in our privacy norms – the 'need' to know versus the 'need' to withhold information – cannot be resolved by law, only reflected in it.[15]

Just as social research itself changes, it is likely that public and political attitudes towards social research will fluctuate. Further research is needed into public attitudes towards surveys, censuses and record-keeping for research purposes.[16] The future is unpredictable. As this is written, for instance, it is not clear what the public reaction will be to the forthcoming round of population censuses in many countries in 1980/1. Will they be less publicly controversial, as controversial or more controversial than the 1970 round proved to be? What is abundantly clear, however, is that to an even greater extent than in the past social researchers and social statisticians depend for the success of their activities upon public co-operation. They must, therefore, take active steps to provide the public with the necessary assurances about the integrity of their work. Indeed, as already indicated, a substantial degree of 'overkill' seems to be required to provide the necessary degree of assurance.

Privacy and confidentiality, it is clear, are on the public agenda, often in somewhat sensational and over-dramatised form. This will affect social research to some extent, and has already done so. The goodwill, co-operation and trust of the public in social research, though extensive, is perhaps somewhat fragile. Increasing general concern about privacy as a social issue is likely to increase that fragility rather than diminish it. The social research community has taken, and will need to take further, real steps to provide the public with assurances about the conduct of research and confidentiality of data, consistent with the preservation of access. Statements of good intention are not enough. Social researchers need to make clear not just that they are concerned to provide adequate technical solutions (important though these are), but that they regard privacy and confidentiality as the serious social issue which it is.

16 Strengthening Public Confidence in Social Survey Research: the British Case*

SCPR Working Party

The Present Structure of Survey Research Activity

The bulk of survey research in Britain is currently undertaken by commercial organisations, of which about 150 are listed in a current Market Research Society publication. Not all these listed firms carry out complete surveys, since many are primarily engaged in consultancy work, or use secondary information sources in preference to engaging in the collection of new data. Others concern themselves only with limited aspects of the survey process such as card punching. Nevertheless, there remains a substantial number which can be described as sample survey research agencies. About sixteen of the largest of these belong to the Association of Market Survey Organisations (AMSO), which has a comprehensive code of practice. It is the responsibility of its member organisations to ensure that their staff abide by all provisions of this code.

Probably a majority of market researchers, whether or not they

* ©1974 Social and Community Planning Research, London. The conclusion, with policy recommendations, to 'Survey Research and Privacy' by the SCPR Working Party, Chapter 5 in this volume.

work for AMSO companies, belong as individuals to the Market Research Society (MRS), to whose code of practice they thereby subscribe. This code is closely similar to AMSO's.

Survey research by government is normally channelled through the Social Survey Divison of the Office of Population, Censuses and Surveys, which maintains the highest standards of ethical behaviour and whose actions are answerable to Parliament. As a recent Ditchley conference pointed out, there is a further hoop through which most government survey research must pass before it is approved:

> By a recent decision of the Prime Minister, before any central government survey of a statistical kind was made, the Central Statistical Office had to be consulted; the greatest care was taken to see that the information sought would contribute really significantly to Government activities; and in so far as the enquiries could not be undertaken by the Government Social Survey itself, but were contracted out, only those market research organisations were employed in whose confidentiality the Government has complete trust. There was ground for criticism that the purely voluntary nature of these enquiries was not always made as clear as it should be, but consideration was being given to the need to draw attention to this in the future, even though this might prejudice to some degree the response to the enquiry and so the reliability of the results.

There are still some semi-government agencies outside Whitehall and there are still the nationalised industries which fall outside the ambit of the Survey Control Unit. Nevertheless, as far as most commercial and central government reseach is concerned, there is undoubtedly a fair degree of control. This is not nearly as true of either local authorities or academic institutions. Neither has an accessible and common source of advice or standards. Individuals engaged in research in either local authorities or universities may well be members of professional associations, but the coverage is by no means complete, despite the existence of codes such as LAMSAC's recent recommendations on computer privacy. Moreover, since local authority research in particular is a large 'growth area' in surveys of the public — with transportation studies, social-service studies and planning studies all becoming commonplace — some form of overall co-ordination is clearly desirable. The existence of democratic control and public scrutiny of local authority research is not sufficient.

Survey research is also carried out by public corporations, manufacturers, firms and by charitable institutes. Amongst the latter, a new organisation, the Association of Social Research Organisations, has recently been formed. Although it does not yet have a code of practice of its own, it is almost certain to have one in the near future.

Weaknesses in the Present Situation

It will be evident from the foregoing cursory review that survey research is engaged in by extremely diverse groups of people and organisations, with widely differing backgrounds and preoccupations. Yet only two published codes *dealing specifically with surveys* exist in this country (the MRS and AMSO codes) and these are centred on, though not confined to, commercial research activity. Nevertheless, there are other bodies with codes of practice which, although not focused primarily on sample survey research, set ethical standards and prescribe codes of behaviour which afford a similar protection against misuse of surveys. Two which have been mentioned are the British Sociological Association's and the British Psychological Society's.

There are, therefore, several disparate attempts being made to ensure the maintenance of good research practice and to protect the public from the hazards which survey research may offer. And there is, as the Younger Committee found, very little complaint about survey research, perhaps largely because of the achievement of high professional standards. Indeed, as we have mentioned, for a large proportion of those interviewed the interview is probably a welcome diversion and an opportunity to express, however indirectly, views for which there is often no other obvious outlet.

The sheer volume of surveys is, of course, still growing rapidly, and we are sporadically warned that sooner or later saturation point will be reached, public co-operation will dry up and we will have to think of new ways of obtaining data. There has, however, been little sign so far that this is imminent.

However little current abuse there may be (apart from the well-known incidents where salesmen have masqueraded as researchers), the public is still open to abuse by being misled about the purposes of surveys, by being cajoled or bullied into responses that it does not wish to make, or by volunteering personal information that is at least in theory capable of misuse.

There are, in fact, four principal weaknesses in the present situation:

(1) *Lack of enforcement*: Despite the existence of several codes of practice, little is done to monitor their effectiveness or to ensure their enforcement.

(2) *Lack of public involvement*: The public is almost wholly unaware of their existence and of the complaints procedures on which the codes must depend if breaches are to be discovered and acted upon.

(3) *Lack of coverage*: There is clearly a large and (currently) uncontrollable minority of survey research undertaken by individuals with no professional or legislative constraints on their activity.

(4) *Lack of co-ordination*: There is no co-ordination of the various bodies concerned with the administration and enforcement of codes of practice and no single source for the public to identify for complaints, guidance or arbitration.

It was on these four weaknesses that the Working Party's attention was focused and to which its recommendations relate. These are discussed below in turn together with suggestions for action. We must stress, however, that the aim of the Working Party was to offer guidance, not solutions. There can be no foolproof, rigid or unchanging formulae. Judgement will always be needed and circumstances will always alter cases. The highest skills and best experience of those already expert in the field (and the associations they have formed) will always be needed. Our aim in presenting guidelines is to provide a structure for more effective action, better communication and closer contact with the public. In discussing the principal four weaknesses in the present situation, we are also aware that the remaining weaknesses referred to earlier will still exist and will (at best) be dealt with only indirectly by the measures we propose.

Enforcement

Most codes of practice are, of course, administered by professional associations and are 'enforceable' by means of sanctions against members who do not comply. Yet this is very rarely done and in any case there is nothing to stop sanctioned members from continuing their malpractices outside the association. So the safeguard for the public is not really effective. In the absence of constraints imposed by legislation, the only sanctions that can be applied to those who do not maintain standards are those which *the public itself can apply.* As far as goods and services are concerned, it is, for example, open to the public not to buy the goods or services of those who will not join an association with declared standards, for example, the British Insurance Association. Similarly, in survey research it is conceivable that, in time, a situation could be reached in which the public could distinguish between those survey research organisations which conform to a recognised code and those which do not.

But public sanctions are workable only if they can be based on generally accepted standards which some organisations reliably uphold. And this distinction can be maintained only if there are adequate inspections and, if necessary, enforcement procedures which ensure that membership of this category is not a mere formality. The 'seal of approval' must be withdrawn from those who do not comply; a complaints procedure has to exist; and a panel of 'judges' has to administer it.

This is not to say that there should necessarily be *one* code covering all survey research activity. A monolithic control is not necessarily the most efficient or the most desirable form of enforcement procedure. *What is clear, however, is the desirability of ensuring that certain minimum standards are almost universally recognised by survey practitioners and almost universally applied.*

There will be different codes, but they must have certain basic elements in common. And they must, between them, cover the great bulk of survey research activity in this country if they are to be effective in affording the kind of protection which we believe to be necessary.

Public involvement

As we have said, one of the problems with existing codes is that they are directed almost entirely at the profession alone. The public is unaware of their content – even where the codes seek to protect their interests. If we are thinking of safeguarding the rights of potential respondents, it is clearly not enough simply to rely on professionals to carry out the task. The public's 'rights' in relation to survey research would have to be widely publicised and widely understood: a 'seal of approval' would be no sort of safeguard unless the public knew that they should ask the person on the doorstep for evidence of it; a complaints procedure would be only a gesture unless its existence were widely recognised.

A possible starting-point to the solution of this problem might be the formulation of a *'respondents' charter'*, containing the basic elements of public protection which would be essential features of all codes. To be at all effective, however, it would have to be widely publicised by the usual means of promotion – newspapers, television etc. But even publicity of this kind would be of limited value in portraying the detail and in emphasising the public's own role.

Survey researchers do, however, possess a unique method of distribution: the survey itself. An idea might be that a copy of the 'charter' should be given to *every* respondent in *every* survey. Assuming wide acceptance of this idea amongst survey researchers, it would not take long for the 'charter' to have reached an appreciable proportion of British households. Even this would, of course, be no guarantee of public response, but it would go some way towards it.

In any event, the idea of a simplified and accessible version of the main elements of survey research ethics is an important one. *For any effective protection to be practicable, the public must itself be aware of its 'rights' in relation to survey research and must be encouraged to be vigilant in its exercise of those rights.*

Inasmuch as public involvement entails the pursuit of complaints against professional practitioners, it can be achieved only if complainants have confidence in a body (or bodies) through which their criticisms will be channelled. This implies the need for an organisation which, unlike the existing organisations, includes representatives of the public and has effective access to the press and possibly to Parliament.

Coverage

It would almost certainly be fair to say that the majority of *individuals* involved in survey research in the United Kingdom have never seen any code of practice, let alone signed one. In the first place it is usually only professionals in agencies and universities who are members of associations which possess such codes. Yet survey research is carried out by a much wider group of organisations and individuals within both the public and private sectors.

In the second place, it is only the *research* staff within those organisations who are normally members of professional associations. Interviewers, coders, punchers and large numbers of clerical staff, *all of whom have access to identified data records*, are rarely if ever made to sign a confidentiality pledge or indeed any other aspects of the code. (The exceptions are OPCS staff and other civil servants who sign the Official Secrets Act.)

Ultimately there can, of course, be no complete safeguard against the abuse of trust by people in positions of responsibility, but it is certainly possible to narrow down the range of people who have access to confidential records and to eliminate almost entirely the chance of accidental disclosures. It is not difficult to envisage agreement on practices of dealing with data records which give good safeguards against such disclosures. *But an essential starting point is that signatories to codes of practice must comprise all individuals who have access to confidential records.* The view of the Working Party is that no individual who has not signed a code should have any access whatever to identified documents. And this should be as true of individuals in sub-contracting organisations as of those whose responsibility it is to carry out the research.

We have not been able to establish the proportion of survey research within the United Kingdom which is carried out by individuals or organisations who are currently outside the scope (or simply not members) of any association which administers a code of practice. We cannot, therefore, estimate the size of the problem. It does, however, warrant a very much closer examination since, if it is sizeable, it clearly needs action.

This also implies a body or group which has as its responsibility the inspection and co-ordination of the field; and this is discussed below.

Co-ordination

There is at present no body which could satisfactorily undertake the task of co-ordinating progress towards the goal of universally applied standards for survey research. The work done by associations already active in this direction is of the greatest value, but – as each of them would be the first to admit – their respective interests cover too limited a part of the field to be capable of sufficient expansion. Moreover, these associations have many other functions besides the maintenance of standards, and it would be unreasonable to suggest that they should abandon these by transforming themselves into watch-dogs for the whole survey field.

Of organisations other than professional associations, perhaps the one most suitably placed to exercise this function is the Central Statistical Office, which does not itself carry out surveys, but is technically equipped to appraise them and already exercises supervision over government work of this kind. It seemed to the Working Party, however, that this additional burden was one which the CSO might well be unwilling to assume. Apart from staffing and other administrative aspects, the CSO could clearly not allow itself to be put in a position where it might be required to apply public sanctions to other government departments, however unlikely it is that such a situation would arise. For these and other reasons, we believe that the body concerned must stand entirely outside the framework of the Civil Service, yet at the same time we are sure that it must have official standing and not be merely another voluntary body – an 'association of associations' – with enforcement problems far greater than those faced by the present associations individually.

It seems to us that *there is one body to which this task would be uniquely suited, namely the Standing Commission which was proposed by the Younger Committee to review computer applications.* The summary (on page 16 of their report) of the terms of reference of the Commission very closely fits the kind of role we envisage for the field of surveys generally. For the proposed Commission to perform the role we have in mind requires only an extension of the boundaries of its operations, but no basic change in its character. It is already to be a body with official standing but outside the framework of the Civil Service (its responsibility lying directly to Parliament); its purview already includes the basic issues of privacy which in any case cut across different disciplines; and its role as a co-ordinator and watch-dog without specific powers is just the kind of role which is needed to enlist the co-operative support of the various 'sub co-ordinators' already working in the field; its ultimate and only 'power' is its annual report to Parliament, which will not only receive publicity but may also recommend legislation.

We believe that the proposed Commission's functions should therefore be expanded to include survey research activity and the problems arising from it. It is a natural extension and, we believe, both practicable and desirable.

In any event, the proposed Commission would be concerned about the storage of data emanating from survey research. And this impinges substantially on the whole subject of data collection and the balance which needs to be struck between minimising fresh intrusions into the home and minimising the sharing of data (with its problems of access). The less access there is to data already collected, the more need there is to collect fresh data. Which is it most important to inhibit – fresh data collection, with consequent intrusions into the home and relatively inefficient use of resources, or the sharing of data, with its increased risk of breaches of confidentiality?

There is no simple answer to this question, but the Commission may wish to examine the arguments over time and to make suggestions about the balance to be struck. For example, it may be that the present level of intrusion into the home seems low enough to cause very little annoyance. There are few known cases of breaches of confidentiality, whereas systems for ensuring confidentiality are currently less well developed. Thus at present it may be desirable to err on the side of restricting access in favour of fresh data collection. In any case, if respondents were told that data would be accessible, response rates might suffer and the process might be counterproductive.

In the future the situation may change. The volume of surveys will increase, and may begin to reach saturation point so that resistance builds up. At the same time, if the proper steps are taken now, very nearly foolproof methods of protecting confidentiality may be developed. The emphasis could then swing towards restricting data collection and making better use, by multiple access, of each set of data which becomes available.

The proposed Commission would be ideally suited to monitor and pronounce on this type of conflict and would have a general duty to encourage and ensure the most stringent precautions against undue intrusion or loss of privacy at whatever stage they may occur on the survey research continuum.

How the Commission Would Work

Our proposal – like that of Younger – is that the Commission's function should be primarily that of a co-ordinator and instigator of 'good practice' where deficiencies exist. It would not have powers to compel or to license; it would not have as its role the enforcement of sanctions against individuals or associations; it would issue no directives. The view of the Working Party is that its role would be quite the opposite because, by and large, there is the will amongst professionals engaged in survey research to improve their practices and to co-operate in realistic attempts to safeguard the public's interests. The Commission would therefore be a forum for discussion and investigation of the key issues involved in the protection of privacy; a channel of communication between the disparate groups of survey research practitioners; and a form of greater access between the public and professionals.

The only 'sanction' proposed is the annual report to Parliament. If the Commission were to feel that legislation was needed, it could recommend it; if it felt that there were loopholes in the existing provisions – which could not be plugged by co-operative action – it could recommend ways and means of eradicating them. But essentially this would be a last resort. If the Commission is to be successful in its aims, it would need the enthusiastic co-operation of professionals and public alike, not merely the grudging consent of practitioners who doubted its competence and suspected its aims.

To achieve this, the Commission would require a permanent standing committee of professional advisers comprising representatives of market research, government, the academic community, foundations, research institutes, local authorities and industry. This committee would advise the Commission on such matters as a set of definitive practical procedures for ensuring confidentiality; methods of encouraging acceptance of such procedures; for example, publicity, sanctions etc.; methods and priorities for reviewing practices; issues (if any) which require parliamentary action, for example, whether or not survey data should be 'privileged' for the purposes of evidence and police scrutiny, whether or not legislation was necessary to prohibit salesmen from masquerading as researchers, and so on.

The existence of an advisory committee of practitioners would also increase the likelihood that improvements in standards would be generated by co-operative pressure from within the profession rather than imposed from above.

The role of the Commission would therefore be a co-ordinating one:

(1) If a complaint were to be made by a member of the public, the Commission would not itself investigate it but would ask the relevant professional body to do so and to report back.
(2) It would publicise malpractices which were felt to be damaging to the proper conduct of survey research.

(3) It would encourage the principal funders of survey research, government departments, local authorities, foundations and industry, not to award grants or contracts to organisations or individuals who were not 'signatories' to one or other code of conduct.

(4) It would encourage the insertion of appropriate safeguards in all codes of conduct.

(5) It would encourage the formation of new associations to maintain standards if and when it became clear that a body of research was being carried out by individuals or organisations who belonged to none of the current professional groups or associations.

(6) It would investigate ways and means of improving standards and achieving agreed measures of implementation.

(7) In the last resort it would recommend legislation on issues which need action but which were incapable of resolution by co-operative measures.

17 Protecting Statistical and Research Data from Improper Use*

UK Data Protection Committee

The Committee on Data Protection, set up to advise the British government on legislation to protect personal data handled in computers, published its report in December 1978. This recommended that the function of a law on data protection should be different from a law on privacy; rather than establishing rights, it should provide a framework for finding a balance between the interests of three different parties – the individual citizen, the user of the data and the community at large. Legislation (the report suggested) should be introduced to cover all automatic handling in the United Kingdom of personal data by any user, including both the public and private sectors.

The legislation would declare a set of principles and establish a Data Protection Authority to implement them. The seven principles suggested include five to reflect the interests of data subjects, one to protect the interests of users and one to reflect the interests of the community at large. The Data Protection Authority (DPA) should be required to ensure that, so far as is practicable, personal data are handled with adequate safeguards for the interests (and especially the privacy) of the data subjects. The DPA, it is suggested, would carry out its task princi-

pally by making rules for data users, maintaining a register of personal data applications, investigating complaints and enforcing compliance with the rules.

At the time of writing, these proposals have been published but no government response to them has been made. They therefore represent an authoritative blueprint for future data protection in Britain, if government decides to implement them. Whether implemented or not, the committee's report is a most important survey of the whole of the data-protection field and a statement of principles which could guide policy. This chapter comes from that part of the committee's report dealing with the special problems of protecting statistical and research data.

* * *

The 1975 White Paper on *Computers and Privacy*[1] devoted five paragraphs to statistics and, by implication, research. It makes the point that 'Statistical work carries few risks for privacy because it gives information about groups of people, even though the original data related to identifiable individuals'. Later it says that 'What is important, however, is that the output of statistics should guard against revealing information about identified or identifiable individuals'. About handling research data it says that '. . . it is necessary to take special precautions against risks for the privacy of the individual, especially as the data may be very sensitive indeed'. Finally, it says that 'Safeguards are needed to ensure that statistics are presented in a way that does not reveal details of an identified or identifiable individual'.

Statistics

The essential characterisitic of statistical data is that they are concerned with groups of individuals and not with individuals themselves. Although usually compiled from records relating to individual persons, households, businesses, and so on, statistical information relates only to groups and is not intended to reveal information about the identifiable individuals of which the groups are composed. It follows that the use of personal information for statistical purposes carries few risks for privacy, provided that precautions are taken, appropriate to the type of statistical activity, to prevent the disclosure of personal information about identifiable individuals.

Statisticians have always had a strong interest in preserving the confidentiality of their records of personal information if only to help maintain the co-operation of the members of the public from whom the information is obtained. Many techniques have been developed to facilitate this purpose and there is a large literature on the subject. Indeed a bibliography recently prepared for the United States Bureau of the Census [2] lists over a thousand items.

We readily accept that statistical information about people need not be personal information. We have concluded that 'personal data' are 'any data which relate, or which can be related, to an identified or identifiable individual, including the information whereby he can be identified'. It is the last part of this definition which is particularly relevant to the use of personal data in statistics and research work. Where information cannot be related to an identified or identifiable individual, then the way in which it is handled, transferred, disseminated or published is not a matter of concern to us – nor, we believe, to a future DPA. Disidentified data about health, wealth and behaviour may be used for good or bad ends about which individuals or groups may wish to take action. But a cause for that action cannot be invasion of privacy or loss of data protection if the safeguards employed prevent individual identification. Our concern in this chapter is therefore to consider only those matters relating to statistics and research which require some regulation because there is a danger that an individual may be identified, and some data may be related to him.

Subject access

If information is to be used only for statistical purposes, and the safeguards to prevent identification are sufficient, we see no need for data subjects to be given access. Great efforts should, of course, be devoted by those responsible to ensuring the accuracy of statistical data, but we accept that it is not always essential, and often not cost-effective for statistical purposes, to attempt to ensure absolute accuracy. In consequence, we see no need for individuals to have a general right to correct errors in data held about them for statistical purposes alone. It is difficult to see how an individual can be harmed by the use of inaccurate data about him in a statistical analysis in which he cannot be identified.

Anonymity

It follows that those responsible for producing statistics should ensure that it is impossible to infer information about individuals from the published data. Where these take the form of the number of individuals falling into specified cells or categories, anonymity can generally be achieved by aggregation or by stipulating minimum numbers within groups, though the size of these will depend on what other informaton is available to assist identification. However, the Central Statistical Office, IBM and the Office for Population Censuses and Surveys thought it was only realistic to say that even when this is done the risk of identification cannot always be completely eliminated,[3] and the Royal Statistical Society said that aggregation methods may render certain types of statistical analysis difficult. We are informed that an alternative technique which is sometimes preferable is to add or subtract random integers in such a way that the true sizes of some cell entries are disguised while marginal totals are substantially unaffected. A variant of this which has some advantages is the 'random rounding' technique developed by Statistics Canada.[4] This consists of rounding all tabulated entries to the next higher or lower multiple of a predetermined small number (for example, 5), the probabilities of rounding up or down being so arranged that the expected value of the entry in each cell is left unchanged. Thus the entry for a cell for which the original entry was 3 would be given the value 0 with probability $\frac{2}{5}$ and 5 with probability $\frac{3}{5}$, and an original entry of 26 would be replaced by 25 selected with probability $\frac{4}{5}$ or 30 selected with probability $\frac{1}{5}$. The method has the advantage of being completely automatic. Tabulations can be run off for external users with random rounding, and for internal users without random rounding, without any modification of the data base itself.

However, if suitable precautions are not observed the presentation of statistics can lead to the identification of an individual. An example of this, which we have permision to use, is in the Department of Education and Science *Statistics of Education 1975*; Table 33 of Volume 4 (Teachers) purported to show the number of Polytechnic staff by grade who do not have a degree. Among those listed is one Director, who is a distinguished designer: the total number of Directors (or equivalent) of Polytechnics is thirty. As it happens this information could have been retrieved from other published sources, but we have no doubt that the general rule should be to maintain anonymity for individuals in all published statistics; where there is any relaxation of this requirement – and this must be in a very limited number of cases – then the consent of those involved or, in exceptional circumstances provided for in the appropriate code of practice, the specific permission of the DPA, should be obtained. We understand that a requirement of this sort is already current practice with Inland Revenue: statistics about narrow and potentially identifiable income groups are not published without the consent of the groups of taxpayers concerned or, in special circumstances, the authorisation of a Minister.

The Office of Population Censuses and Surveys has told us that it seems likely that the release for public use of anonymised individual records (on, say, magnetic tape) will be more widely adopted. Information from the General Household Survey is already disseminated in this form, on the grounds that it gives the user greater flexibility in statistical analysis without compromising the confidentiality of information about identifiable individuals. We see no objection to this development – provided adequate precautions are taken to prevent identification. However, it is important to recognise that mere deletion of names and addresses may not suffice to ensure anonymity. If, for example, information is included on locality, profession and age it might be quite easy to infer the identities of particular individuals. Thus it is desirable that those responsible for releasing the data should adopt some appropriate technique, such as to delete or 'broadband' (that is, give information in broad rather than narrow categories) as many further items as are necessary to ensure anonymity, taking account of whatever other information may be available from other sources. An alternative technique that might be preferable for some items is to disguise them by adding random variables. The conditions under which anonymised individual data may be released should form part of appropriate codes of practice.

In addition to developing methods for preserving confidentiality in published records, statisticians have also devised techniques for conducting surveys on highly sensitive topics in which the respondent's privacy is preserved even in relation to the interviewer conducting the survey. They are called 'randomised response techniques' and our attention has been drawn to a useful review of them which has recently been published,[5] where many developments of the basic idea are discussed. Devices can be used to disguise the answers to sensitive questions when passing individual data from one organisation to another. Such a device can indeed be applied for this purpose entirely automatically in the computer. Modification of the original data in this way constitutes a special case of what are called privacy transformations. These are transformations of individual data which are designed to disguise or conceal data on the original record. With randomisation procedures we understand that it is impossible to deduce the original data from the transformed data. A general discussion of privacy transformations in the statistical context has been given by Dalenius.[6]

Transfer of identifiable data

It is sometimes necessary, for statistical purposes, for information to be passed from the collector of the information to third parties. The Yorkshire Regional Health Authority, the Royal Statistical Society and the British Association for the Advancement of Science suggested to us that, where possible, the name and address or other data directly identifying individuals should be detached and stored separately when this is done.However, in some cases the required statistical analysis will not be possible unless the collector passes data identifying the individual so that the recipient can link the information with other data about the same individual. In such cases the circumstances under which the transfer is legitimate should be specified by the appropriate code of practice. The code should contain provisions for ensuring both that the data are held securely and that the undertakings on confidentiality given by the original collector of the data are maintained by those to whom the data are passed. Departures from this requirement should be permissible only if either the written permission of the individuals concerned or, in exceptional circumstances in accordance with the code of practice, the specific permission of the DPA has been obtained. Responsibility for preserving anonymity in the published record must rest with the organisation producing the published data.

Special problems can arise when identifiable individual data from several sources are merged in order to tabulate a wider range of statistics or to analyse the relations between the various sets of data. For instance, the British Steel Corporation has commissioned a health hazards study, by the Institute of Industrial Medicine, based on data supplied voluntarily by subjects, data from pension fund files and data from other outside agencies. It is sometimes suggested that confidentiality can be preserved when files are merged by giving to an independent body the task of linking identifying information from the different files, users being provided only with disidentified merged files. However, although this process may asssist in preserving confidentiality, it does not guarantee it absolutely. For the organisation which originally requested the merging could take the disidentified merged file and by using modern computer search techniques could match up data about individuals in its own identified file with individual data in the disidentified merged file, and hence deduce identifiers of individuals in the merged files. Even if this could not be done for all individuals there remains the risk of a breach of confidentiality for some. We understand that one technique for dealing with this problem is micro-aggregation. Instead of the merged file being passed to the user in individualised form the data are grouped, and only grouped data are transferred, the groups being chosen to be large enough to ensure confidentiality, but otherwise as small as possible so as to preserve the maximum amount of information for analysis. Thus the classification into groups for this purpose need not correspond to that used in the resulting publications. Randomisation methods of the kind mentioned earlier can also be used. A detailed discussion of methods of preserving confidentiality when files are merged has been given by Campbell and others.[7] We repeat that, whatever the source of the underlying information, the organisation which produces the published statistics should be held responsible for ensuring that individuals cannot be identified from the published data. The National Council for Civil Liberties thought that when files are merged, any further contact with the subject, for follow-up action perhaps, should come from the body responsible for maintaining the link file and not from the organisations contributing the original files. However, while we agree that this might be appropriate in some cases we do not think it should be universally required in all circumstances. All these matters will require very careful consideration by the DPA when developing the appropriate codes of practice.

Sampling frames

Where data are collected for statistical purposes the information is sometimes also used for the construction of registers for future statistical inquiries; for example, such a register may be used to provide a sampling frame from which samples of individuals may be drawn for further surveys. In such cases we do not believe that it is normally enough for the collector to assure the subject that the information is required 'for statistical purposes', or 'to compile statistics' etc, since follow-up surveys, if unexpected by the data subject, can cause understandable and needless alarm. This is illustrated by the concern which was expressed when a number of women who had disclosed in the 1971 Census that they were former nurses were subsequently, at the request of the Briggs Committee on Nursing,[8] asked to give further information about their reasons for leaving the profession.[9] (In fact, this survey was conducted by the Office of Population Censuses and Surveys, and we were told that none of the information obtained about identifiable individuals was passed outside that office, and that there was no breach of census confidentiality.) In our view, the fact that information will be used to construct registers for further inquiries should normally be made clear at the time the information is collected. The Royal Statistical Society suggest that the subject's specific consent to this practice should be obtained, either at the time of original collection or subsequently. We would propose that if the possible use of the information for such purposes is envisaged at the time of collection, subject agreement should be sought then. This point should be covered in the appropriate code of practice.

Where information is collected purely for statistical analysis we believe that, in order to let the subject know why the data are required and how they will be handled, it is sufficient for him to be told that the information is required 'for statistical purposes' or 'to compile statistics', and so on, and to be informed in general terms about the overall purpose of the inquiry. The subject should also be given assurances on confidentiality. We think it is unnecessary for the subject to be given comprehensive details, at the time of collection, about how the information will be used and who will have access to it – though he should have the right to obtain this knowledge in general terms on request insofar as it is known at the time. Details on procedures to be followed when collecting statistical information should form part of the appropriate code of practice. In this context Social and Community Planning Research thought that a charter of respondents' rights should be drawn up and a copy given to every subject who participates in a survey. We do not, however, believe that this need be a universal requirement.

Time limits

Since it is often difficult or impossible to specify in advance all the analyses which might in the future be made of a particular set of data,

we think the requirement that information should be kept only for as
long as is needed for the specific purpose for which the data are collected, cannot normally be applied to data used for statistical purposes. Both the Royal Statistical Society and the Record Users Group
thought that there should be no time limit for the retention of data.
We agree that the need for particular analyses might well not emerge
until future events have taken place, but the need for retention should
be reviewed from time to time in each particular case.

In most cases it would be impossible to specify at the time of collection of the data all the tabulations or analyses that might subsequently be undertaken. Moreover, it would not be feasible to
approach each individual for his permission to use data whenever a
new analysis is contemplated. While we accept that the individual
should be able to find out in general terms what use has been made of
information provided by him, it must be recognised that when the information is used for statistical purposes it would often be extremely
costly, or even impossible, to specify in detail all the uses that have
been made of a particular piece of information. Moreover, such use
cannot directly affect the individual concerned. In a statistical context, therefore, there is no need to allow the subject to find out what
has been done with the information.

Statistics and administration

The Royal Statistical Society suggest, and we agree, that there should
be no objection to the use for statistical purposes of administrative
and other data not originally obtained for these purposes, provided
appropriate provisions on confidentiality and security are set out in
the relevant codes of practice and are adhered to. Indeed, much of the
statistical information published by government departments is
derived from data obtained as a by-product of administration. The
Central Statistical Office (CSO) has given as examples the unem-
ployment and vacancy statistics, which are derived from information
arising from the functions performed by the Employment Services
Agency, and the statistics of motor vehicles, which are based on the
registration of these vehicles for tax purposes. We commend the use
where possible of administrative and other data for statistical purposes, both on grounds of economy and also in order to minimise the
burden of form-filling on the public, provided that there are adequate
safeguards to preserve confidentiality. Appropriate codes of practice

covering this area should be agreed between the DPA and representative statistical organisations.

While the use of administrative information for statistical purposes is generally acceptable, with proper safeguards, the use of statistical data for administration is not. The Scottish Office told us that 'By definition statistical data are intended to be used only for statistical purposes. No other use is permissible because then it would not be possible to proffer security and confidentiality reassurances to the individual, nor could the credibility of the Government Statistical Service be maintained.' This view is also taken by the CSO who suggested that where information may be used for other than strictly statistical purposes these should be stated on the collecting form. The British Association for the Advancement of Science said that data banks for statistical purposes should be quite separate from those for administrative use. We share the view of the majority of those who mentioned this point; we believe that any code of practice should ensure that the strongest measures are included to prevent the use for any other purpose of information gathered for statistical work unless this is made clear at the time of collection, or the data subject's specific permission is obtained subsequently.

Our discussions with the CSO have given us very useful information on the progress being made in the Government Statistical Service towards the production of the set of internal guidelines for privacy protection which is mentioned in the White Paper (paragraph 22). We were impressed by the thoroughness with which the CSO had approached this matter and the extent to which consultations within the Government Statistical Service were taking place. We wish to record our appreciation for the CSO's co-operation in allowing us to examine their proposals; we are satisfied that the direction taken in this work is in accordance with our own views. We propose that this guidance, or code of practice, should be subject to agreement by the future DPA. It would be right, in our view, for any monitoring function required by such a code to be within the purview of the DPA.

Research

The problems of privacy and data protection arising in research are similar to those found in statistical work, although the collection of data for statistical work is primarily carried out by governmental organisations, while research may be undertaken in both the public and private sectors. In the following paragraphs we will consider the similarities and differences in the two processes and how they affect protection of privacy in the research field.

Research on personal data is mostly carried out by sociologists, market researchers, historians, economists and the medical profession, all of whom use the same basic approach. In many cases their aim is to collect data directly from the subject to solve a particular problem. Such data may be obtained by questionnaires, by observation of the activities of others, or by physical measurements. The results are presented in statistical tables, or if specific cases are described, in a way which prevents identification of an individual.

We believe the same precautions should be taken in the use of research data as have been described for statistical data. When information is collected directly from the subject an explanation of the study should be given. At the same time it must be clear that the data may be used for other research studies (but not for administrative purposes). In the analysis of data collected to provide an answer to one particular question, unexpected associations are often found which contribute to a new understanding of some other human process. It would be wasteful of resources, and perhaps irritating to the subject, if permission had to be obtained each time a research team wished to perform a new analysis. However, we received various opinions on this matter. The British Medical Association thought that only the consent of the patient's doctor should be required for disclosure of medical data for clinical use, but it also said that the patient's consent should be sought for other disclosures, including that for research purposes. On the other hand the Record Users Group said that the use of records for a new purpose in connection with historical archive research was essential to historians; for them it was often too late to obtain the subject's consent. Other witnesses (as for instance, the North Western Regional Health Authority and the Oxford Regional Health Authority) thought it would be impracticable to obtain a patient's consent for each new research use of data from medical records. Several suggested that approval by the DPA would be more realistic than attempting to approach possibly thousands of subjects on each occasion of new use. In research work there is obviously a problem in notifying purpose to subjects; we believe that special guidance to prevent serious conflict between the needs of researchers and the individual would be required from the DPA when a code of practice was defined. It seems appropriate that the DPA should perform a monitoring function when individual agreement by the subject is not practical.

Subject access

A subject's claim to have access to his own data presents particular problems in research. We believe the same solution should be applied to this as that suggested for statistical data. Where information for research is held in a disidentified form the risks to data protection will not differ from those for any other anonymous statistical data, and there is no reason to provide a subject with access to his own data. On the other hand, where information relates to identifiable persons this rule should be interpreted to ensure proper protection for an individual in a way which would not unreasonably prejudice research activity. There must be some situations when to allow the subject access to base data could be very expensive both in terms of time and cost. The DPA should have a special role in adjudicating on cases where the subject may be at a disadvantage if denied access to his data.

Time limits

We also believe that the rules about the length of time data are retained should be similar both for statistics and research, and that only in exceptional circumstances should a limit be explicitly stated. Furthermore, as with statistical data, research data should not be used for administrative purposes, for example by a local authority or the police. The flow should be in one direction only so that administrative data could be used for research, but research data could not be used for identifying individuals for administrative action.

Sampling frames

Research projects may involve the creation of registers, and these should be treated as described earlier in this chapter.

Linkage and minimum data collection

There are two other aspects of data privacy in research: the problems arising from linkage of data on separate files, and collection of the minimum amount of data necessary for the stated objectives.

Problems arising from the linkage of data files occur in research when data obtained by different organisations are merged. Data can be collected by an organisation, such as a cancer registry, and be required for use by independent research workers for their own analyses. Part of this process may include the linking of several records about the same individual in order to gain broader understanding of a sociological or medical problem.

Both the British Association for the Advancement of Science and the British Psychological Society have told us that there should be no linkage without the subject's consent. The latter acknowledged that it would be inconvenient to obtain permission for access and linkage, but thought that it was necessary for ethical reasons because research could be controversial and a subject may have ethical objections. Nevertheless such restrictions could halt many medical and sociological investigations in which survey data are linked to data collected for statistical or administrative purposes. We think that the extent of subject consent should be determined by the nature of the investigation, and prescribed in the code of practice under which the research was carried out. This could range from none, as in the case of death certificates (there are already strict rules for the dissemination of such data), to direct consent, as required when a research worker wishes to obtain information about a patient from his doctor.

Because research is frequently on the borders of current knowledge and the exact data set for achieving a specified purpose is not known, it is often necessary to collect more data than, in retrospect, might be regarded as the minimum. A broad interpretation of the principle of collecting only what is required for a particular purpose would be necessary. So far no method has been devised for defining the minimum data necessary for a project, and it would seem unwise to attempt to limit the scope for scientific inquiry in this way when no clear infringement of privacy is involved.

Codes of practice

Most investigators work under the guidance of some code of practice. These have already been established by the Market Research Society, the British Sociological Association, the Medical Research Council and others. Few sanctions for breaking these codes of practice exist, though a notable exception is that for medical doctors who have to be registered before being allowed to practice, and are re-registered annually. The threat of withdrawal of the practising licence for un-ethical behaviour towards a patient helps to maintain a high standard of professional conduct. It is also some assurance to the public that confidentiality and ethical practice are safeguarded. We believe that a similar type of assurance should cover all research workers through adherence to codes of practice devised by the DPA.

Research is carried out in a variety of institutions or organisations; for example market-research companies, departments of behavioural science, medical schools and pharmaceutical companies. Because it is carried out on groups it is expensive and must therefore be financed through institutions which attract adequate funds: it is rare for re-search on personal data files to be carried out by an individual who has no allegiance to a particular organisation. We think, therefore, that any registration of research applications with the DPA should not be by individuals or single projects, but by the organisations in which the research is undertaken which must accept responsibility for ensuring that the requirements of the relevant codes of practice are observed. Should a worker associated with an organisation infringe the code then the DPA's powers of enforcement should be directed at the organisation concerned and not the individual worker. The organ-isation might suitably discipline the erring researcher, and perhaps a register of persistent offenders might prove to be necesssary.

18 Methods for Assuring Personal Integrity in Social Research: an Introduction*

Robert F. Boruch

Individual dignity and human rights have been a matter of fundamental concern to Americans since the colonial period. That interest is reflected generally in explicit law, including the Constitution, and in social custom. The recent growth of applied social research, especially research on the evaluation of social programmes, is in many ways entirely consistent with that interest. For research seeks in its broader efforts to understand better the nature of economic, social and mental disability, and to verify the effectiveness of social programmes designed to ameliorate these problems. Insofar as disabilities influence the individual's control over his own destiny, that research will, at its best, enhance human dignity and freedom of choice.

In other respects, however, the rigorous conduct of social research may conflict directly with law and social ethics. This discord is at times specious, based less on interests in human rights than on wilful ignorance, institutional arrogance and promiscuous suspicion. At least as often, the conflicts are legitimate and involve fundamental problems which must be resolved to understand human behaviour and to produce research which has some social value. Sample surveys, and field tests of social programmes, for example, often involve a depreciation in the respondent's privacy, at least in principle. This exchange of information at the individual level is a small and imper-

* Original material©1979 Robert F. Boruch.

fect reflection of a generalised conflict between social needs for information and a parallel need to recognise individual rights. Similarly, though random assignment of eligible individuals to one of two or more programme variations in a controlled social experiment represents one of the best vehicles for learning about the relative effects of such programmes, the process engenders a variety of ethical and legal issues. They include deciding whether informed consent to participate is necessary, and establishing its meaning, and understanding how to assure the individual's right to enter the experimental programme, to reject or drop out of the programme, without degrading the quality of the test. Regardless of whether the research involves randomised assignment, there are difficulties of determining when, under what conditions, and to what degree control over research participants is necessary. The possibility of feedback and reward systems to establish a parity of relation between researcher and research subject must also be considered.

Many of these problems appear in small-scale research efforts, but they are most visible in large-scale contemporary research funded by government. That they are not confined to domestic borders is readily evident from the media and professional journal coverage of the problems at the international level and from support for discussion of the problems, for example, by the National Institute of Education and the National Science Foundation in the United States, by Volkswagen Foundation in Germany, and by the Swedish Council for Social Science Research.

The main objective of this chapter is to introduce, to an interdisciplinary audience, methods which are being developed to reconcile conflicts of the sort described.[1] Attention is devoted primarily to privacy and confidentiality in research, especially multiple methods of attenuating problems in this area. The treatment is very brief and is based on a detailed review of the topic by Boruch and Cecil in *Assuring Confidentiality in Social Research*.[2]

The Role of the Methodologist

The community of methodologists is meeting the challenge to reconcile conflicting interests in a variety of ways. Methodological innovations designed to ameliorate problems cut across every stage of the research process, from design of the research question (to reduce blame-laying, scapegoating, and so on) to design of statistical methods for assuring privacy of response, which are discussed later, and methods of assuring equity of participation in research. There is a rapidly developing state of the art in ethical design of the research plan. Possible statistical alternatives to randomised experiments (which are at times ethically unacceptable or illegal) are being developed: play-the-winner procedures, so-called one-armed-bandit approaches, and regression discontinuity techniques, to determining the relative impact of social programmes. In understanding ways to adjust classical experimental designs in the interest of ethical or legal standards, the emphasis has been on development of planned variation studies which may involve no 'control' condition, on development and appraisal of component-wise experiments to test small features of a large programme, and on the use of simulation and role-playing as substitutes for ethically dubious approaches which involve deception of human subjects.[3]

These methods are designed to accomplish research goals to a fair degree, without needless abridgement of personal dignity or rights of the research participant. They often stem from live conflicts between law or ethics and the need for rigorous research in education, psychology, sociology, epidemiology and medicine. Many of the older methods have been field-tested but are largely unknown because of their methodological complexity. Still others, especially newer developments, have not yet been field-tested but offer considerable promise as a technological fix to the social problems generated by social research. The contributions to this arena are many and international in character. Research on methods for assuring confidentiality in social research, for example, has been undertaken in Germany, Sweden, Denmark, the United Kingdom, Israel, Spain and Holland, as well as in the United States.

Assuring Privacy and the Confidentiality of Data

The problem of minimising degradation of privacy in social research, of assuring confidentiality of data elicited from respondents, is a persistent one. It has been dramatised most recently during the Negative Income Tax Experiment, in which a county prosecutor forced economic researchers to yield research records on identified subsidy recipients (research participants). The case illustrates that the researcher may be cast unwillingly into the role of informant if he does not anticipate the possibility of judicial or legislative appropriation of his records for prosecuting some of his research subjects. Similar incidents are not difficult to find in other social research endeavours. A dozen such episodes, occurring in criminal research, health-related investigations, sociological and psychological research, are analysed in small case-study form by Boruch and Cecil.[4] These are samples of a larger population of episodes in survey research and field experiments, being compiled independently by Carroll and Knerr.[5]

The general implication of these episodes is that we take as an objective, reducing depreciation of privacy without severe abridgement of research goals. That is, we must articulate strategy for reconciling differing standards on need for information and need for respecting individual privacy. Accommodating this joint task is difficult, but there have been a variety of efforts mounted recently to do so. The major approaches can be grouped into four broad categories – procedural, statistical, statutory and empirical – which are considered below. In discussing these, we adhere to a simple outline:

    direct interviews
    direct impersonal inquiry
    indirect inquiry: unobtrusive measures
    record linkage
    approaches based on law
    field research and development

Direct interviews

In many surveys or experiments, direct interviews with identified respondents are essential. The identification of the respondent generally serves only as an accounting device, to permit long-term follow-up of respondents and is not normally used to make evaluative judgements about the individual. The researcher or interviewer, moreover, usually offers to the respondent a promise that the information he or she supplies will remain confidential. Though most such inquiries are innocuous, the respondent may, in some instances, be exposed to some notable risk despite the promise. If the inquiry concerns very sensitive topics, the respondent may be embarrassed or discomfited by the request to respond whether response is voluntary or not, a difficulty which bears on social and professional ethic to reduce or eliminate the negative effects of inquiry. Where the inquiry bears on illegal or socially deviant behaviour, the risk may be more serious. The researcher's records on identified respondents may be subpoenaed or used in other legal proceedings, an event which may involve not only a breach of the original promise but disruption and destruction of the research as well.

To ameliorate and, in some cases, to eliminate such problems, a variety of statistical procedures have been developed. They permit one to elicit data even in an interview setting without actually gaining information about a particular respondent's state. They do, moreover, permit the statistician to develop elementary statistical summaries for the sample and the question at hand.

The best-known class of approaches is the randomised response tactic currently under development by Greenberg, Abernathy, Horvitz[6] and others in the United States, by Dalenius,[7] Lanke, Swensson, Svensson and Ericksson[8] in Sweden, by Warner[9] in Canada, Moors in Holland, and by others. In the simplest variation of the approach, the social scientist simultaneously presents a sensitive inquiry to an individual, for example, 'Did you cheat on your income taxes this year?', and an insensitive one, for example, 'Do you prefer potatoes over noodles?' The individual is then instructed to roll a dice and to respond to the first question if a one or two shows up, and to the second question if a three, four, five or six shows. He is also told to refrain from giving the interviewer any indication of which question was answered. When the process is carried out on two large samples of individuals, the odds on asking each question being changed from one sample to the next, and the instructions are followed by the respondent, it is possible to estimate the proportion of individuals in the sample who have cheated on their income-tax forms and the proportion who prefer noodles. In particular, knowing some fundamental laws of probability, given the odds on answering one or the other question in each sample, and given the observed proportion of 'yes' responses, the estimation is a simple matter of solving two independent equations in two unknowns.

The technique permits us to establish the statistical character of sensitive properties of groups of individuals. And, moreover, it does so *without* disclosing to the social scientist any information about a particular individual. Variations on the method are being field-tested in research on drug use, fertility control, gambling, use of alcohol and other sometimes sensitive topics in the United States, Canada and

Sweden. The basic method is being refined to make it more efficient in a statistical sense, more acceptable to the respondent in a social-psychological sense, and less vulnerable to corruption.

A related class of approaches is based on aggregation of response. The individual is asked not to respond to each item in a set of questions, but to respond in aggregated form to the set. In one variation, for example, the respondent may add up numerical values corresponding to each answer of each question in a set. If 'yes' is assigned a value of 1 and 'no' a value of −1, for example, the answer provided to a set of three questions each answerable with a yes or no is a single number whose permissible range is −3 to +3. In a second independent sample of the same population, respondents are asked to subtract item 1 from the sum of items 2 and 3, rather than add the numerical value of all responses. And in a third subsample, another linear combination is used, for example, subtracting item 2 from the sum corresponding to items 1 and 3. Given the yes responses in each sample, one needs only a little algebra − notably methods for solving a system of three simultaneous equations − to estimate the proportions of individuals in the total sample who have each of the three properties. The statistical properties of the estimates can also be derived easily.

Again, the technique permits one to elicit even sensitive information in direct interview situations without any deterministic linkage between an identified response to the researcher's question and the actual status of the individual. Deductive disclosure of an individual response is possible for some combinations of traits, but the possibility of that can be eliminated in more elaborate variations on the method. With some technical improvements, it probably can be applied to some longitudinal studies in which average relations among properties are essential.

The third class of statistical techniques which has received some attention is aggregation of the sample. The technique requires that one obtain data not on single identified individuals, but rather on very small and carefully constructed clusters of individuals. If the cluster's composition remains the same over time, each cluster can, under certain conditions, be regarded as a synthetic person, a composite of all the properties of the small set of individuals it comprises. Some informative data analyses can be conducted on those aggregates and, insofar as aggregation helps to assure anonymity of individual response, there is no depreciation of individual privacy.

The applications of sample microaggregation have so far been limited to economic research in commercial units. Banks, for example, may be reluctant to release information about their operations to any outside economist. They are willing, however, to have the social scientist analyse aggregates of banks in the interest of reconciling bank privacy with the need for the research. And, indeed, a major system of data maintenance and dissemination has been built up on this theme at the University of Wisconsin.[10]

Statistical methods such as these almost invariably increase the cost and complexity of research. At worst, they may occasionally reduce rather than enhance candour in reporting and restrict the types of analyses which can be done. Nonetheless, they are a promising vehicle for assuring the confidentiality of response without severe impairment of research quality.

Direct impersonal inquiry

Still other approaches are possible if the research is based on more impersonal forms of inquiry, such as mailed questionnaires, telephone surveys and the like. To the extent that inquiry can be depersonalised, the anxiety or embarrassment of a respondent *may* be attenuated, satisfying at least some ethical requirements for reducing the respondent's discomfort. To the extent that depersonalisation also involves breaking the linkage between a respondent's report and his identification, the approaches may help to eliminate conflicts between, say, government demands for identified records on respondents and the researcher's interest in sustaining a promise of confidentiality.

For instance, in longitudinal data collected periodically on the same sample of respondents, the simple device of using alias identifiers is obvious if under-utilised. Either numeric or nominal aliases may be created by the respondent and used consistently in response to permit intrasystem linkage. It may be created by social scientists, provided to the respondent, then purged from the social scientists' files to achieve the same ends. To decentralise the process, some neutral brokerage agency (a census bureau, a non-governmental agency) may similarly create an alias for the respondent and destroy its own records of any linkage between clear identification and alias. To assure validity of sampling and validity of response, special methods have been developed. The respondent may be asked to verify, at some other time, that he had in fact completed and returned the anonymous questionnaire, for example.

The alias-based strategies have been field-tested only occasionally, but with some success, in United States drug studies, political-attitude surveys and the like. Aside from mechanical problems, their major shortcoming is that they limit the researcher's ability to link the data provided under an alias with any other existing data on the same individuals for research purposes.

To accommodate some logistical problems as well as the limitation on intersystem linkage, procedures such as the link-file system have been developed (by, for example, Astin and Boruch[11]). In this technique, a dictionary of double aliases is created by the social scientist and given over for safekeeping to an independent agency. The decentralisation of the process enhances physical security and, if the dictionary custodian is legally entitled to resist governmental appropriation of files, the procedure assures that identifiable records are secure from even governmental interrogation. The dictionary is used as a basis for linking information which is periodically obtained from individuals. The main benefit of the strategy is that it reduces the social scientist's need to maintain longitudinal records on identified individuals, in general. It also reduces the time during which the social scientist has access to any given wave of data containing identifiers to an arbitrarily short period.

Indirect inquiry: unobtrusive measures

Methodological approaches under this rubric are focused on 'asking the right question', that is, so that risk to the respondent is reduced and, at the same time, the purpose of the research is at least partially accommodated. Pertinent tactics include rephrasing or transforming the inquiry and the response to minimise ethical or legal conflicts and substituting direct and intrusive inquiry with indirect questions that provoke fewer threats of third-party interest or social sanction.

There are several ways to transform the inquiry itself, depending on the sensitivity of the information and the way in which acquiring the data may conflict with ethical values. Time, for example, can be a vehicle for transformation. Retrospective reports are more likely than are reports about contemporary behaviour to be innocuous and less likely to be vulnerable to sanctions, if the information falls outside a legal or social statute of limitations. For example, it is very unlikely that disclosure of a college student's report that he drank beer during high-school years will subject the respondent to embarrassment, and almost certainly not to punitive action (in the United States at any rate).

Another simple device in transforming the inquiry is to make the question general rather than specific. The respondent who gives information about the exact time, place and circumstance in which he smoked marijuana is obviously more open to social harassment and legal prosecution than is the student who simply answers that he has at some time smoked marijuana.

Other and more indirect methods of acquiring valuable research information require no direct response from a subject (see Webb *et al.*, *Unobtrusive Measures*,[12] for a comprehensive description of some of these). They typically involve methods for collecting data that supplement or approximate the direct question to a respondent and are based on archival or incidental indicators of respondent behaviour and on unobtrusive observation. The methods have been described chiefly in the context of multiple operationism and social indicators, but there is no reason why they cannot be applied to the kinds of social research where direct inquiry and response may run some risk of disclosure of individually identifiable records, increased anxieties of respondents and similar problems.

Indirect measures of local marijuana and drug usage, for example, can be used as either strictly statistical indexes of environmental variables or as direct information on specific individuals. In either case, administrative, judicial, journalistic or police records may be used in statistical form as one index of local factors which affect an individual's use of marijuana. To the extent that such records are legally defined as public information, they are an economical and non-reactive measure of an individual's personal attributes. Rather than rely on archival records, the researcher can employ other indirect measures. He can, for example, observe retail sales or stock depletion in cigarette papers, mechanical cigarette-rolling devices and books (for example, *How to Grow Your Own*). An even less direct and more equivocal index of usage is local beer sales (see, for example, *New York Times*, 9 August 1970, 'Marijuana Turning Some Youths Away from Beer').

Other unobtrusive measures and translation methods can be developed. But for the moment we would be satisfied to have some good documentation on the uses of these strategies in social research, their success and the scientific problems they engender. In some cases, they may provoke further ethical conflicts (for example, unobtrusive measures), and we need to identify general conditions under which this will occur. Clearly, some methods degrade quality of information: asking a rather general question may be less intrusive, but responses will be less reliable on account of memory lapse, for example.

Record linkage

In some research, it is necessary or desirable that records maintained on the same individuals by different archives be linked. The linkage of hospital records with those of a researcher conducting long-term studies of the ageing process, for example, might be justified on grounds of economy, or on the grounds that hospital data are more accurate than retrospective reporting by respondents, and so on. Similarly, it may be desirable to link records from different administrative archives, hospitals or orphanages, for instance, to consolidate data on the young and disabled, so as to better plan support services. In either case, assurances of confidentiality made to the individual or to a vicar may be violated by such linkage. That violation may be questionable on grounds of social ethics, or law, as indeed it has been.

For those cases in which records from different archives must be linked, a variety of methods have been developed to permit linkage without violating the customs or law governing linkage. Among the better known systems for doing so is the 'mutually insulated file approach', used by Schwartz and Orleans.[13] Basically, the system involves two files of records operated under different auspices; all records are identified and there is some overlap between the samples of individuals on which the records are maintained. To accomplish the linkage, the first archive (assume it is the social scientist) cryptographically encodes the information portion of each record, producing a new file without meaning to any outsider, which is then transmitted to the second archive. This archive then matches the encoded file with its own records, based on the clear identifiers appearing in each record in both files. Upon completion of the match, identifiers are deleted and the linked records are returned to the social scientist. Initially, encoded sections of the merged record are then decoded and statistical analysis of the anonymous records conducted. The linkage, moreover, is accomplished without violating institutional regulations on disclosure and without violating the researcher's promise of confidentiality.

There are a large variety of simple procedural approaches such as these.[14] In some cases, they are vulnerable to corruption. Nonetheless, they are useful in a variety of research settings to assure confidentiality of data with respect to the researcher and outsiders, and they can be tailored to accommodate longitudinal or correlational studies. Their refinement has been undertaken by both research community and the government agencies to enhance the procedures' flexibility and protection level. Some of the refinements depend on statistical approaches considered earlier.

The linkage of records maintained on the same individuals by different government or private agencies has, of course, been a matter of consistent public concern, especially since the middle 1960s. Governmental regulation may prevent linkage even for research purposes where clear identifiers are used as a basis for linkage, for example, merging Internal Revenue Service data and Veterans Administration records is prohibited by each of the respective agencies. New law, such as the Privacy Act of 1974 and the Tax Reform Act of 1976, generally make linkage for research purposes even more difficult. Regardless of law, public reaction to linkage based on clear identifiers may be negative. As a consequence, there may be a natural judicial reluctance to tolerate any research based on record linkage. In *Roe vs. Ingraham* (403 F. Supp. 931 SDNY 1975), for example, psychiatric patients and parents testified as to the negative impact of state-wide reporting, that is, linkage and consolidation of records from regional psychiatric clinics, and data-bank requirements on their choices of treatments. Likewise in *Volkman vs. Miller* (383 NYS 2d 95 (App. Div. 3d Dept. 1976)), clients of a mental health outpatient clinic testified that they would not have entered therapy if they had known of a requirement that their names and certain treatment information would be compiled in a state-wide electronic data bank.[15] A few strategies for record linkage circumvent this kind of problem by using a consistent alpha-numeric alias for the patient, created by the patient or his clinician, as a basis for linking longitudinal records maintained by the state. That is, the local clinic uses the alias in all its dealings with the higher level of organisation and with the computerised data bank, rather than clear identifiers.

Approaches based on law

A distinctive approach to enhancing the privacy of the respondent in social research concerns formal legal action by legislators, the courts or governmental executive agencies. Such action is taken to ensure that when identifiable data must be collected for research purposes, the data will not be used for purposes other than research. As a practical matter, this means not only strengthening legal sanctions against theft or casual interrogation of research records, but also defining bounds on governmental appropriation of records. The actions are taken to reduce the likelihood that research records on identifiable individuals will be used to depreciate privacy any more than is normally required by research, and to isolate that research from temporary threats, legal or otherwise, when the potential benefits of research justify this course of action. The forms which such protection may take vary considerably; the major stereotypes are described here very briefly.

In some of the United States, a few public officials such as the governor are empowered by the state constitution or by other legislation to offer testimonial privilege to a social researcher. That privilege entitles the recipient to legally resist any legal effort to appropriate research records on identifiable individuals. The threat of appropriation may stem from a prosecutor's idea that he may use even an unwilling researcher as a criminal investigator. It may stem from arbitrary exercise of subpoena power by legislatures or the courts. In order to legally assure that data will not be so appropriated and possibly to increase the likelihood that individuals will co-operate in the research, a governor may then provide testimonial privilege on an *ad hoc* basis. For example, the governor of Vermont gave such privilege to researchers *and* respondents who participated in special roadside surveys of drivers. The survey objectives were to estimate the proportion of drinking drivers (blood tests were given to drivers), and the privilege was essential in getting a high co-operation rate. Drivers who were legally intoxicated were driven home by a policeman. No record of any identified individual's condition was lodged with any law-enforcement agency or other government archive, though drivers would normally be prosecuted under the law.

This sort of privilege can be applied in special cases where potential benefits of the survey are high and the relevant government executive is well enough informed to recognise the fact. However, we cannot always rely on expected benefits of research for, although some research may be quite important, its result may be uncertain. Nor can we always rely on the good offices of the public official, for the awarding of such privilege is discretionary and political factors may argue against it. In any event, discretionary privilege may be as susceptible to abuse from the researcher, just as it has been abused occasionally by some government executives.

Judicial discretion is another potential source of support for social scientists who, having collected identifiable data and having established a need for its maintenance, wish to secure it against non-research uses. At times, it has been possible for the scientist to legally resist a court-issued subpoena on grounds that the disclosure of identified records to the court would badly disable a major research effort. Evidence that breaches of confidentiality can be harmful to research efforts is sometimes available and can be used effectively to show cause why the records should not be used except in anonymous form. In fact, a similar line of argument has been used in a case involving the Negative Income Tax Experiments in New Jersey: the suspicion of fraud among people who happened to participate in the research led to a grand jury investigation and subpoena of research records on identified individuals.[16] Judicial discretion, like executive discretion, is by definition a bit arbitrary at best, and wildly unpredictable at worst. So its usefulness in protecting the confidentiality of data is not especially promising.

Legislative action in the form of concrete law is both feasible and, from the point of view of clarity and uniformity, very desirable. In particular, it is possible to build law to grant testimonial privilege to legitimate social scientists under well-defined conditions and uniformly-applied criteria. It is also possible to build into such law, sanctions against the fraudulent researcher or the corrupt social scientist or the public official who might attempt to appropriate research data for research purposes.

The 1970 Drug Abuse Act and the 1970 Alcohol Abuse Acts, for example, each carry a provision which permits the Attorney General to accord privilege to social scientists who are funded by the government to conduct research on those topics. Under the Public Health Services Act, persons engaged in research on mental health, including the use of alcohol and other proactive drugs, can be accorded privilege by the Secretary of Health, Education and Welfare to protect the privacy of individuals who are subjects of such research.[17]

These are new laws, enacted specifically to assure the confidentiality of social research records on identifiable individuals. They represent a limitation on the power of governmental access to social research records and a specification of the conditions under which the researcher may act. They represent a spirit of support for the social sciences as well as an appreciation for the negative impact which even legal appropriation of research records may exert on policy-relevant research. At least one such law has been tested by the courts, and its intent has been reaffirmed in that arena as well.

Field research and development

The strategies discussed here represent a few of the design solutions to the confidentiality-related problems encountered in social research. Some are under-utilised even by expert methodologists. Most solutions need to be engineered for the particular evaluation, to be field-tested along with other research methods, and to be refined in the interest of better research design.

More generally, there have been a variety of efforts undertaken recently to better understand the empirical nature of privacy, especially public reaction to the use of novel confidentiality-assuring procedures and to sensitive inquiry. The results of such are likely to contribute greatly to what we know about the process of eliciting social-research data.

Singer, for example, has mounted a well thought-out experiment, under the support of the National Science Foundation, to determine the extent to which response rate and validity of response in surveys are affected by level of information provided to the respondent, by requirements for a respondent signature and by promises of confidentiality.[18] That study will add a great deal to what is known already about those factors, especially for questions concerning sexual behaviour. Under the auspices of the National Academy of Sciences Commission of Federal Statistics, Panel on Privacy and Confidentiality, the United States Census Bureau is also conducting experiments along related but different lines. One experiment is designed to elicit badly-needed information about respondents' attitudes, and how their willingness to co-operate is affected by governmental rather than university sponsorship. A second experiment which, like the first, is based on large national probability samples, is designed to establish how co-operation rates in censuses are affected by a promise of confidentiality and the time at which census data may become accessible to scholarly researchers.[19]

Case studies of the matter are also being undertaken. The largest of such efforts, nearing completion, has been mounted by Carroll and Knerr[20] as a vehicle for documenting the incidence and character of disruption of social research, especially those generated by conflicts between research standards and law. The authors have managed, through a postal survey, to accumulate information on a large number of such incidents. One of the objectives of that study, to better understand how professional associations might affect the conduct of sensitive research and the outcome of such conflicts, is also being attacked by a Bureau for Social Science Research project under Robert Bower.[21] The latter effort involves consolidation and analysis of codes of ethics, ethical-policy papers etc., which have been produced by the various social, behavioural and related professional organisations.

Further Reading

The literature on privacy is a large and growing one. The following *short* and *highly selective* list of suggestions for further reading is intended as an introduction to that literature, but it cannot hope to be in any way comprehensive. The interested reader is advised to use a 'snowball' technique, as many of the works cited themselves contain further bibliographies. Particularly useful items are marked with an asterisk *. The selection reflects particularly the themes of the present volume and the interests and biases of the editor. It begins with general works on privacy and then goes on to those more specifically concerned with social research and privacy.

Introductory Reading

The following ten titles have been selected as together providing the best general overview of different aspects of the subject of privacy, both in general and in relation to social research.

*A. F. WESTIN, *Privacy and Freedom*, New York, Atheneum, 1967.

*S. WHEELER, *On Record: files and dossiers in American life*, New York, Russell Sage Foundation, 1969.

* *Report of the Committee on Privacy* (Chairman, Kenneth Younger), Cmnd. 5012, London, HMSO, 1972.

* *Records, Computers and the Rights of Citizens*, Cambridge, Mass., MIT Press, 1973.

*J. RULE, *Private Lives and Public Surveillance*, London, Allen Lane, 1973.

*J. M. ADAMS and D. H. HADEN, *Social Effects of Computer Use and Misuse*, New York, Wiley, 1976.

*PRIVACY PROTECTION STUDY COMMISSION, *Personal Privacy in an Information Society*, Washington DC, US Government Printing Office, 1977.

*J. C. YOUNG (ed.), *Privacy*, Chichester, Wiley, 1978.

*D. H. FLAHERTY, *Privacy and Government Data Banks*, London, Mansell Scientific, 1979.

*R. F. BORUCH and J. S. CECIL, *Assuring Confidentiality in Social Research*, Philadelphia, University of Pennsylvania Press, 1979.

Bibliographies

*T. DALENIUS, *Information Privacy and Statistics: a topical bibliography*, Washington DC, US Department of Commerce, Bureau of the Census Working Paper 41, 1978 (includes a bibliography of bibliographies).

*D. H. FLAHERTY, E. H. HANIS and S. P. MITCHELL, *Privacy and Access to Government Data for Research: an international bibliography*, London, Mansell Scientific, 1979.

*R. T. BOWER and P. DE GASPARIS, *Ethics in Social Research: protecting the interests of human subjects*, New York, Praeger, 1978.

H. A. LATIN, *Privacy: a selected bibliography and topical index of social science materials*, New Jersey, Fred B. Rothman, 1976.

M. MACCAFFERTY, *The Right to Know*, London, Aslib, 1976.

1. Popular Works on Privacy

H. BRENTON, *The Privacy Invaders*, New York, Coward-McCann, 1964.

M. ERNST and A. SCHWARZ, *Privacy: the right to be let alone*, London, MacGibbon and Kee, 1968.

P. HEWITT, *Privacy: the information gatherers*, London, National Council for Civil Liberties, 1977.

M. JONES (ed.), *Privacy*, Newton Abbot, David and Charles, 1974.

A. LEMOND and R. FRY, *No Place to Hide*, New York, St Martin's Press, 1975.

D. MADGWICK and T. SMYTHE, *The Invasion of Privacy*, London, Pitman, 1974.

V. PACKARD, *The Naked Society*, New York, McKay, 1964.

J. M. ROSENBURG, *The Death of Privacy*, New York, Random House, 1969.

L. A. SOBEL (ed.), *War on Privacy*, New York, Facts on File, 1976.

A. A. THOMPSON, *Big Brother in Britain Today*, London, Joseph, 1970.

General works on privacy

I. ALTMAN, 'Privacy: a conceptual analysis', *Environment and Behaviour*, **8**, 1976, pp. 7–29.

A. BRITTAN, *The Privatised World*, London, Routledge, 1978.

M. CRANSTON, *The Right to Privacy*, London, Liberal Publications for the Unservile State Group, 1975.

S. Dash et al., *The Eavesdroppers*, New Brunswick, New Jersey, Rutgers University Press, 1959.

D. H. Flaherty, *Privacy in Colonial New England*, Charlottesville, University Press of Virginia, 1972.

P. Halmos, *Solitude and Privacy: a study of social isolation*, London, Routledge, 1952.

E. Josephson, 'Notes on the sociology of privacy', *Humanitas*, **11**, February 1975, pp. 1–25.

H. Kalven Jr., 'The problem of privacy in the year 2000', *Daedalus*, **96**, 1962, pp. 876–82.

E. V. Long, *The Intruders*, New York, Praeger, 1966.

R. P. Lowry, 'Towards a sociology of secrecy and security systems', *Social Problems*, **19**, 1972, pp. 437–50.

*S. T. Margulis (ed.), 'Privacy', in D. H. Carson (general ed.), *Man-Environment Interactions: Evaluation and Applications, Part II*, Stroudsberg, Penn., Dowden Hutchinson and Ross, 1974, pp. 1–124.

A. R. Miller, *The Assault on Privacy*, Ann Arbor, University of Michigan Press, 1971.

*Privacy Protection Study Commission, *Personal Privacy in an Information Society*, Washington DC, US Government Printing Office, 1977.

Report of the Committee on Privacy, Cmnd. 5012, London, HMSO, 1972.

J. Rule, *The Politics of Privacy*, New York, New American Library, 1979.

*J. Rule, *Private Lives and Public Surveillance*, London, Allen Lane, 1973.

B. Schwarz, 'The social psychology of privacy', *American Journal of Sociology*, **73**, 1968, pp. 741–52.

E. Shils, *The Torment of Secrecy*, Glencoe, Ill., Free Press, 1956.

E. Shils, 'Privacy: its constitution and vicissitudes', *Law and Contemporary Problems*, **31**, 1966, pp. 281–306.

A. Simmel, 'Privacy', in *International Encyclopaedia of the Social Sciences*, New York, Macmillan, 1968.

C. Warren and B. Laslett, 'Privacy and secrecy: a conceptual comparison', *Journal of Social Issues*, **33**, 1977, pp. 43–51.

*A. Westin, *Privacy and Freedom*, New York, Atheneum, 1967.

*S. Wheeler (ed.) *On Record: files and dossiers in American life*, New York, Russell Sage Foundation, 1969.

*J. B. Young (ed.), *Privacy: a multidisciplinary study*, Chichester, Wiley, 1978.

Computers, data banks and privacy

*J. M. Adams and D. H. Haden, *Social Effects of Computer Use and Misuse*, New York, Wiley, 1976 (includes bibliography).

W. G. Collin, *Computers and Privacy*, Manchester, National Computing Centre, 1976.

Computers and Privacy, Cmnd. 6353, London, HMSO, 1975.

Computers: Safeguards for Privacy, Cmnd. 6354, London, HMSO, 1975.

O. E. DIAL and E. M. GOLDBERG, *Privacy, Security and Computers: guidelines for public information systems*, New York, Praeger, 1975.

A. S. DOUGLAS, *Computers and Society*, London School of Economics, 1973.

*C. C. GOTLEIB and A. BORODIN, *Social Issues in Computing*, New York, Academic Press, 1973.

M. GREENBERGER (ed.), *Computers, Communications and the Public Interest*, Baltimore, Johns Hopkins University Press, 1975.

L. J. HOFFMAN, *Modern Methods for Computer Security and Privacy*, Englewood Cliffs, Prentice Hall, 1977.

C. JENKINS and B. SHERMAN, *Computers and the Unions*, London, Longman, 1977.

J. MARTIN, *Security, Accuracy and Privacy in Computer Systems*, Englewood Cliffs, Prentice Hall, 1973.

J. MARTIN and A. R. NORMAN, *The Computerised Society*, Harmondsworth, Penguin, 1973.

*A. R. MILLER, *The Assault on Privacy: computers, data banks and dossiers*, Ann Arbor, University of Michigan Press, 1971.

Policy Issues in Data Protection and Privacy: concepts and perspectives, OECD Informatics Studies 10, Paris, OECD, 1976.

Privacy and Computers, Ottawa, Information Canada, 1972.

Records, Computers and the Rights of Citizens (US Department of HEW Advisory Committee), Cambridge, Mass., MIT Press, 1973.

B. C. ROWE (ed.), *Privacy, Computers and You*, Manchester, National Computer Centre, 1972.

*P. SIEGHART, *Privacy and Computers*, London, Latimer, 1976.

C. TAPPER, *Computers and the Law*, London, Weidenfeld, 1973, esp. chapter 3.

*I. TAVISS (ed.), *The Computer Impact*, Englewood Cliffs, Prentice Hall, 1970.

M. WARNER and M. STONE, *The Data Bank Society: computers, organisation and social freedom*, London, Allen and Unwin, 1970.

A. E. WESSELL, *The Social Use of Information: ownership and access*, New York, Wiley, 1976.

A. F. WESTIN, 'Computers and the protection of privacy', *Technological Review*, **71**, 1969, pp. 32–7.

A. F. WESTIN (ed.), *Information Technology in a Democracy*, Cambridge, Mass., Harvard University Press, 1971.

*A. F. WESTIN and M. A. BAKER, *Data Banks in a Free Society: computers, record-keeping and privacy*, New York, Quadrangle, 1972.

S. WHEELER (ed.), *On Record: files and dossiers in American life*, New York, Russell Sage Foundation, 1969.

Report of the Committee on Data Protection (chairman, Sir Norman Lindop), Cmnd. 7341, London, HMSO, 1978.

The law and privacy

There is a very large literature on the law and privacy in different societies. This section only contains a very few general references. A useful survey, by the International Commission of Jurists, is

"The Legal Protection of Privacy: a comparative study of ten countries', *International Social Science Journal*, **24, 1972, pp. 417–583.

C. F. O. CLARKE, *Private Rights and the Freedom of the Individual*, Oxford, Ditchley Foundation, 1972.

*G. DWORKIN, 'Privacy and the Law', in J. B. Young (ed.), *Privacy*, Chichester, Wiley, 1978, pp. 113–36.

S. H. HOFSTADTER and G. HOROWITZ, *The Right of Privacy*, New York, Central Book, 1964.

*JUSTICE, *Privacy and the Law*, London, Stevens, 1970.

L. LUSKY, 'Invasion of privacy: a clarification of concepts', *Columbia Law Review*, **72**, 1972, pp. 693–710.

'Protecting confidentiality of pre-trial psychiatric disclosures', *New York University Law Review*, **51**, 1976, pp. 409–45.

S. STROMHOLM, *Rights of Privacy and Rights of Personality*, Stockholm, P. A. Norstedt and Soners, 1967.

C. TAPPER, *Computers and the Law*, London, Weidenfeld, 1973, esp. chapter 3.

*S. D. WARREN and L. D. BRANDEIS, 'The Right to Privacy', *Harvard Law Review*, **4**, 1890, pp. 193–220.

*A. WESTIN, *Privacy and Freedom*, New York, Atheneum, 1967.

2. Social Science and Privacy in General

J. A. BARNES, *Who Should Know What? social science, privacy and politics*, Harmondsworth, Penguin, 1979.

*R. F. BORUCH and J. S. CECIL, *Assuring Confidentiality in Social Research*, Philadelphia, University of Pennsylvania Press, 1979.

R. T. BOWER *et al.*, *Ethics in Social Research*, New York, Praeger, 1978.

*T. DALENIUS and A. KLEVMARKEN (eds), *Personal Integrity and the Need for Data in the Social Sciences* (proceedings of the Hasselby Slott symposium), Stockholm, Swedish Council for Social Science Research, 1976.

E. DIENER and R. CRANDALL, *Ethics in Social and Behavioural Research*, University of Chicago Press, 1978.

*D. FLAHERTY, *Privacy and Government Data Banks: an international perspective*, London, Mansell Scientific, 1979.

J. F. GALLIHER, 'The protection of human subjects', *American Sociologist*, **8**, 1973, pp. 93–100.

T. E. HEDRICK *et al.*, 'On ensuring the availability of evaluative data for secondary analysis', *Policy Sciences*, **9**, 1978, pp. 259–80.

E. JOSEPHSON, 'Notes on the sociology of privacy', *Humanitas*, **11**, February 1975, pp. 1–25.

H. C. KELMAN, *A Time to Speak: on human values and social research*, San Francisco, Jossey Bass, 1968.

H. C. KELMAN, 'Privacy and research with human beings', *Journal of Social Issues*, **33**, 1977, pp. 163–95.

Limits of Scientific Inquiry, special issue of *Daedalus*, Spring 1978.

P. NEJELSKI (ed.), *Social Research in Conflict with Law and Ethics*, Cambridge, Mass., Ballinger, 1976.

O. OYEN, 'Social research and the protection of privacy', *Acta Sociologica*, **19**, 1976, pp. 249–61.

*Policy Issues in Data Protection and Privacy: concepts and perspectives, OECD Informatics Studies 10, Paris, OECD, 1976.

'Privacy and Behavioural Research: report of the panel on privacy and behavioural research', *American Psychologist*, **22**, 1967, pp. 345–9.

'Privacy as a Behavioural Phenomenon', special issue of the *Journal of Social Issues*, **33**, no. 3, 1977.

O. M. RUEBHAUSEN and O. G. BRIM JR., 'Privacy and behavioural research', *American Psychologist*, **21**, 1966, pp. 423–37.

E. SHILS, 'Privacy and Power', in *Center and Periphery*, University of Chicago Press, 1975, pp. 317–44.

*E. SHILS, 'Social Inquiry and the Autonomy of the Individual', in D. Lerner (ed.), *The Human Meaning of the Social Sciences*, New York, Meridian, 1959, pp. 114–57.

M. USEEM and G. T. MARX, 'Ethical Dilemmas and Political Considerations in Social Research', in R. B. Smith (ed.), *A Handbook of Social Science Methods: Qualitative Methods*, New York, Irvington Press, 1978.

Social surveys and privacy

B. A. BAILOR and C. N. LANPHIER, *Development of Survey Methods to Assess Survey Practices*, Washington DC, American Statistical Association, 1978.

R. F. BORUCH, 'Assuring confidentiality of responses in social research', *American Sociologist*, **6**, 1971, pp. 308–10.

R. F. BORUCH, 'Educational research and the confidentiality of data', *Sociology of Education*, **44**, 1971, pp. 59–85.

R. W. CONANT and M. A. LEVIN (eds), *Problems of Research on Community Violence*, New York, Praeger, 1969.

H. S. CONRAD, 'Clearance of questionnaires with respect to invasion of privacy', *American Psychologist*, **22**, 1967, pp. 356–9.

E. D. GOLDFIELD *et al.*, 'Privacy and confidentiality as factors in survey response', *Proceedings of the American Statistical Association: Social Statistics Section, Part 1, 1977*, Washington DC, American Statistical Association, pp. 219–29.

G. HAWKER, 'Privacy and Survey Research', *SSRC Newsletter*, **18**, March 1973, pp. 7–8.

A. J. KING and A. J. SPECTOR, 'Ethical and legal aspects of survey research', *American Psychologist*, **18**, 1963, pp. 204–8.

*MARKET RESEARCH SOCIETY WORKING GROUP, 'Response rates in sample surveys', *Journal of the Market Research Society*, **18**, 1976, pp. 113–42.

*D. MONTERO, 'Research among racial and cultural minorities', *Journal of Social Issues*, **33**, 1977, pp. 1–10 (contains bibliography).

National Central Bureau of Statistics and the Public, Survey Research Institute of the Swedish National Central Bureau of Statistics, Stockholm, 1977, mimeo.

*P. REDFERN, 'The Different Roles of Population Censuses and Interview Surveys, especially in the UK context', *International Statistical Institute Proceedings 1973*, 4.2, pp. 1–18.

*O. M. RUEBHAUSEN and O. G. BRIM JR., 'Privacy and behavioural research', *American Psychologist*, **21**, 1966, pp. 423–37.

*E. SINGER, 'Informed Consent', *American Sociological Review*, **43**, 1978, pp. 144–62.

G. F. STREIB, 'Privacy in the research interview', *Journal of Comparative Family Studies*, **4**, 1973, pp. 276–85.

H. WARE and J. C. CALDWELL, 'Confidentiality, privacy and sensitivity in household surveys', *Australian Journal of Statistics*, **14**, 1972, pp. 197–203.

D. I. WARREN, 'Some observations from post-riot Detroit: the role of social research in contemporary racial conflict', *Phylon*, **34**, 1973, pp. 171–86.

Population censuses and privacy

F. BANFIELD, '1971 Census: voluntary survey on income', *Population Trends*, **12**, 1978, pp. 18–21.

J. BLAKE, 'Census under censure', *New Society*, 16 March 1972, pp. 541–2.

D. V. GLASS, *Numbering the People: the eighteenth century population controversy and the development of census and vital statistics in Britain*, Farnborough, Saxon House, 1973.

C. HAKIM, *Census Confidentiality, Microdata and Census Analysis*, London, OPCS Occasional Paper No. 3, 1978.

T. LINEHAN, 'Problems of confidentiality with particular reference to population censuses', *Statistical Reporter*, Autumn 1972, pp. 17–21.

H. P. MILLER, 'Considerations determining the content of the 1970 Census', *Demography*, **4**, 1967, pp. 744–52.

1976 Census of Population, Cmnd. 5906, London, HMSO, 1975. (Three months later this census was cancelled for reasons of economy.)

* *1981 Census of Population*, Cmnd. 7146, London, HMSO, 1978.

*C. W. PARSONS (ed.), *America's Uncounted People: report of the Advisory Committee on problems of census enumeration*, Washington DC, National Academy of Sciences, 1972, esp. chapters 4 and 5.

*P. REDFERN, 'The Different Roles of Population Censuses and Interview Surveys, especially in the UK context', *International Statistical Institute Proceedings 1973*, 4.2, pp. 1–18.

* *Security of the Census of Population*, Cmnd. 5365, London, HMSO, 1973, containing the *Report* by the British Computer Society, the *Report* by the nominees of the Royal Statistical Society, and the government's response.

Statistical data and privacy

*AMERICAN STATISTICAL ASSOCIATION, 'Report of the Ad Hoc Committee on Privacy and Confidentiality', *American Statistician*, **31**, 1977, pp. 59–78.

*O. AUKRUST and S. NORDBOTTEN, 'Files of individual data and their potentialities for social research', *Review of Income and Wealth*, **19**, 1973, pp. 189–201.

R. BACHI and R. BARON, 'Confidentiality problems related to data banks', *Journal of the International Statistical Institute*, 1969.

R. L. BISCOE (ed.), *Data Bases, Computers and the Social Sciences*, New York, Wiley, 1970.

R. F. BORUCH, 'Strategies for eliciting and merging confidential research data', *Policy Sciences*, **3**, 1972, pp. 275–97.

R. F. BORUCH, 'Record Linkage in Longitudinal and Correlational Research: its justification and implications for individual privacy', in T. Dalenius and A. Klevmarken (eds), *Personal Integrity and the Need for Data in the Social Sciences*, Stockholm, Swedish Council for Social Science Research, 1976, pp. 139–73.

*R. F. BORUCH and J. S. CECIL, *Assuring Confidentiality in Social Research*, Philadelphia, University of Pennsylvania Press, 1979.

*D. T. CAMPBELL, R. F. BORUCH *et al.*, 'Confidentiality-preserving modes of access to files and interfile exchange for useful statistical analysis', *Evaluation Quarterly*, **1**, 1977, pp. 269–300.

T. DALENIUS, 'The invasion of privacy problem and statistics production: an overview', *Sartryck ur Statistisk Tidskrift*, **3**, 1974, pp. 213–25.

J. W. DUNCAN, 'The impact of privacy legislation on the federal statistical system', *Review of Public Data Use*, **3**, 1975, pp. 51–3.

J. W. DUNCAN, 'Confidentiality and the future of the US statistical system', *American Statistician*, **30**, 1976, pp. 54–9.

Federal Statistics: Report of the President's Commission, 2 vols, Washington DC, US Government Printing Office, 1971, esp. Privacy and Confidentiality, **I**, pp. 195–218, and Statistics and the Problem of Privacy, **II**, pp. 339–66.

I. P. FELLEGI, 'On the question of statistical confidentiality', *Journal of the American Statistical Association*, **67**, 1972, pp. 7–18.

C. M. FIRTH, 'Confidentiality of personal information supplied to public authorities', *GLC Research and Intelligence Quarterly Bulletin*, **10**, March 1970, pp. 5–11.

D. H. FLAHERTY, *Final Report of the Bellagio Conference 1977 on Privacy, Confidentiality and the Use of Government Microdata for Research and Statistical Purposes*, reprinted in *Statistical Reporter*, **78-8**, May 1978, pp. 274–8, and *Journal of the Royal Statistical Society, Series A*, **141**, 1978, pp. 401–6.

*D. H. FLAHERTY, *Privacy and Government Data Banks: an international perspective*, London, Mansell Scientific, 1979.

L. FRANKEL, 'Statistics and People: the statistician's responsibilities', *Journal of the American Statistical Association*, **71**, 1976, pp. 9–16.

R. I. HOFFERBERT and J. M. CLUB, *Social Science Data Archives*, London, Sage, 1977.

SIR CLAUS MOSER, 'The role of the Central Statistical Office in assisting public policy makers', *American Statistician*, **30**, 1976, pp. 59–67.

SIR CLAUS MOSER, 'The environment in which statistics offices will work in ten years' time', *Statistical News*, **38**, 1977, pp. 1–6.

*OFFICE OF FEDERAL STATISTICAL STANDARDS AND POLICY, *A Framework for Planning US Federal Statistics in the 1980s*, Washington DC, US Government Printing Office, 1978, chapter 21 on confidentiality of statistical and research data, pp. 255–83.

J. TUKEY, 'Methodology and the statistician's responsibility for both accuracy and relevance', *Statistical Reporter*, **76**, 1976, pp. 253–62.

H. P. WYN, 'Freedom of Statistical Information', *Journal of the Royal Statistical Society, Series A*, **141**, 1978, pp. 1–13.

Health records and health statistics: an example

E. D. ACHESON, *Medical Record Linkage*, Oxford University Press, 1967.

E. D. ACHESON (ed.), *Record Linkage in Medicine*, Edinburgh, Livingstone, 1968.

AMERICAN PSYCHIATRIC ASSOCIATION, 'Position statement on the need for preserving confidentiality of medical records in any health care system', *American Journal of Psychiatry*, **128**, April 1972.

R. DOLL, 'Public benefit and personal privacy: the problems of medical investigation in the community', *Proceedings of the Royal Medical Society*, **67**, December 1974.

D. H. FLAHERTY, *Privacy and Government Data Banks*, New York, Science Associates/International, 1979.

E. M. LASKA (ed.), *Safeguarding Psychiatric Privacy: computer systems and their uses*, New York, Wiley, 1975.

MEDICAL RESEARCH COUNCIL, 'Responsibility in the use of medical information for research', _British Medical Journal_, 27 January 1973.

*_Report of the Committee on Privacy_, Cmnd. 5012, London, HMSO, 1972, pp. 108–15.

D. P. RICE, 'The role of statistics in the development of health care policy', _American Statistician_, **31**, 1977, pp. 101–6.

ROYAL COLLEGE OF PSYCHIATRISTS, 'Confidentiality of psychiatric data in medical information systems', _British Journal of Psychiatry_, **128**, 1976.

*US NATIONAL BUREAU OF STANDARDS, _Computers, Health Records and Citizens Rights_ (by A. F. Westin), Washington DC, NBS Monograph 157, 1976.

*A. F. WESTIN, _Health Care and the Right to Privacy_, New York, Quadrangle, 1976.

The proposed United States National Data Centre

The Computer and Invasion of Privacy: US Government hearings on the proposed National Data Centre, New York, Arno, 1966.

E. S. DUNN JR., 'Review of Proposals for a National Data Centre', _Statistical Evaluation Report no. 6_, Washington DC, US Office of Statistical Standards, 1965.

E. S. DUNN JR., 'The idea of a National Data Centre and the issue of personal privacy', _American Statistician_, **21**, 1967, pp. 21–7.

E. S. DUNN JR., _Social Information Processing and Statistical Systems: change and reform_, New York, Wiley, 1974.

E. GLASER _et al._, 'The design of a federal statistical data centre', _American Statistician_, **21**, 1967, pp. 11–20.

C. KAYSEN, 'Data Banks and Dossiers', _The Public Interest_, **7**, 1967, pp. 52–60.

C. KAYSEN (CHAIRMAN), 'Report of the task force on storage of and access to government statistics', _American Statistician_, **23**, 1969.

R. RUGGLES (CHAIRMAN), _Report of the Committee on the Preservation and Use of Economic Data_, New York, SSRC, 1965.

J. SAWYER and H. SCHECHTER, 'Computers, privacy and the National Data Centre', _American Psychologist_, **23**, 1968, pp. 810–18.

Informed consent in social research

G. J. ANNAS, L. H. GLANTZ and B. F. KATZ, _Informed Consent to Human Experimentation: the subject's dilemma_, Cambridge, Mass., Ballinger, 1977.

*B. BARBER _et al._, _Research on Human Subjects_, New York, Russell Sage Foundation, 1973.

S. BOK, 'Freedom and Risk', _Daedalus_, Spring 1978, pp. 115–27.

*R. BOWER _et al._ (eds), _Ethics in Social Research: protecting the interests of human subjects_, New York, Praeger, 1978.

L. H. FRANKEL, 'Statistics and People – the statistician's responsibility', *Journal of the American Statistical Association,* **71,** 1976, pp. 9–16.

B. H. GRAY, *Human Subjects in Medical Experimentation,* New York, Wiley, 1975.

B. H. GRAY, 'Complexities of Informed Consent', *Annals of the American Academy of Political and Social Science,* May 1978, pp. 37–48.

L. HUMPHRIES, *Tearoom Trade,* Chicago, Aldine, revised edition 1975, esp. appendix with contributions by D. P. Warwick and others.

H. C. KELMAN, 'The rights of the subject in social research', *American Psychologist,* **27,** 1972, pp. 989–1016.

P. NEJELSKI (ed.), *Social Research in Conflict with Law and Ethics,* Cambridge, Mass., Ballinger, 1976.

L. RAINWATER and D. J. PITTMAN, 'Ethical problems in studying a politically sensitive and deviant community', *Social Problems,* **14,** 1967, pp. 357–66.

Responsibility in Investigations on Human Subjects, London, Medical Research Council, 1963.

P. D. REYNOLDS, 'On the protection of human subjects and social science', *International Social Science Journal,* **24,** 1972, pp. 693–719.

A. M. RIVLIN and P. M. TIMPANE (eds), *Ethical and Legal Issues in Social Experimentation,* Washington DC, Brookings Institution, 1975.

*E. SINGER, 'Informed consent: consequences for response rate and response quality in social surveys', *American Sociological Review,* **43,** 1978, pp. 144–62.

J. P. SWAZEY, 'Protecting the "animal of necessity": limits to inquiry in clinical investigations', *Daedalus,* Spring 1978, pp. 129–45.

Trials of War Criminals before the Nuremberg Military Tribunals under Control Council law no. 10, the Medical Case (US v. Brandt), Vol. II, Washington DC, US Government Printing Office, 1949.

D. P. WARWICK, 'Social scientists ought to stop lying', *Psychology Today,* **8,** February 1975, pp. 38ff.

W. WOLFENSBERGER, 'Ethical issues in research with human subjects', *Science,* **155,** no. 3758, 6 January 1967, pp. 47–51.

Codes of professional ethics: examples

AMERICAN ANTHROPOLOGICAL ASSOCIATION, *Principles of Professional Responsibility,* Washington DC, 1971.

AMERICAN ASSOCIATION FOR PUBLIC OPINION RESEARCH, 'Code of Professional Ethics and Practices', *Public Opinion Quarterly,* **24,** 1960, pp. 529–30.

AMERICAN PSYCHOLOGICAL ASSOCIATION, AD HOC COMMITTEE ON ETHICAL STANDARDS IN PSYCHOLOGICAL RESEARCH, *Ethical Principles in the Conduct of Research with Human Participants,* Washington DC, 1973.

ASSOCIATION OF MARKET SURVEY ORGANISATIONS, LONDON, *Code of Standards*.
BRITISH COMPUTER SOCIETY, *Code of Good Practice*, London, 1972.
BRITISH SOCIOLOGICAL ASSOCIATION, *Statement of Ethical Principles and their application to sociological practice*, London, 1973.
MARKET RESEARCH SOCIETY OF GREAT BRITAIN, *Code of Conduct*, London, 1976.

For a review, see:
R. T. BOWER *et al.* (eds), *Ethics in Social Research*, New York, Praeger, 1978.
J. KATZ, *Experimentation with Human Beings*, New York, Russell Sage, 1972.

Social-research data and the law

R. F. BORUCH and J. S. CECIL, *Assuring Confidentiality in Social Research*, Philadelphia, University of Pennsylvania Press, 1979.
*R. T. BOWER (ed.), *Ethics in Social Research: protecting the interests of human subjects*, New York, Praeger, 1978.
J. E. CARROLL and C. R. KNERR, 'A report of the APSA confidentiality in social research project', *Political Science*, Summer 1975, pp. 258–61.
F. W. HONDIUS, *Emerging Data Protection in Europe*, Amsterdam, North Holland, 1975.
*D. N. KERSHAW and J. C. SMALL, 'Data confidentiality and privacy: lessons from the New Jersey Negative Income Tax Experiment', *Public Policy*, **20**, 1972, pp. 257–80.
*P. MULLER (ed.), *Emerging Data Protection and the Social Sciences need for access to data*, Cologne, CESSDA/IFDO, 1978.
N. L. NATHANSON, 'Social science, administrative law and the Information Act of 1966', *Social Problems*, **21**, 1973, pp. 21–37.
P. NEJELSKI and K. FINSTERBUSCH, 'The Prosecutor and Researcher', *Social Problems*, **21**, 1973, pp. 3–21.
P. NEJELSKI and L. M. LERMAN, 'A researcher-subject testimonial privilege: what to do before the subpoena arrives', *Wisconsin Law Review*, 1971, pp. 1085–1148.
*P. NEJELSKI (ed.), *Social Research in Conflict with Law and Ethics*, Cambridge, Mass., Ballinger, 1976.

Notes and References

Chapter 1

1. *Report of the Committee on Privacy* (Chairman Sir Kenneth Younger), Cmnd. 5012, July 1972, London, HMSO, pp. 229–30.

2. Alan F. Westin, *Privacy and Freedom*, London, Bodley Head, 1970, p. 7.

3. US Department of Health Education and Welfare, *Records, Computers and the Rights of Citizens*, Cambridge, Mass., MIT Press, 1973, pp. 40–1.

4. Although this book discusses censuses, which are compulsory, the same consideration applies, hence census-takers are particularly careful, in their planning, to ensure that the questions which they ask will secure public acceptability. The mutuality of the relationship is taken into account at the planning stage.

5. Quoted below, p. 136.

6. Cf. *Security of the Census of Population*, Cmnd. 5365, HMSO, 1973.

7. Cf. E. Shils, 'Privacy: its constitution and vicissitudes', *Law and Contemporary Problems*, **31**, 1966, p. 283, note 1.

8. It has been argued that there is also a 'private' realm of secrecy. Cf. C. Warren and B. Laslett, 'Privacy and secrecy: a conceptual comparison', *Journal of Social Issues*, **33**, 1977, pp. 43–51, who discuss stigmatised or disadvantaged minorities that use secrecy to conceal their behaviour. However, the examples used of sexual minorities are doubtfully generalisable.

9. For a recent British example, cf. H. P. Wyn, 'Freedom of statistical information', *JRSS, A*, **141,** 1978, pp. 1–13.

10. For a discussion of this trend, cf. M. Bulmer (ed.), *Social Policy Research*, London, Macmillan, 1978, Chapter 1.

11. For an historical survey, see C. A. Moser and G. Kalton, *Survey Methods in Social Investigation*, London, Heinemann, 1971, Chapter 1.

12. Cf. J. M. Adams and D. H. Haden, *Social Effects of Computer Use and Misuse*, New York, Wiley, 1976, Chapter 3, 'The history of computation'.

13. D. Madgwick and T. Smythe, *The Invasion of Privacy*, London, Pitman, 1974, p. 20.

14. For a succinct introduction to computers and privacy in general, see Alan F. Westin and M. A. Baker, *Data Banks in a Free Society: computers, record-keeping and privacy*, New York, Quadrangle Books, 1972, Chapter 1.

15. Cf. *Computers and Privacy*, Cmnd. 6353, HMSO, 1975, p. 4.

16. For general surveys, see Westin and Baker, op. cit.; US Department of Health Education and Welfare, *Records, Computers and the Rights of Citizens*, op. cit.; C. C. Gotlieb and A. A. Borodin, *Social Issues in Computing*, New York, Academic Press, 1973; A. R. Miller, *The Assault on Privacy*, Ann Arbor, Michigan, University of Michigan Press, 1971; I. Taviss (ed.), *The Computer Impact*, Englewood Cliffs, Prentice Hall, 1970.

17. See *1981 Census of Population*, Cmnd. 7146, London, HMSO, 1978, p. 3.

18. For full details, see Bibliography, pp. 250–2.

19. For full details, see Bibliography, pp. 251–2.

20. *Report of the Committee on Privacy*, op. cit.

21. A. F. Westin and M. A. Baker, op. cit., pp. 465–85.

22. Privacy Protection Study Commission, *Personal Privacy in an Information Society*, Washington DC, US Government Printing Office, July 1977, pp. 3, 14.

23. American Statistical Association, 'Report of Ad Hoc Committee on Privacy and Confidentiality', *The American Statistician*, **31**, May 1977, p. 60.

24. O. M. Ruebhausen and O. C. Brim, 'Privacy and Behavioural Research', *The American Psychologist*, **21**, 1966, p. 426.

25. M. Rein, *Social Science and Public Policy*, Harmondsworth, Penguin, 1977, p. 259.

26. 'Privacy and Behavioural Research: preliminary summary of the Report of the Panel on Privacy and Behavioural Research', *The American Psychologist*, **22**, 1967, pp. 347–8.

27. Ruebhausen and Brim, op. cit., p. 428.

28. Ibid.

29. H. C. Kelman, 'The Rights of the Subject in Social Research', *The American Psychologist*, **27**, 1972, p. 989. See also H. C. Kelman, 'Privacy and Research with Human Beings', *Journal of Social Issues*, **33**, 1977, pp. 169–95.

30. *Trials of War Criminals before the Nuremberg Military Tribunals under Control Council Law number 10, the Medical Case* (United States v. Brandt), vol. II, Washington DC, US Government Printing Office, 1949.

31. J. P. Swazey, 'Protecting the "Animal of Necessity": limits to inquiry in clinical investigation', *Daedalus*, Spring 1978, pp. 129–45.

32. Ibid, and B. J. Culliton, 'Science's restive public', *Daedalus*, Spring 1978, pp. 147–56.

33. Cf. 'Privacy and Behavioural Research . . .', op. cit. and Ruebhausen and Brim, op. cit.

34. 'Privacy and Behavioural Research . . .', op. cit., p. 347.

35. For a discussion of one such case, see D. N. Kershaw and J. C. Small, 'Data Confidentiality and Privacy: Lessons from the New Jersey Negative Income Tax Experiment', *Public Policy*, **20**, 1972, pp. 257–80.

36. For a fuller exposition and analysis, see E. Shils, 'Privacy and Power', in *Center and Periphery: Essays on Macrosociology*, University of Chicago Press, 1975, pp. 317–44.

Chapter 4

1. M. Useem and G. T. Marx, 'Ethical dilemmas and political considerations in social research', in R. B. Smith (ed.), *A Handbook of Social Science Methods: Qualitative Methods*, New York, Irvington Press, 1978.

2. Cf. M. Abrams, *Social Surveys and Social Action*, London, Heinemann, 1951; Pauline V. Young, *Scientific Social Surveys and Research*, Englewood Cliffs, Prentice-Hall, 1939.

3. Cf. M. G. Kendall, 'Measurement in the study of society', in W. Robson (ed.), *Man and the Social Sciences*, London, Allen and Unwin, 1972, pp. 141–3.

4. F. Teer and J. D. Spence, *Political Opinion Polls*, London, Hutchinson, 1973, Chapter 1.

5. Descriptions of the technical operations involved in a social survey are available in a number of standard works: for example, C. A. Moser and G. Kalton, *Survey Methods in Social Investigation*, London, Heinemann, 1971; E. R. Babbie, *Survey Research Methods*, Belmont, California, Wadsworth, 1973; G. Hoinville *et al.*, *Survey Research Practice*, London, Heinemann, 1978.

6. E. Josephson, 'Notes on the sociology of privacy', *Humanitas*, **XI**, February 1975, p. 21.

7. P. Redfern, 'The different roles of population censuses and interview surveys, especially in the UK context', *International Statistical Institute Proceedings*, 1973, paper 4.2.

8. H. Ware and J. C. Caldwell, 'Confidentiality, Privacy and Sensitivity in Household Surveys', *Australian Journal of Statistics*, **14**, 1972, pp. 197–203.

9. Sir Claus Moser, 'The role of the Central Statistical Office in Assisting Public Policy Makers', *The American Statistician*, **30**, May 1976, p. 66.

10. S. Bok, 'Freedom and Risk', *Daedalus*, Spring 1978 (special issue on *Limits of Scientific Inquiry*), p. 117.

11. D. I. Warren, 'Some Observations from post-riot Detroit: the role of the social researcher in contemporary racial conflict', *Phylon*, **34**, June 1973, pp. 171–86 at p. 173.

12. Useem and Marx, op. cit.

13. H. C. Kelman, 'Privacy and Research with Human Beings', *Journal of Social Issues*, **33**, 1977, pp. 169–195, esp. pp. 173–6. See also D. Montero, 'Research among racial and cultural minorities', *Journal of Social Issues*, **33**, 1977,

pp. 1–10.

14. Josephson, op. cit., p. 14.

15. 'Response rates in sample surveys: report of a working party', *Journal of the Market Research Society*, **18**, 1976, pp. 113–42.

16. Ibid., p. 126.

17. A. B. Atkinson and A. J. Harrison, *The Distribution of Personal Wealth in Britain*, Cambridge University Press, 1978; Appendix 1, Sample Survey Evidence, pp. 268–75.

18. Ware and Caldwell, op. cit.

19. E. Singer, 'Informed Consent: consequences for response rate and response quality in social surveys', *American Sociological Review*, **43**, 1978, pp. 144–62.

20. 'Human Subject Guidelines at the University of Delaware', in K. W. Eckhardt and M. D. Ermann, *Social Research Methods*, New York, Random House, 1977, pp. 350–5.

Chapter 7

1. This is a revised version of a paper presented at the Annual Meeting of the American Association for Public Opinion Research, Lake George, NY, 1969. The author is obliged to Ann Brunswick, Patricia Collette and Jack Elinson for their helpful comments on an earlier version of this chapter.

2. L. Rainwater and D. J. Pittman, 'Ethical problems in studying a politically sensitive and deviant community', *Social Problems*, **14**, 1967, pp. 357–66.

3. J. W. Moore, 'Political and ethical problems in a large-scale study of a minority population', in G. Sjoberg (ed.), *Ethics, Politics and Social Research*, Cambridge, Mass., Schenkman, and London, Routledge, 1967.

4. B. M. Smith, 'Conflicting values affecting behavioural research with children', *Children*, **14**, March–April 1967.

5. C. Gell and J. Elinson (eds), 'The Washington Heights Master Sample Survey', *The Milbank Memorial Fund Quarterly*, **47**, 1969, Part 2.

6. G. Nash and C. Epstein, 'Harlem views Columbia University', unpublished ms., New York, July 1968.

7. Executive Office of the President, *Privacy and Behavioural Research*, Office of Science and Technology, Washington DC; US Government Printing Office, 1967, p. 21.

8. D. Wolfle, 'Editorial', *Science*, **159**, February 1968, p. 3817.

9. I. L. Horowitz, *The Rise and Fall of Project Camelot*, Cambridge, Mass., MIT Press, p. 363.

10. J. W. Moore, op. cit., p. 242.

Chapter 9

1. Cf. W. S. Holt, *The Bureau of the Census*, Washington DC, Brookings Institution, 1929; H. Alterman, *Counting People: the census in history*, New York, Harcourt, Brace and World, 1969; and A. H. Scott, *Census U.S.A.: Fact-Finding for the American People 1790–1970*, New York, Seabury Press, 1968.

2. D. V. Glass, *Numbering the People*, Farnborough, Saxon House, 1973.

3. D. V. Glass, op. cit.

4. Cf. H. S. Shryock and J. S. Siegel, *The Methods and Materials of Demography*, Washington DC, US Government Printing Office, 1975, Chapter 2.

5. *1981 Census of Population*, Cmnd. 7146, London, HMSO, 1978, p. 2.

6. *1976 Census of Population*, Cmnd. 5906, London, HMSO, 1975.

7. For a major study of this phenomenon, see C. W. Parsons (ed.), *America's Uncounted People: report of the advisory committee on census enumeration*, Washington DC, National Academy of Science, 1972. British evidence is contained in P. Gray and F. A. Gee, *A Quality Check on the 1966 Census*, London, HMSO, OPCS Social Survey Division Report SS 391, 1972.

8. H. P. Miller, 'Considerations in determining the content of the 1970 Census', *Demography*, **4**, 1967, p. 744.

9. For an analysis of the content of recent British censuses, see B. Benjamin, *The Population Census*, London, Heinemann with SSRC, 1970.

10. *1981 Census of Population*, op. cit., paras 24 and 25; K. K. Sillitoe, 'Ethnic Origin: the search for a question', *Population Trends*, **13**, 1978, pp. 25–30.

11. P. Redfern, 'The different roles of population censuses and interview surveys, especially in the UK context', *International Statistical Institute Proceedings, 1973*, Paper 4.2, p. 6.

12. For a review of these in the British context, see *Security of the Census of Population*, Cmnd. 5365, London, HMSO, 1973.

13. Ibid., p. 29.

14. T. Linehan, 'Problems of Confidentiality with particular reference to population censuses', *Statistical Reporter*, August 1972, p. 18. For a review of the history of American practices, see R. C. Davis, 'Confidentiality and the Census 1790–1929', in US Department of HEW, *Records, Computers and the Rights of Citizens*, Cambridge, Mass., MIT Press, 1973, pp. 178–201.

15. P. Redfern, op. cit., p. 2; T. Linehan, op. cit., p. 17; J. Blake, 'Census under Censure', *New Society*, 16 March 1972, pp. 541–2.

16. P. Hewitt, *Privacy: the information gatherers*, London, National Council for Civil Liberties, 1977, pp. 11–13.

17. Ibid.

18. D. Madgwick and T. Smythe, *The Invasion of Privacy*, London, 1974, p. 96.

19. *Security of the Census of Population*, op. cit.

20. P. Redfern, op. cit., p. 2.

21. Ibid., p. 7.

22. *Security of the Census of Population*, op. cit., p. 28.

23. Dr J. Dunwoody, *Hansard (House of Commons)*, **796**, col. 339.

24. R. H. S. Crossman, *Diaries of a Cabinet Minister, Vol. 2, Lord President of the Council*, London, H. Hamilton and J. Cape, 1976, pp. 657–8 and 664.

25. Mr Bruce Millan, *Hansard*, **796**, col. 351.

26. F. Banfield, '1971 Census: Voluntary Survey on Income', *Population Trends*, **12**, 1978, pp. 18–21.

27. P. Redfern, op. cit., p. 4.

Chapter 10

1. The term Census Office is used for convenience to refer to the organisation responsible for conducting the census in England and Wales, that is the GRO and, since 1970, the Office of Population Censuses and Surveys. Where the plural is used, the reference includes the General Register Office (Scotland). Responsibility for taking the census in Great Britain lay with the General Register Office in 1841 and 1851. After a separate GRO was established in Scotland in 1855, each GRO was responsible for the census in its area. In 1970, the Government Social Survey and the GRO were merged to form the Office of Population Censuses and Surveys (OPCS), which retained responsibility for taking the census in England and Wales. The census confidentiality policy of the General Register Office (Scotland) is broadly the same as that of OPCS. The main reference of this paper is to OPCS policy and practice.

2. Alan F. Westin, *Privacy and Freedom*, New York, Atheneum, 1976, Part 1. But see also the discussions of privacy in Stephen T. Margulis (ed.), 'Privacy as a Behavioural Phenomenon', *Journal of Social Issues*, **33**, no. 3, Summer 1977, and by Walter M. Carlson, 'Privacy', in Martha E. Williams (ed.), *Annual Review of Information Science and Technology*, **12**, New York, Knowledge Industry Publications Inc. for American Society for Information Science, 1977, pp. 279–305. A discussion of privacy and confidentiality with reference to government statistical offices, and the population census in particular, is given in David H. Flaherty, *Privacy and Government Databanks: An International Perspective*, London, Mansell Scientific, 1979.

3. *Computers and Privacy*, Cmnd. 6353, HMSO, 1975, para. 8.

4. The topics covered by the 1981 Census and the uses of census statistics in policy formulation, planning and research are outlined in *1981 Census of Population*, Cmnd. 7146, HMSO, 1978, paras 15–30.

5. Ibid, para. 19.

6. *Security of the Census of Population*, Cmnd. 5365, HMSO, 1973.

7. Bulmer's review in the next chapter of Parliamentary debates and Parliamentary questions on the census since 1920 shows that until recently the census itself was a minor issue without much political attraction. The current interest in the census seems to derive almost entirely from the emergence of privacy and confidentiality as public issues.

8. For a complete list of assurances given on householders' forms at each census 1851–1971, see C. Hakim, *Census Confidentiality, Microdata, and Census Analysis*, Occasional Paper No. 3, London, OPCS, 1977, Appendix A. This publication is hereafter referred to as *Census Confidentiality*.

9. In the United States, for example, assurances of confidentiality have varied somewhat between censuses, but have become increasingly restrictive. See J. W. Duncan, 'Confidentiality of Statistical and Research Data', *Statistical Reporter*, no. 77–4, January 1977, pp. 115–36, at p. 131; Robert C. Davis, 'Confidentiality and the Census, 1790–1929', Appendix C in US Department of Health, Education and Welfare, *Records, Computers and the Rights of Citizens*, Cambridge, Mass., MIT Press, 1973.

10. Hakim, *Census Confidentiality*, op. cit., p. 12.

11. Duncan, op. cit., p. 117. This view is also implicit in the assurances about census confidentiality given in *1981 Census of Population*, op. cit., paras 10 and 12.

12. An outline of the information collected at each census can be found in OPCS and GRO(S), *Guide to Census Reports 1801–1966, Great Britain*, HMSO, 1977. Information on the data collected by other European censuses can be found in Judith Blake and Jerry J. Donovan, *Western European Censuses, 1960*, Institute of International Studies, University of California, Berkeley, 1971.

13. The increase in the volume and range of census output is described in C. Hakim, *Data Dissemination for the Population Census*, Occasional Paper No. 11, London, OPCS, 1978.

14. *Security of the Census of Population*, op. cit., paras 1.9 and 3.2.2.

15. Ibid, paras 3.2.2 and 4.6. The figures quoted are for England and Wales.

16. Ibid, paras 3.2.1–3.2.5 and 4.1–4.14.

17. *1981 Census of Population*, op. cit., para. 37.

18. While this is generally true, some of the early returns have survived. For example, most of the original census returns for 1821 and 1831 for Poplar, Middlesex, are held (in bound volumes) at the Central Library, Bancroft Road, London E1. See I. R. Harrison, 'Poplar Genealogy: The Resources of a Dockland Parish', *The Genealogists Magazine*, **18**, no. 7, September 1976, pp. 352–3.

19. Duncan, op. cit., p. 131; David H. Flaherty, 'Access to Historic Census Data in Canada, A Comparative Analysis', *Canadian Public Administration*, **20**, no. 3, Fall 1977, pp. 481–98.

20. The Scottish census returns up to 1891 are open to the public, but

returns for the 1901 and subsequent censuses are subject to the 100 years' closure period, as stated by the Secretary of State for Scotland in reply to a question from Mr Buchanan, *Hansard*, **874,** 23 May 1974, cols. 272–3.

21. Research and other uses of early census records are described in Hakim, *Data Dissemination for the Population Census*, op. cit., section 3.1.

22. Hakim, *Census Confidentiality*, op. cit., pp. 4–5.

23. The constraints on searches of census records have varied over the decades, but in general only a limited amount of information has been released to the person concerned, or his immediate relatives or descendants. In England and Wales, a seventy years' rule is now applied, and the information released is restricted to age and place of birth; in Scotland, a fifty years' rule is applied. See Hakim, *Census Confidentiality*, op. cit., p. 5; Secretary of State for Social Services in reply to Mr Stainton, *Hansard*, **846,** 1972–3, 13 to 24 November, cols. 357–8; Baroness Stedman in reply to Lord Teviot, House of Lords, *Hansard*, **390,** no. 57, 6 April 1978, col. 314; *1981 Census of Population*, op. cit., para. 12.

24. The United States Bureau of the Census will release identifiable information to an individual who supplied it, or to their heirs, largely for the purpose of verifying age or to establish eligibility for a benefit. See Duncan, op. cit., p. 119.

25. *Security of the Census of Population*, op. cit., para. 1.5.

26. Duncan, op. cit., p. 131.

27. Dennis Newman, *Techniques for Ensuring the Confidentiality of Census Information in Great Britain*, Occasional Paper No. 4, London, OPCS, 1978.

28. The type of microdata collected in Britain (including census information), policies on the release of public-use sample data, and the potential applications of microdata in research and statistical analysis are described in more detail in Flaherty's comparative study of policy and practice in Canada, the United States, the Federal Republic of Germany, Sweden and the United Kingdom. See David H. Flaherty, *Privacy and Government Databanks: An International Perspective*, London, Mansell Scientific, 1979. The Bellagio Conference on government microdata concluded that a number of important fields of research required access to microdata, especially from government sources, and that public-use samples were the single most important way in which central statistical agencies could assist the research community. See David H. Flaherty, 'Final Report of the Bellagio Conference on Privacy, Confidentiality, and the Use of Government Microdata for Research and Statistical Purposes', *Statistical Reporter*, no. 78–8, May 1978, pp. 274–9, reprinted in the *Journal of the Royal Statistical Society*, Series A, **141,** Part 3, 1978, pp. 401–6.

29. See, for example, the consultative paper presented to the Research Interests Advisory Committee on the 1981 Census, OPCS and GRO(S), *1981 Census: Datatapes*, CEN (RES) (77)9, July 1977; Census Division, OPCS, 'Planning for the 1981 Census of Population', *Population Trends*, no. 10, Winter

1977, p. 9.

30. The data-censoring techniques being evaluated include variants of those discussed by Donald T. Campbell *et al.* in 'Confidentiality-Preserving Modes of Access to Files and to Interfile Exchange for Useful Statistical Analysis', *Evaluation Quarterly*, **1,** no. 2, May 1977, pp. 269–99, such as the deletion of identifiers; the use of crude report categories; the restriction of 'public' variables; microaggregation; and error inoculation.

31. Philip Redfern, 'Office of Population Censuses and Surveys', *Population Trends*, no. 4, Summer 1976, pp. 21–3.

32. P. Gray and F. A. Gee, *A Quality Check on the 1966 Ten Per Cent Sample Census of England and Wales*, HMSO, 1972.

33. Results of these surveys are reported in Judy Sadler and Tony Whitworth, *Reserves of Nurses*, HMSO, 1975; OPCS, *1971 Census Income Follow-up Survey*, OPCS Studies on Medical and Population Subjects No. 38, HMSO, 1978; Faith Banfield, '1971 Census: Voluntary Survey on Income', *Population Trends*, no. 12, Summer 1978, pp. 18–21. Some results of the survey on qualified manpower are reported in 'Employment of the Highly Qualified 1971–1986', *Department of Employment Gazette*, **86,** no. 5, May 1978, pp. 531–9.

34. *Security of the Census of Population*, op. cit., paras. 3.2.6 and 3.2.7.

35. *1981 Census of Population*, op. cit., paras. 31–4.

36. OPCS, *Cohort Studies: New Developments*, Studies in Medical and Population Subjects No. 25, HMSO, 1973, p. 4.

37. *Security of the Census of Population*, op. cit., para. 5.6.

38. A description of the applications of the Longitudinal Study is given in OPCS, *Cohort Studies: New Developments*, op. cit., pp. 5–12.

39. *Computers and Privacy*, op. cit., para. 21.

40. In the United States, for example, census data is matched with individual social-security records, and (separately) with tax records on individuals and businesses, for statistical purposes, as described in Duncan, op. cit., pp. 119, 125. See also the discussion of data-linkage techniques while preserving confidentiality in Campbell *et al*, 'Confidentiality-Preserving Modes of Access to Files and to Interfile Exchange for Useful Statistical Analysis', op. cit., pp. 283–95.

41. W. F. F. Kemsley, 'Family Expenditure Survey: A study of differential response based on a comparison of the 1971 sample with the census', *Statistical News*, no. 31, November 1975, pp. 16–21.

42. The results of the two post-census surveys are summarised in *Security of the Census of Population*, op. cit., paras. 5.1–5.9.

43. Hakim, *Census Confidentiality*, op. cit., describes the implications for census data analysis of the procedures adopted to protect confidentiality in census output.

44. *Security of the Census of Population*, op. cit., para. 5.6.

45. Secretary of State for Social Services in reply to Mr John Moore,

Hansard, **954,** no. 164, 28 July 1978, cols. 710–11.

46. *Third Report of the Parliamentary Commissioner for Administration, Session 1971–72*, HMSO, June 1972; *1981 Census of Population*, op. cit., para. 12.

47. See Duncan, op. cit., p. 117.

48. The only case in which a census form would appear in legal proceedings would be where the census office has prosecuted a person for non-compliance with the census. In this case, it is the absence of any response to questions on the census form that is the subject of discussion, not the information provided (if any) in response to questions.

49. For a history of the controversy, see D. V. Glass, *Numbering the People: The eighteenth-century controversy and the development of census and vital statistics in Britain*, Farnborough, Hants, Saxon House, 1973.

50. Rt Hon K. Younger, *Report of the Committee on Privacy*, HMSO, 1972; *Computers and Privacy*, op. cit.; *Computers: Safeguards for Privacy*, Cmnd. 6354, HMSO, 1975.

51. Among the data-censoring techniques considered so far is the random deletion of (correct) response codes and their replacement by the automated editing process. See Barry Werner, 'The Development of Automatic Editing for the Next Census of Population', *Statistical News*, no. 37, May 1977, pp. 10–14.

52. W. H. Mason, K. E. Taeuber and H. H. Winsborough (eds), *Old Data for New Research*, Report of a Workshop on Research Opportunities and Issues in the Design and Construction of Public Use Samples from the 1940 and 1950 Censuses and from Current Population Surveys from 1960 Forward, held in Madison, Wisconsin, 28–30 June 1976, University of Wisconsin-Madison, Centre for Demography and Ecology, February 1977.

53. Hakim, *Data Dissemination for the Population Census*, op. cit., Section 2.4.

54. For example, the release of census statistics showing that certain local authorities had high proportions of households with lodgers in council housing might lead those authorities to increase their degree of inspection and identify the households, even though the *personal* information they supplied had been fully protected by the census office. This point is made by Linehan, 'Problems of Confidentiality with Particular Reference to Population Censuses', *Statistical Reporter*, August 1972, p. 17.

55. Herbert C. Kelman, 'Privacy and Research with Human Beings', *Journal of Social Issues*, **33,** no. 3, 1977 pp. 173–6. See also Bulmer, Chapter 4 above, pp. 61–3; Josephson, Chapter 7 above, *passim*; and Petersen, Chapter 13 below, pp. 178–81.

56. Hakim, *Census Confidentiality*, op. cit., pp. 10–11.

57. C. Hakim, *INSEE: Data Dissemination for the French Censuses*, London, OPCS, July 1977, p. 5.

58. See, for example, the descriptions by Davis and Flaherty of the development of census confidentiality in North America. Davis, 'Confidentiality

and the Census 1790–1929', op. cit.; Flaherty, 'Access to Historic Census Data in Canada: A Comparative Analysis', op. cit. Recent legislation on data privacy in Western Europe is described in *Computers: Safeguards for Privacy*, op. cit., paras 69–85.

59. Sir Claus Moser, 'The Environment in which Statistical Offices will Work in Ten Years' Time', *Statistical News*, no. 38, August 1977, p. 4.

Chapter 11

1. For a fuller discussion, see B. Benjamin, *The Population Census*, London, Heinemann, 1970.

2. 10 and 11 GEO 5, Census Act 1920.

3. See *1976 Census of Population*, Cmnd. 5906, London, HMSO, February 1975.

4. Census Act 1920, op. cit.

5. *Hansard*, House of Commons, **132,** col. 2587.

6. Ibid., col. 2586.

7. Ibid., **796,** cols. 329–41.

8. Ibid., **622,** cols. 1193–8.

9. Ibid., **889,** cols. 423–9.

10. Dr J. Dunwoody, Parliamentary Under-Secretary of State, Department of Health and Social Security, ibid., **796,** col. 340.

11. Mr Niall MacPherson, Joint Under-Secretary of State, Scottish Office, ibid., **622,** col. 1197.

12. Ibid., **622,** col. 1192.

13. Ibid., **889,** col. 427.

14. D. V. Glass, *Numbering the People: the C18th population controversy and the development of census and vital statistics in Britain*, Farnborough, Saxon House, 1973, esp. chapters 2 and 3.

15. *Security of the Census of Population*, Cmnd. 5365, London, HMSO, July 1973.

Chapter 13

1. Ranging, thus, from Alan F. Westin, *Privacy and Freedom*, New York, Atheneum, 1967; Samuel Dash *et al.*, *The Eavesdroppers*, Rutgers Univ. Press, New Brunswick, NJ, 1959; and Edward V. Long, *The Intruders*, New York, Praeger, 1966, through such works as Myron Brenton, *The Privacy Invaders*, New York, Coward-McCann, 1961, down to Vance Packard, *The Naked Society*, New York, McKay, 1964.

2. See, for example, 'Special Inquiry on Invasion of Privacy', Hearings

before a Sub-committee of the Committee on Government Operations, House of Representatives, 89th Congress, 1st Session, 1965, Washington DC, US Government Printing Office, 1966.

3. Office of Science and Technology, Executive Office of the President, *Privacy and Behavioral Research*, Washington DC, US Government Printing Office, 1967.

4. New Jersey omitted race or colour from its certificates of birth, death and fetal death in 1962, restoring it again later that year or, in effect, the following year; see US Public Health Service, *Vital Statistics of the United States, 1963*, II, Part A, Section 6, Washington DC, US Government Printing Office, 1965, pp. 6–9. In all of the national compilations by race, thus, this one state is omitted for 1962 and 1963. I wrote to several New Jersey officials for details on this interesting switch but received no responsive reply.

5. Albert Mindlin, 'The Designation of Race or Color on Forms', *Public Administration Review*, 26, 1966, pp. 110–18. See also Earl E. Huyck, 'White–Nonwhite Differentials: Overview and Implications', *Demography*, 3, 1966, pp. 548–65.

6. Henry Lee Moon, speaking before the 1962 meeting of the American Statistical Association; quoted in Mindlin, op. cit.

7. The same title calls for a census 'count of persons of voting age by race, color, and national origin'; there is no indication of how the implied contradiction should be resolved.

8. Cf. William Petersen, 'Religious Statistics in the United States', *The Politics of Population*, Garden City, NY, Doubleday, 1964, pp. 248–70.

9. Herman P. Miller, 'Considerations in Determining the Content of the 1970 Census', *Demography*, 4, 1967, pp. 744–52.

10. The laws and administrative rulings guarding privacy are quoted in Conrad Taeuber, 'Invasion of Privacy', Chapter 12 above; some of the court cases in which these rules have been upheld are discussed in Petersen, op. cit. A prime instance of the Census Bureau's probity, even under intense pressure from other government agencies and despite a prevailing mood of hysteria, was its refusal in 1941 to disclose the names and addresses of Japanese Americans. 'To its everlasting credit the Bureau of the Census demonstrated a higher devotion to the Constitution than did many of those who were responsible for the creation of detention camps for our fellow citizens who happened to be of Japanese ancestry' (Representative Cornelius E. Gallagher, Dem., NY, as quoted in the *New York Times*, 9 May 1969). For the general background, see W. Petersen, *Japanese Americans*, New York, Random House, 1971, esp. Chapter 4.

11. 'Census Programs Attacked as Invasions of Privacy', *American Statistician*, 22, April 1968, pp. 12–13; 'Attacks on Census Increase', 22, June 1968, p. 11; 'The Census Inquisition', *Population Bulletin*, 25, May 1969; John Kantner, 'The Census under Attack', *American Sociologist*, 4, 1969, p. 256.

12. One question (repeated virtually verbatim from the 1960 Census) was, 'Do you have a bathtub or shower?' with a choice among three answers: 'Yes, for this household only'; 'Yes, but shared with another household'; and 'No bathtub or shower'. In the publicity attacking the census, this effort to measure the quality of America's housing was paraphrased as 'Do you take your shower with other persons?'

13. One official of the Census Bureau asked me, if I were testifying before a congressional committee, fully aware that the allocation of sufficient funds depended in large part on its goodwill, how I would respond to this comment: One congressman admitted the justice of the witness's remarks that the collection of population data was useful but asked why the government had to be involved in it. When he wanted to know how many persons live in a certain city, he said, he looked up the fact in an almanac; why could not everyone else do the same and save the government many millions of dollars?

Chapter 14

1. This quotation comes from the general explanatory leaflet circulated with copies of the 1971 Census schedule.

2. D. V. Glass, *Numbering the People*, Saxon House, 1973.

3. *Security of the Census of Population*, Cmnd. 5365, HMSO, 1973.

4. C. Hakim, *Census Confidentiality, Microdata and Census Analysis*, Occasional Paper no. 3, Office of Population Censuses and Surveys, 1978.

5. K. Sillitoe, *Ethnic Origins, 1, 2 and 3*, Occasional Papers Nos. 8, 9 and 10, Office of Population Censuses and Surveys, 1978.

6. *1981 Census of Population*, Cmnd. 7146, HMSO, 1978, p. 3.

7. *Report of the Committee on Privacy*, Cmnd. 5012, HMSO, 1972.

8. Ibid., p. 228.

9. *Computers and Privacy*, Cmnd. 6353, and *Computers, Safeguards for Privacy*, Cmnd. 6354, HMSO, 1975.

10. Alan F. Westin, *Privacy and Freedom*, Bodley Head, 1970.

11. These are different methods of treating statistical tables to prevent them revealing data on identifiable individuals. The best discussions of the problems and techniques are *Confidentiality in Statistical Tables*, Stockholm, National Central Bureau of Statistics, 1974 and *Destruction, Anonymization and Ciphering: Privacy and Confidentiality Protection Measures in Statistics Production*, Investigation Report No. 8, Stockholm, National Central Bureau of Statistics, 1976.

12. Letter to the Editor, *The Times*, 12 April 1971.

13. *Report of the Committee on Privacy*, op. cit.; *Response Rates in Sample Surveys*, Report of a Working Party of the Market Research Society Research and Development Committee, 1976; *Survey Research and Privacy*, this book, Chapters 5

and 16.

14. Cf. *Report of the Committee on Privacy*, op. cit., p. 230.

15. This term is used in the sense described in W. Solesbury, 'The Environmental Agenda', *Public Administration*, **54**, Winter 1976, p. 379.

16. Judith Thompson, 'The Right to Privacy', *Philosophy and Public Affairs*, **4**, no. 4, Summer 1975, pp. 295–314; J. H. Reiman, 'Privacy, Intimacy and Personhood', *Philosophy and Public Affairs*, **6**, no. 1, Fall 1976, pp. 26–44.

17. See Bibliography, pp. 250ff.

18. Richard Sennett, *The Fall of Public Man*, Cambridge University Press, 1977.

19. Cf., for example, the discussion in Chapter 4 of J. Busfield and M. Paddon, *Thinking about Children*, Cambridge University Press, 1977.

20. S. T. Margulis, 'Conceptions of Privacy: Current Status and Next Steps', *Journal of Social Issues*, **33**, no. 3, 1977, pp. 5–21 and L. C. Velecky, 'The Concept of Privacy', in J. B. Young (ed.), *Privacy*, Chichester, Wiley, 1978.

21. As described in *Report of the Committee on Privacy*, op. cit., p. 17.

22. See C. Bell and H. Newby, *Community Studies*, London, Allen and Unwin, 1971, especially chapter 2.

23. For a further discussion of the distinction, see C. Hakim, op. cit.

24. I. Altman, 'Privacy: A Conceptual Analysis', *Environment and Behavior*, **8**, no. 1, March 1976, pp. 7–29.

25. S. T. Margulis, op. cit.

26. A. F. Westin, op. cit., p. 25. See also the discussion in E. Shils, 'Privacy: Its Constitution and Vicissitudes', *Law and Contemporary Problems*, **31**, 1966, pp. 281–306.

27. I. Altman, 'Privacy Regulation: Culturally Universal or Culturally Specific?', *Journal of Social Issues*, **33**, no. 3, 1977, pp. 66–84.

28. P. H. Klopfer and D. I. Rubenstein, 'The Concept *Privacy* and its Biological Basis', *Journal of Social Issues*, **33**, no. 3, 1977, pp. 52–65.

29. A. F. Westin, op. cit., p. 14.

30. Address by the Prime Minister, Herr Thorbjörn Fälldin, at the meeting of the Centre Party's Representative Council, New Parliament Building, Stockholm, 22 April 1977. For details of the Swedish 'personnummer' system, see S. Lundeborg, 'The Personal Identity Number in Sweden', Stockholm, National Central Bureau of Statistics, 1978.

31. For example, the debate over the British 1971 Census was very similar in nature to that which had preceded the 1970 US Census. See 'The Census Inquisition', *Population Bulletin of the Population Reference Bureau*, **25**, no. 2, May 1969.

32. I am grateful for this information to Dr Lennart Törnqvist of the National Central Bureau of Statistics, Stockholm.

33. *The Times*, 24 April 1971, p. 2.

34. The technique, widely used in interview surveys, of 'tail-end loading'

sensitive questions, so that should the respondent jib at them there is still the majority of the question replies available, is not useable in inquiries such as the census.

35. In Newcastle-upon-Tyne, where there have been two local surveys to date, refusal rates were 11 per cent in 1975 and 13 per cent in 1976, *Urban Trends 1975* and *Urban Trends, City of Newcastle upon Tyne*, Newcastle-upon-Tyne City Council, Management Services Department, 1976 and 1978. Unfortunately, few of the published reports of other local surveys give details of refusal rates. Several of them have had total non-response rates, which include non-contacts as well as refusals, which have been much higher than the non-response rates in the Newcastle surveys.

36. Letter to the Editor, *The Times*, 14 April 1971; letter to the Editor, *Guardian*, 19 July 1978.

37. There was a sample census in 1966, which enumerated 10 per cent of households. The census proposed for 1976, which would have been a full 100 per cent inquiry, was cancelled in the 1975 Budget.

38. Most of the studies on the topic were carried out during the Second World War, such as G. W. Allport and L. Postman, *The Psychology of Rumour*, Henry Holt, 1948.

39. Chief among these must be the practice known as 'sugging' – selling under the guise of market research or social-survey activity, which the Market Research Society is attempting to stamp out.

40. B. Benjamin, 'Public Needs and Personal Privacy', paper presented to the Census Research Group conference on Privacy, Confidentiality and the Census, London, 1976.

41. Cf. Chapter 4.

42. Cf. Chapter 4.

43. There have been suggestions that recipients of schedules may swop them with people to whom they think the questions on their particular schedule are more relevant.

44. See, for example, the Report of the IFDO/CESSDA Conference on Emerging Data Protection and the Social Sciences' Need for Data, Köln, August 1978.

45. I. Altman, op. cit., p. 12.

Chapter 15

1. 'Confidentiality of statistical and research data', in US Department of Commerce, Office of Federal Statistical Policy and Standards, *A Framework for Planning U.S. Federal Statistics in the 1980s*, Washington DC, US Government Printing Office, 1978, pp. 255–83.

2. Cf. R. Bower *et al.*, *Ethics in Social Research*, New York, Praeger, 1978.

3. Privacy Protection Study Commission, *Personal Privacy in an Information Society*, Washington DC, US Government Printing Office, 1977, pp. 13–21.

4. Cf. sources listed on p. 258.

5. O. Aukrust and S. Nordbotten, 'Files of Individual Data and their Potentials for Social Research', *The Review of Income and Wealth*, **19**, 1973, pp. 189–201.

6. Another such inquiry is the British Longitudinal Study, described in *Cohort Studies: New Developments*, OPCS Studies in Medical and Population Subjects no. 25, 1973, London, HMSO.

7. Cf. S. Akerman, in T. Dalenius and A. Klevmarken (eds), *Personal Integrity and the Need for Data in the Social Sciences*, Stockholm, Swedish Council for Social Science Research, 1976, pp. 104–5.

8. *The Personal Identity Number in Sweden*, National Central Bureau of Statistics, Sweden, paper 1978–01–17, mimeo.

9. Cf. the systems described by James Rule in *Private Lives and Public Surveillance*, London, Allen Lane, 1973.

10. Cf. A. F. Westin and M. A. Baker, *Databanks in a Free Society*, New York, Quadrangle Books, 1972, pp. 30–45, and 396–400; United States Department of Health, Education and Welfare, *Records, Computers and the Rights of Citizens*, Cambridge, Mass., MIT Press, 1973, pp. 108–35.

11. Westin and Baker, op. cit., pp. 398–9.

12. Sir Claus Moser, 'The Role of the Central Statistical Office in Assisting Public Policy Makers', *The American Statistician*, **30**, May 1976, p. 66.

13. United States Department of Health, Education and Welfare, *Records, Computers and the Rights of Citizens*, Cambridge, Mass., MIT Press, 1973, p. 89. For background to the internment of Japanese Americans during the Second World War, see W. Petersen, *Japanese Americans*, New York, Random House, 1971, especially chapter 4.

14. See the sources listed on pp. 256–8.

15. E. Josephson, 'Notes on the sociology of privacy', *Humanitas*, **XI**, February 1975, p. 25.

16. For an illuminating example of such a study, see *The National Central Bureau of Statistics and the Public*, Stockholm, National Central Bureau of Statistics Survey Research Institute, 1977.

Chapter 17

1. Cmnd. 6353, December 1975, London, HMSO.

2. T. Dalenius. *Information, Privacy and Statistics. A Topical Bibliography*, United States Bureau of the Census, Working Paper No. 41, 1978, Washington DC, US Government Printing Office.

3. The conditions under which individual information is disclosed in

published tables of aggregate figures have been investigated by I. P. Fellegi, 'On the question of statistical confidentiality', *Journal of the American Statistical Association*, **67**, no. 337, March 1972, pp. 7–18, and by T. Dalenius, 'Towards a methodology for statistical disclosure control', *Sartryck ur Statistisk tidskrift*, **5**, 1977, pp. 429–44.

4. I. P. Fellegi and J. L. Phillips, 'Statistical confidentiality: some theory and applications to data dissemination', *Annals of Economic and Social Measurement*, **3**, 1974, pp. 339–409.

5. D. G. Horvitz, B. G. Greenberg and J. R. Abernathy, 'Randomised response: a data-gathering device for sensitive questions', *International Statistical Review*, **44**, no. 2, 1976, pp. 181–96. The same issue contains six further articles on randomised response together with a printed discussion.

6. T. Dalenius. 'Privacy transformations for Statistical Information Systems', *Journal of Statistical Planning and Inference*, **1**, 1977, pp. 73–86.

7. D. T. Campbell, R. F. Boruch, R. D. Schwartz and J. Steinberg, 'Confidentiality-preserving modes of access to files and to interfile exchange for useful statistical analysis', *Evaluation Quarterly*, **1**, 1977, pp. 269–300.

8. Cmnd. 5115, pp. 227–9.

9. *Hansard*, 26 October 1971 (Parliamentary question by Mr Leslie Huckfield, MP to Sir Keith Joseph, Secretary of State for Social Services). The government have undertaken that in future, whenever census data are to be used for a voluntary survey, this will be announced in Parliament: *Security of the Census of Population*, Cmnd. 5365, para. 4.22.

Chapter 18

1. Background research on the topic has been supported by National Science Foundation Grant APR77–00349.

2. R. F. Boruch and J. S. Cecil, *Assuring Confidentiality in Social Research*, Philadelphia, University of Pennsylvania Press, 1979.

3. H. W. Riecken, R. F. Boruch, D. T. Campbell, N. Caplan *et al.*, *Social Experimentation: a method for planning and evaluating social programs*, New York, Academic Press, 1974, provides a basic description of ethical, legal and institutional problems engendered by experimental tests of social programmes, and suggests some solutions to those problems. A. M. Rivlin and P. M. Timpane (eds), *Ethical and Legal Issues in Social Experimentation*, Washington DC, Brookings Institution, 1975, covers legal issues in economic experiments alone, using problems in medical research as a basis for comparison.

4. Boruch and Cecil, op. cit.

5. J. E. Carroll and C. R. Knerr, 'A report of the APSA confidentiality in social research project', *Political Science*, Summer 1975, pp. 258–61.

6. B. G. Greenberg, J. R. Abernathy and D. G. Horvitz, 'A new survey

technique and its applications in the field of public health', *Millbank Memorial Fund Quarterly*, **68**, 1970, pp. 38–55; D. G. Horvitz, B. G. Greenberg and J. R. Abernathy, 'Recent developments in randomised response design', in J. N. Srivastara (ed.), *A Survey of Statistical Design and Linear Models*, Amsterdam, North-Holland, 1975.

7. T. Dalenius, 'The invasion of privacy problem and statistics production: an overview', *Sartryck ur Statistisk Tidskrift*, **3**, 1974, pp. 213–25.

8. In T. Dalenius and A. Klevmarken (eds), *Personal Integrity and the Need for Data in the Social Sciences*, Stockholm, Swedish Council for Social Science Research, 1976.

9. S. L. Warner, 'Linear randomised response model', *Journal of the American Statistical Association*, **66**, 1971, pp. 884–8.

10. R. A. Bauman, M. H. David and R. F. Miller, 'Working with complex data files', in R. L. Biscoe (ed.), *Data Bases, Computers and the Social Sciences*, New York, Wiley, 1970.

11. A. W. Astin and R. F. Boruch, 'A link file system for assuring confidentiality of research data in longitudinal studies', *American Educational Research Journal*, **7**, 1970, pp. 615–24.

12. E. J. Webb, D. T. Campbell, R. D. Schwarz and L. Sechrest, *Unobtrusive Measures: non-reactive research in the social sciences*, Chicago, Rand McNally, 1966.

13. R. D. Schwarz and S. Orleans, 'On legal sanctions', *University of Chicago Law Review*, **34**, 1967, pp. 382–400.

14. Cf. R. F. Boruch, 'Strategies for eliciting and merging confidential social research data', *Policy Sciences*, **3**, 1972, pp. 275–97; D. T. Campbell, R. F. Boruch, R. D. Schwarz and J. Steinberg, 'Confidentiality-preserving modes of access to files and interfile exchange for useful statistical analysis', *Evaluation Quarterly*, **1**, 1977, pp. 269–99.

15. E. Scott *et al.*, *Privacy interests and statutes providing for governmental collection and compilation of personally identified mental health information*, Report to the American Psychological Association Committee on Privacy and Confidentiality, Washington DC, APA, 1976, mimeo.

16. D. N. Kershaw and J. C. Small, 'Data confidentiality and privacy: lessons of the New Jersey Negative Income Tax Experiment', *Public Policy*, **20**, 1972, pp. 257–80.

17. More recent legislation has strengthened the assurance given to participants in special types of research. The Crime Control Act of 1973 (Public Law 93–83), for example, limits judicial and executive agency access to the criminal researcher's records on identifiable individuals.

18. E. Singer, 'Informed consent: consequences for response rate and response quality in social surveys', *American Sociological Review*, **43**, 1978, pp. 144–62.

19. E. D. Goldfield, A. G. Turner, C. D. Cowan and J. C. Scott, 'Privacy

and confidentiality as factors in survey response', *Proceedings of the American Statistical Association: Social Statistics Section, Part 1*, Washington DC, ASA, 1977, pp. 219–29.

20. Carroll and Knerr, op. cit.

21. R. T. Bower *et al.* (eds), *Ethics in Social Research: protecting the interests of human subjects*, New York, Praeger, 1978.